Fombombo

Thomas Sigismund Stribling

Alpha Editions

This edition published in 2022

ISBN : 9789356081451

Design and Setting By
Alpha Editions
www.alphaedis.com
Email - info@alphaedis.com

As per information held with us this book is in Public Domain.
This book is a reproduction of an important historical work. Alpha Editions uses the best technology to reproduce historical work in the same manner it was first published to preserve its original nature. Any marks or number seen are left intentionally to preserve its true form.

Contents

CHAPTER I .... - 1 -

CHAPTER II .... - 6 -

CHAPTER III .... - 11 -

CHAPTER IV .... - 17 -

CHAPTER V .... - 21 -

CHAPTER VI .... - 32 -

CHAPTER VII .... - 39 -

CHAPTER VIII .... - 50 -

CHAPTER IX .... - 59 -

CHAPTER X .... - 67 -

CHAPTER XI .... - 75 -

CHAPTER XII .... - 82 -

CHAPTER XIII .... - 89 -

CHAPTER XIV .... - 100 -

CHAPTER XV .... - 109 -

CHAPTER XVI .... - 117 -

CHAPTER XVII .... - 122 -

CHAPTER XVIII..- 137 -

CHAPTER XIX ....- 143 -

CHAPTER XX..- 154 -

CHAPTER XXI ....- 164 -

CHAPTER XXII ....- 172 -

CHAPTER XXIII..- 186 -

CHAPTER XXIV ....- 195 -

CHAPTER XXV...- 199 -

CHAPTER XXVI ....- 207 -

CHAPTER XXVII ....- 222 -

CHAPTER XXVIII...- 233 -

CHAPTER I

In Caracas, Thomas Strawbridge called at the American Consulate, from a sense of duty. The consul, a weary, tropic-shot politician from Kentucky, received him with gin, cigars, and a jaded enthusiasm. He glanced at Mr. Strawbridge's business card and inquired if his visitor were one of the Strawbridges of Virginia. The young man replied that he lived in Keokuk, Iowa, and that his father had moved there from somewhere East. Upon this statement the consul ventured the dictum that if any family didn't know they had come from Virginia, they hadn't.

Having exhausted their native states as a topic of conversation, they swung around, in their talk, to the relatively unimportant Venezuela which sweltered outside the consulate in a drowse of endless summer. The two Americans damned the place, with lassitude but thoroughness. They condemned the character of the Venezuelan, his lack of morals, honesty, industry, and initiative. The Venezuelan was too polite; he was cowardly. He had not the God-given Anglo-Saxon instinct for self-government. But the high treason named in this joint bill of complaint was that the Venezuelan was unbusinesslike.

"I'm no tin angel," proceeded Mr. Strawbridge, emphatically, "but you know just as well as I do, Mr. Anderson, that the fellow who pulls slick stuff in a business deal has hit the chutes for the bowwows. Business methods and strict business honesty will win in the long run, Mr. Anderson."

The consul nodded a trifle absent-mindedly at this recommendation of his nation's widely advertised virtue.

"In fact," continued Mr. Strawbridge, with an effect of having begun to recite some sort of creed he could not stop until he reached the end, "in fact, continual aggressive business policies coupled with an incorruptible honesty are bound to land the American exporter flat-footed on the foreign trade. And, moreover, Mr. Anderson—" Strawbridge had the traveling salesman's habit of repeating a companion's name over and over in the course of a conversation, so he would not forget it—"moreover, Mr. Anderson, we American traveling business men have got to set an example to these people down here; show 'em what to do and how to do it. Snap, vim, go, and absolute honesty."

"Yes, ... yes," agreed the consul, still more absently. He was holding Mr. Strawbridge's card in his fingers and apparently studying it. Presently he broke into the homily:

"Speaking of business, how do you find the gun-and-ammunition business in Venezuela, Mr. Strawbridge?"

"Rotten. I've hardly booked an order since I landed in the country."

The consul lifted his brows.

"Have you booked any at all?"

"Well, no, I haven't," admitted Strawbridge.

The consul smiled faintly and finished off his glass of gin and water.

"I thought perhaps you hadn't."

"What made you think that?"

"No one does who just passes through the country offering them to any and every merchant."

"Why not?"

"Isn't allowed."

Strawbridge stared at his consul—a very honest blue-eyed stare.

"Not allowed? Who doesn't allow it, Mr. Anderson? Why, look here—" he straightened his back as there dawned on him the enormity of this personal infringement of his right to sell firearms whenever and wherever he found a buyer—"why the hell can't I sell rifles and—"

"Forbidden by the Government," interposed Mr. Anderson, patly.

Strawbridge was outraged.

"Now, isn't that a hell of a law! No reason at all, I suppose. Like their custom laws. They don't tax you for what you bring into this God-forsaken country; they tax you for the mistakes you make in saying what you've brought in. They look over your manifest and charge you for the errors you've made in Spanish grammar. Venezuela's correspondence course in the niceties of the Castilian tongue!"

The consul again smiled wearily.

"They have a better reason than that for forbidding rifles—revolutions. You know in this country they stage at least one revolution every forty-eight hours. The minute any Venezuelan gets hold of a gun he steps out and begins to shoot up the Government. If he wings the President, he gets the President's place. It's a very lucrative place, very. It's about the only job in this country worth a cuss. So you see there's a big reason for forbidding the importation of arms into Venezuela."

Mr. Strawbridge drew down his lips in disgust.

"Good Lord! Ain't that rotten! When will this leather-colored crew ever get civilized? Here I am—paid my fare from New York down here just to find out nobody buys firearms in this sizzling hell-hole; can't be trusted with 'em!"

In the pause at this point Mr. Anderson still twirled his guest's card. He glanced toward the front of his consulate, then toward the rear. The two Americans were alone. With his enigmatic smile still wrinkling his tropic-sagged face, the consul said in a slightly lower tone:

"I didn't say no one bought firearms in Venezuela, Mr. Strawbridge. I said they were not allowed to be sold here."

"O-o-oh, I se-e-e!" Mr. Strawbridge's ejaculation curved up and down as enlightenment broke upon him, and he stared fixedly at his consul.

"All I meant to say was that the trade is curtailed as much as possible, in order to prevent bloodshed, suffering, and the crimes of civil war."

Mr. Strawbridge continued his nodding and his absorbed gaze.

"But, still, some of it goes on—of course."

"Naturally," nodded Strawbridge.

"I suppose," continued the consul, reflectively, "that every month sees a considerable number of arms introduced into Venezuela, as far as that goes."

Strawbridge watched his consul as a cat watches a mouse-hole—for something edible to appear.

"Yes?" he murmured interrogatively.

"Well, there you are," finished the consul.

Strawbridge looked his disappointment.

"There I am?" he said in a pained voice. "Well, I must say I am not very far from where you started with me; am I?"

"It seems to me you are somewhat advanced," began the diplomat, philosophically. "You know why you haven't sold anything up to date. You know why you can't approach a Venezuelan casually to sell him guns, as if you were offering him stoves or shoe-polish." The consul was still smiling faintly, and now he drew a scratch-pad toward him and began making aimless marks on it after the fashion of office men. "In fact, to attempt to sell guns at all would be quite against the law, as I have explained, for the reasons I have stated. It's a peculiar and I must say an unfortunate situation."

As he continued his absent-minded marking his explanation turned into a soliloquy on the Venezuelan situation:

"You may not know it, Mr. Strawbridge, but there are one or two revolutions which are chronic in Venezuela. There is one in Tachira, a state on the western border of the country. There is another up in the Rio Negro district, headed by a man named Fombombo. They never cease. Every once in a while the federal troops go out to hunt these insurrectionists, a-a-and—" the consul dragged out his "and" after the fashion of a man relating something so well known that it isn't worth while to give his words their proper stress—"a-a-and if they kill them, more spring up." His voice slumped without interest. He continued marking his pad. "Then there are the foreign juntas. About every four or five years a bunch of Venezuelans go abroad, organize a filibustering expedition, come back, and try to capture the presidency. Now and then one succeeds." The consul yawned. "Then the diplomatic corps here in Caracas have to get used to a different sort of ... of ... President." He paused, smiling at some recollection, then added, "So, you see, one can hardly blame the powers that be for wanting to keep rifles out of the country."

The young man was openly disappointed.

"Well, ... that's very interesting historically," he said with a mirthless smile, "and I am sure when I send in my expense account for this trip my house will be deeply interested in the historical reasons why I blew in five hundred dollars and landed nothing."

"Well, that's the state of affairs," repeated the consul, with the sudden briskness of a man ending an interview. "Insurrectionists in Tachira, old Fombombo raising hell on the Rio Negro, and an occasional flyer among the filibusters." He rose and offered his hand to his caller. "Be glad to have you drop in on me any time, Mr. Strawbridge. Occasionally I give a little soirée here for Americans. Send you a bid." He was shaking hands warmly now, after the fashion of politicians. His air implied that Mr. Strawbridge's visit had been sheer delight. And Mr. Strawbridge's own business-trained cordiality picked up somewhat even under his unexpressed disappointment. In fact, he was just loosing the diplomat's hand when he discovered there was a bit of paper in Mr. Anderson's palm pressing against his own. When the consul withdrew his hand he left the paper in his countryman's fingers.

"Well, good-by; good luck! Don't forget to look me up again. When you leave Caracas you'd better give me your forwarding address for any mail that might come in."

The consul was walking down the tiled entrance of the consulate, floating his guest out in a stream of somewhat mechanical cordiality. Strawbridge moved into the dazzling sunshine, clenching the bit of paper and making confused adieus.

He walked briskly away, with the quick, machine-like strides of an American drummer. After a block or two he paused in the shade of a great purple flowering shrub that gushed over the high adobe wall of some hidden garden. Out of the direct sting of the sun he found opportunity to look into his hand. It held a sheet of the scratch-pad. This bore the address, "General Adriano Fombombo, No. 27 Eschino San Dolores y Hormigas." Inside the fold was the sentence, "This will introduce to you a very worthy young American, Mr. Thomas Strawbridge, a young man of discretion, prompt decision, strict morals, and unimpeachable honesty." It bore no signature.

Strawbridge turned it over and perused the address for upward of half a minute. Now and then he looked up and down the street, then at the numbers on the houses, after the fashion of a man trying to orient himself in a strange city.

CHAPTER II

In the capital of Venezuela, ancient usage has given names to the street corners instead of to the streets. This may have been very well in the thinly populated days of the Spanish conquest, but to-day this nomenclature forms a hopeless puzzle for half the natives and all the foreigners.

To Mr. Thomas Strawbridge the address on the consul's note was especially annoying. He hardly knew what to do. He could not go back and ask Mr. Anderson where was Eschino San Dolores y Hormigas, because in a way there was a tacit understanding between the two men that no note had passed between them. On the other hand, he felt instinctively that it was not good revolutionary practice to wander about the streets of Caracas inquiring of Tomas, Ricardo, and Henrico the address of a well-known insurrectionary general. However, he would have to do just that thing if he carried out the business hint given him by the consul. It was annoying, it might even be dangerous, but there seemed to be no way out of it. It never occurred to the drummer to give the matter up. The prospect of a sale was something to be pursued at all hazards. So he put the note in his pocket, got out a big silver cigar-case with his monogram flowing over one of its sides, lit up, frowned thoughtfully at the sun-baked streets, then moved off aimlessly from his patch of shade, keeping a weather eye out for some honest, trustworthy Venezuelan who could be depended upon to betray his country in a small matter.

As the American pursued this odd quest, the usual somnolent street life of Caracas drifted past him: a train of flower-laden donkeys, prodded along by a peon boy, passed down the *calle*, braying terrifically; native women in black mantillas glided in and out of the ancient Spanish churches, one of which stood on almost every corner; lottery-ticket venders loitered through the streets, yodeling the numbers on their tickets; naked children played in the sewer along foot-wide pavements; dark-eyed señoritas sat inside barred windows, with a lover swinging patiently outside the bars. Banana peels, sucked oranges, and mango stones littered the *calles* from end to end and advertised the slovenliness of the denizens.

All this increased in Strawbridge that feeling of mental, moral, and racial superiority which surrounds every Anglo-Saxon in his contacts with other peoples. How filthy, how slow, how indecent, and how immoral it all was! Naked children, lottery venders, caged girls! Evidently the girls could not be trusted to walk abroad. Strawbridge looked at them—tropical creatures with creamy skins, jet hair, and dark, limpid eyes; soft of contour, voice, and glance.

A group of four domino-players were at a game just outside a *peluqueria*. A fifth man, holding a guitar, leaned against a little shrine to the Blessed Virgin which some pious hand had built into the masonry at the corner of the adobe. He was a graceful, sunburned fellow, and as he bent his head over the guitar, during his intermittent strumming, Strawbridge was surprised to see that his hair was done up like a woman's, in a knot at the back of his head.

Just why the American should have decided to ask this particular man for delicate information, it is impossible to say. It may have been because he was leaning against a shrine, or because he showed splendid white teeth as he smiled at the varying fortunes of the players. There is a North American superstition that a man with good teeth also possesses good morals. If one can believe the dentifrice advertisements, a good tooth-paste is a ticket to heaven. At any rate, for these or other reasons, the drummer moved across the *calle* and came to a stand, with his own hand resting on the base of the little clay niche that sheltered the small china Virgin. He was so close to the man that he could smell the rank pomade on his knob of hair. He stood in silence until his nearness should have established that faint feeling of fellowship which permits a question to be asked between two watchers of the same scene. Presently he inquired in a casual tone, but not loud enough for the players to hear:

"Señor, can you tell me where is Eschino San Dolores y Hormigas?"

The strumming paused a moment. The man with the knot of hair gave Strawbridge a brief glance out of the corners of his eyes, then resumed his desultory picking at the strings.

"How should I know where is Eschino San Dolores y Hormigas?" he replied in the same nonchalant undertone.

"I thought perhaps you were a native of this town."

"*Pues*, you are a stranger?"

"Yes."

"*Un Americano*, I would say?"

"Yes."

The strumming proceeded smoothly.

"Señor, in your country, is it not the custom in searching for an address to inquire of the police?"

A little trickle of uneasiness went through the American's diaphragm.

"Certainly," he agreed, with a faint stiffness in his undertone, "but when there is no policeman in sight, one can inquire of any *gentleman*."

The man with the knob of hair muted his guitar, then lifted his hand and pointed.

"Yonder stands one, two corners down, señor."

"*Gracias*, señor." Strawbridge had a feeling as if a path he meant to climb along a precipice had begun crumbling very gently under his feet. "*Gracias*; I'll just step down there." He made a little show of withdrawing his attention casually from the game, glanced about, got the direction of the policeman in question, then moved off unhurriedly toward that little tan-uniformed officer.

As he went, Strawbridge tried quickly to think of some other question to ask the police. He wondered if it would be best not to go up to the officer at all. If he knew the man with the hair was not looking after him.... He was vaguely angry at everything and everybody—at Venezuela for making a law that would force an American salesman to go about the important function of business like a thief; at the consul for not giving him complete sailing instructions; at himself for asking ticklish questions of a man with a wad of hair. He might have known there was something tricky about a man like that!

Then his thoughts swung around to the nation again. He began swearing mentally at the basic reason of his slightly uncomfortable position. "Damn country is not run on business principles," he carped in his thoughts. "Looks like they're not out for business. Then what the hell are they out for? Why, they were all trying to pull crooked deals, overcharging, milking the customs! One honest, upright, strictly business American department-store down here in Caracas would grab the business from these yellow sons of guns like a burglar taking candy from a sick baby!" He moved along, pouring the acid of a righteous indignation over his surroundings. However, he was now approaching the policeman, and he stopped insulting the Venezuelan nation, to think of a plan to circumvent it.

He was again beginning to debate whether or not he should make a show of going to the officer at all, when he heard the thrumming of a guitar just behind him. He looked around quickly and saw that the man with the knot of hair had followed him. Then Strawbridge realized that not only would he have to go to the policeman, but he would have to inquire for the actual address in order to maintain an appearance of innocence. Right here he lost his order! He damned his luck unhappily and was on the verge of crossing the street, when the man with the knob of hair continued their conversation, in the same low tone they had used:

"By the way, señor, I just happened to recall an errand of my own at the address you inquired for, if you care to go along with me."

"Why, sure!" accepted Strawbridge, vastly relieved. He drew out a silk handkerchief and touched the moisture on his face. "Sure! Be glad to have your company."

The man began tinkling again.

"I suppose you are going to ... er ... to the house with the blue front?" He lifted his eyebrows slightly.

"I'm looking for Number ... I never was there before, so I don't know what color the house is."

"No?" The guitarist lifted his brows still more. He seemed really surprised. But the next moment his attention broke away. He smote his guitar to a purpose, and broke out in a bold tenor voice:

"Thine eyes are cold, thine eyes are cold to me.

   Would I could kindle in their depths a flame.

I bring my heart, a bold torero's heart to thee."

The American was startled at this sudden outbreak of song, but no one else took any notice of it. That is, no one except a girl inside a barred window, who dropped a rose through the grille and withdrew. As the two men passed this spot, the singer stooped for the flower and in a shaken voice murmured into the window, "Little heaven!" and somewhere inside a girl laughed.

The two men walked on a few paces, when the guitarist shrugged, spread a hand, and said:

"They always laugh at you!"

Strawbridge stared at him.

"Who?" he asked.

"A bride ... that bride ... any bride."

The American had been so absorbed in the matter of the police and the street address that he had followed none of this by-play.

"A bride?" he repeated blankly.

"Yes, she married three nights ago. *Caramba!* The house was crowded, and everybody was tipsy. The guests overflowed out here, into the *calle*...." He broke off to look back at the window, after a moment waved his hand guardedly, then turned around and resumed his observations:

"Don't you think there is something peculiarly attractive ... well, now ... er ... provocative in a young girl who has just been married?"

The American stared at his new acquaintance, vaguely outraged.

"Why—great God!—no!"

CHAPTER III

The man with the knob of hair came to a halt, and pointed on a long angle across the street.

"That big blue house, señor. I'll come on more slowly and pass you. There is no use for two men to be seen waiting outside the door at one time."

This touch of prudence reassured Strawbridge more than any other thing the stranger could have said. The drummer nodded briskly and walked ahead of his companion toward the building indicated. It was one of a solid row of houses all of which had the stuccoed fronts and ornamental grilles that mark the better class of Caracas homes. The American paused in front of the big double door and pressed a button. He waited a minute or two and pushed again.

Nothing happened. A faint breeze moved a delicate silk curtain in one of the barred windows, but beyond that the *casa* might have been empty. The silent street of old Spanish houses, their polychrome fronts, and somewhere the soft, guttural quarreling of pigeons wove a poetic mood in Strawbridge's brain. It translated itself into the thought of a huge order for his house and a rich commission for himself. He began calculating mentally what his per cent. would be on, say, ten thousand cases of cartridges—or even twenty thousand. Here began a pleasant multiplication of twenty thousand by thirty-nine dollars and forty-two cents. That would be ... it would be....

The sonnet of his mood was broken by the guitarist, who walked past him, snarling:

"*Diablo, hombre!* You'll never get in that way! Ring once, then four short rings, then a second long, then three." He walked on.

This brought Strawbridge back to the fact that his order had not yet reached the stage where he could count his profits. He pressed the button again, using the combination the knob-haired man had given him.

Immediately a small panel in the great door opened and framed the head of a negro sucking a mango. The head withdrew and a moment later a whole panel in the door and a corresponding panel in the iron grille opened and admitted the drummer. Strawbridge stepped into a cool entrance of blue-flowered tiles which led into a bright patio. He looked around curiously, seeking some hint of the revolutionist in his *casa*.

"Is your master at home?" he asked of the negro.

The black wore the peculiarly stupid expression of the boors of his race. He answer in a negroid Spanish:

"No, seño', he ain't in."

"When'll he be in?"

The negro lowered his head and swung his protruding jaws from side to side, as though denying all knowledge of the comings and goings of his master.

Strawbridge hesitated, speculated on the advisability of delivering his note to any such creature, finally did draw it out, and stood holding it in his hand.

"Could you deliver this note to your master?"

"If de Lawd's willin' an' I lives to see him again, seño'."

Strawbridge was faintly amused at such piety.

"I don't suppose the Lord will object to your delivering this note," he said.

"No, seño'," agreed the black man, solemnly, and Strawbridge placed the folded paper in the numskull's hands.

The creature took it, looked blankly at the address, then unfolded it and with the same emptiness of gaze fixed his eyes on the message.

"It goes to General Fombombo," explained Strawbridge.

"Gen'l Fombombo," repeated the negro, as if he were memorizing an unknown name.

"Yes, and inside it says that ... er ... ah ... it says that I am an honest man."

"A honest man."

"Yes, that's what it says."

"I thought you was a *Americano*, seño'."

Strawbridge looked at the negro, but his humble expression appeared guileless.

"I am an American," he nodded. "Now, just hand that to your master and tell him he can communicate with me at the Hotel Bolivia." Strawbridge was about to go.

"*Sí*, seño'," nodded the servant, throwing away the mango stone. "I tell him about de *Americano*. I heard about yo' country, seño', *el grand America del Norte*; so cold in de rainy season you freeze to death, so hot in de dry season you drap dead. *Sí*, seño', but ever'body rich—dem what ain't froze to death or drap dead."

"Sounds like you'd been there," said the drummer, gravely.

"I never was, but I wish I could go. Do you need a servant in yo' line o' business, seño'?"

"I don't believe I do."

"Don't you sell things?"

"Sometimes."

"What, seño'?"

"I sell—" then, recalling the private nature of this particular prospect, he finished—"almost anything any one will buy."

This answer apparently satisfied the garrulous black, who nodded and pursued his childish curiosity:

"An' when you sell something do you have it sent from away up in *America del Norte* down here?"

"Sure."

"An' us git it?"

Strawbridge laughed.

"If you're lucky."

The black man scratched his head at this growing complication of the drummer's sketch of the North American export trade. Then he discovered a gap in his information.

"Seño', you ain't said what it is you sell, yit."

"That's right," agreed Strawbridge, looking at the fool a little more carefully. "I have not." Then he added, "A man doesn't talk his business to every one."

The negro nodded gravely.

"Dat's right, but still you's bound to talk your business somewhere, to sell anybody at all, seño'."

"That's true," acceded the American, with a dim feeling that perhaps this black fellow was not the idiot he had at first appeared.

"And how would you git paid, away up there in America?" persisted the black.

The American decided to answer seriously.

"Here's the way we do it. We ship the ... the goods ... down here and at the same time draw a draft on a bank here in Caracas. We get our pay when the goods are delivered, but the bank extends the buyer six, nine, or twelve months' credit, whatever he needs. That is the accepted business method between North and South America."

The drummer was not sure the black man understood a word of this. The fellow stood scratching his head and pulling down his thick lips. Finally he said, speaking more correctly:

"Señor, I was not thinking about the time a person had to pay in. It was how you could get paid at all."

"How I could get paid at all?"

The negro nodded humbly, and his dialect grew a trifle worse:

"You see, if anybody was to go an' put a lot o' money in de banks here in Caracas, most likely de Guv'ment would snatch it right at once."

Strawbridge came to attention and stood studying the African.

"How would the Government ever know?" he asked carefully.

"How would you ever keep 'em from knowin'?" retorted the negro. "How could anybody, seño', even a po' fool nigger like me, drive a string o' ox-carts through de country, loaded wid gold, drive up to the bank do' an' pile out sacks o' gold an' not have ever'body in Caracas know all about it?"

The suggestion of gold, of wagon-loads of gold delivered to banks, sent a sensation through Strawbridge as if he had been a harp on which some musician had struck a mighty chord. As he stood staring at the black man his mouth went slightly dry and he moistened his lips with his tongue.

"I see the trouble," he said in a queer voice.

His vis-à-vis nodded silently.

The negro with the mango juice on his face and the trig white man stood studying each other in the blue entrance.

"Well," said Strawbridge, at last, "how will I get the money?"

"Where?"

"Here."

"Impossible, señor."

Strawbridge was getting on edge. He laughed nervously.

"You seem to know more about ... er ... certain conditions in this country than I do. What would you suggest?"

The black cocked his head a little to one side.

"Seño', did you know that the Orinoco River and the Amazon connect with each other up about the Rio Negro?"

"I think I've heard it. Didn't some fellow go through there studying orchids, or something? A man was telling me something about that in Trinidad."

"He went through studying everything, seño'," said the black man, solemnly. "You are thinking of the great savant, Humboldt."

"M—yes, ... Humboldt." Strawbridge repeated the name vaguely, not quite able to place it.

"I would suggest that you follow Herr Humboldt's route, seño'. You can carry the bullion down in boats and get it exchanged for drafts in Rio."

A dizzy foreshadowing of Indian canoes laden with treasure, pushing through choked tropical waterways, shook the drummer. He drew a long breath.

"Is it a practical route? I mean, does anybody know the way? Do you think it can be done?"

"I would hardly say practical, seño'. It has been done."

The negro and the white man stood looking at each other.

"How do I ... er ... how does any one get to Rio Negro?" asked the drummer, nervously.

"You will need some person to pilot you, seño': some black man would make a good guide."

"Now, I just imagine he would," said Strawbridge, drawing in his lips and biting them. "Yes, sir, I imagine he would—" He broke off and suddenly became direct: "When do we start?"

"When you feel like it, seño'—now, if you are ready."

"I stay ready. How do we get there?" He asked the question with a vague feeling that the black man might climb up to the roof of the blue house and show him a flying-machine.

"I have a little motor around at the garage, seño'."

"Uh-huh? Well, that's good. Let's go."

The negro went into a room for an old hat. He took a key from his pocket, opened the door, and courteously bowed the American into the *calle*. When he had locked the door behind them, he said, "Now you go in front, seño'," and indicated the direction down the street. Strawbridge did so, the negro following a little distance behind. They looked like master and servant set forth on some trifling errand.

They had not gone very far before Strawbridge observed that two or three blocks behind them came the guitarist. This fellow meandered along with elaborate inattention to either the white man or the negro.

CHAPTER IV

Now that his rôle of ignoramus and lout had been played, the black man introduced himself as Guillermo Gumersindo and glided into the usual self-explanatory conversation. He was sure Señor Strawbridge would pardon his buffoonery, but one had to be careful when a police visitation was threatened. He was the editor of a newspaper in Canalejos, "El Correo del Rio Negro," a newspaper, if he did say it, more ardently devoted to Venezuelan history than any other publication in the republic. Gumersindo had been chosen by General Fombombo to make this purchasing expedition to Caracas just because he was black and could drop easily into a lowly rôle.

To the ordinary white American an educated negro is an object of curious interest, and Strawbridge strolled along the streets of Caracas with a feeling toward the black editor much the same as one has toward the educated pony which can paw out its name from among the letters of the alphabet.

Gumersindo's historical interest exhibited itself as he and Strawbridge passed through the *mercado*, a plaza given over to hucksters and flower-venders, in the heart of Caracas. The black man pointed out a very fine old Spanish house of blue marble, with a great coat of arms carved over the door:

"Where Bolivar lived." Gumersindo made a curving gesture and bowed as if he were introducing the building.

The American looked at the house.

"Bolivar," he repeated vaguely.

The editor opened his eyes slightly.

"*Sí*, señor; Bolivar the *Libertador*."

The black man's tone showed Strawbridge that he should have known Bolivar the *Libertador*.

"Oh, sure!" the drummer said easily; "the *Libertador*. I had forgot his business."

The black man looked around at his companion as straight as his politeness admitted.

"Señor," he ejaculated, "I mean the great Bolivar. He has been compared to your Señor George Washington of North America."

Strawbridge turned and stared frankly at the negro.

"Wha-ut?" he drawled, curving up his voice at the absurdity of it and beginning to laugh. "Compared to George Washington, first in war, first in—"

"*Sí, ciertamente,* señor," Gumersindo assured his companion, with Venezuelan earnestness.

"But look here—" Strawbridge laid a hand on his companion's shoulder—"do you know what George Washington did, man? He set the whole United States free!"

"But, *hombre!*" cried the editor. "Bolivar! This great, great man—" he pointed to the blue marble mansion—"set free the whole continent of South America!"

"He did!"

"*Seguramente!* And this man, who freed a continent, was at length exiled by ungrateful Venezuela and died an outcast, señor, in a wretched little town on the Colombian coast—an outcast!"

Strawbridge looked at Bolivar's house with renewed interest.

"Well, I be damned!" he said earnestly. "Freed all of South America! Say! why don't somebody write a book about that?"

Gumersindo pulled in one side of his wide-rolling lips and bit them. The two men walked on in silence for several blocks west. They passed the Yellow House, the seat of the Venezuelan Government. On the south side of this building stands a monument with a big scar on the pedestal, where some name has been roughly chiseled out. The negro explained that this monument had been erected by the tyrant Barranca, who occupied the Venezuelan presidency for eight years, but that when Barranca was overthrown by General Pina, the oppressed people, in order to show their hatred of the fallen tyrant, erased his name from the monument.

Strawbridge stood looking at the scar and nodding.

"Did they have to rise against this man Barranca to get him out of office?" he asked in surprise.

"Rise against him!" cried Gumersindo. "Rise against him! Why, señor, the only way any Venezuelan president ever did go out of office was by some stronger man rising against him! But come: I will show you, on Calvario."

They moved quickly along the street, which was changing its character somewhat, from a business street to a thoroughfare of cheap residences. After going some distance Strawbridge saw the small mountain called Calvario which rises in the western part of the city. The whole eastern face of this mountain had been done into a great flight of ornamental steps. Half-way up was a terrace containing three broken pedestals.

"These," decried Gumersindo, "were erected by the infamous Pina, but when Pina was assassinated and the assassin Wantzelius came into power, the people, infuriated by Pina's long extravagances, tore down the statues he had erected and broke them to pieces." The black man stood looking with compressed lips at the shattered monoliths in the sunshine.

There was a certain incredulity in Strawbridge's face. The American could not understand such a social state.

"And you say they just keep on that way—one president overthrowing another?"

"Precisely. Wantzelius had Pina assassinated, Toro Torme overthrew Wantzelius, Cancio betrayed and exiled Toro Torme...."

The American arms salesman stood on the stairs of Calvario, beneath the broken pedestals, and began to laugh.

"Well, that's a hell of a way to change presidents—shoot 'em—run 'em off—exile 'em! It's just exactly like these greaser Latin countries!" He sat down on the stairs in the hot sunshine and laughed till the tears rolled out of his eyes.

The thick-set negro stood looking at him with a queer expression.

"It ... seems to amuse you, señor?"

Strawbridge drew out his handkerchief and wiped his eyes. He blew out a long breath.

"It is funny! Just like a movie I saw in Keokuk. It was called 'Maid in Mexico,' and it showed how these damned greasers batted along in any crazy old way; and here is the wreckage of just some such rough stuff." He looked up at the broken pedestals again with his face set for mirth, but his jaws ached too badly to laugh any more. He drew a deep breath and became near-sober.

Just below him stood the negro, like a black shadow in the sunshine. He stared with a solemn face over the city with its sea of red-tiled roofs, its domes and campaniles, and the blue peaks of the Andes beyond. Abruptly he turned to Strawbridge.

"Listen, señor," he said tensely, and held up a finger. "My country has lived in mortal agony ever since Bolivar himself fell from his seat of power amid red rebellion, but there is a man who will remedy Venezuela's age-long wounds; there is a man great enough and generous enough—"

At this point some remnant of mirth caused Strawbridge to compress his lips to keep from laughing again. The dark being on the steps stopped his discourse quite abruptly; then he said with a certain severity:

"Let us understand each other, señor. You sell rifles and ammunition; do you not?"

"Yes," said Strawbridge, sobering at once at this hint of business.

Gumersindo took a last glance at the city sleeping in the fulgor of a tropical noon:

"Let's get to the garage," he suggested briefly.

CHAPTER V

Gumersindo's automobile turned out to be one of those cheap American machines which one finds everywhere. Its only peculiarity was an extra gasolene-tank which filled the greater part of the body of the car, and which must have given the old rattletrap a cruising-radius of a thousand or fifteen hundred miles.

Just as the negro and the white man were getting into the car the man with the knot of hair at the back of his head strolled into the garage. He called to Gumersindo that the *Americano* was to take him on the expedition which was just starting.

The black editor looked up and stared.

"Take you!"

"*Sí*, señor, me. This *caballero*—" he nodded at Strawbridge—"promised to take me along for the courtesy of directing him to ... well ... to a certain address."

Strawbridge heard this with the surprise an American always feels when a Latin street-runner begins manufacturing charges for his service.

"The devil I did! I said nothing about taking you along. I didn't know where I was going. I still don't know."

"*Caramba!*" The man with the hair spread his hands in amazement. "Did I not say we would go to the same address, and did not you agree to it!"

"But, you damn fool, you know I meant the address here in Caracas! Good Lord! you know I didn't propose to take you a thousand miles!"

The man with the hair made a strong gesture.

"That's not Lubito, señor!" he declared. "That's not Lubito. When a man attaches himself to me in friendly confidence, I'm not the man to break with him the moment he has served my purpose. No, I will see you through!"

"But—damnation, man!—I don't want you to see me through!"

"*Cá!* You don't! You go back on your trade!"

The American snapped his fingers and motioned toward the door of the garage.

"Beat it!"

The man with the hair flared up suddenly and began talking the most furious Spanish:

"*Diantre! Bien, bien, bien!* I'll establish my trade! I'll call the police and establish my trade! Ray of God, but I'm an honest man!" and he started for the door, beginning to peer around for a policeman before he was nearly out. "Yes, we'll have a police investigation!" He disappeared.

Strawbridge looked at Gumersindo, and then by a common impulse the black editor and the white drummer started for the door, after the man with the hair. The editor hailed him as he was walking rapidly down the *calle*:

"Hold on, my friend; come back!"

Lubito whirled and started back as rapidly as he had departed. His movements were extraordinarily supple and graceful even for Latin America, where grace and suppleness are common.

"We have decided that we may be able to carry you along after all, Señor Lubito. We may even be of some mutual service. What is your profession?"

"I am, señor, a bull-fighter." He tipped up his handsome head and struck a bull-ring attitude, perhaps unconsciously. The negro editor stared at him, glanced at Strawbridge, and shrugged faintly but hopelessly.

"Very good," he said in a dry tone. "We want you. No expedition would care to set out across the llanos without a bull-fighter or two."

If he hoped by voice and manner to discourage Lubito's attendance, he was disappointed. The fellow walked briskly back and was the first man in the car.

The other two men followed, and as the motor clacked away down the *calle* Lubito resumed the rôle of cicerone, cheerfully pointing out to Strawbridge the sights of Caracas. There was the palace of President Cancio; there was an old church built by the Canary Islanders who made a settlement in this part of Caracas long before the colonies revolted against Spain.

"There is La Rotunda, señor, where they keep the political prisoners. It is very easy to get in there." Whether this was mere tourist information or a slight flourish of the whip-hand, which Lubito undoubtedly held, Strawbridge did not know.

"Have they got many prisoners?" he asked casually.

"It's full," declared the bull-fighter, with gusto. "The overflow goes to Los Castillos, another prison on the Orinoco near Ciudad Bolívar, and also to San Carlos on Lake Maracaibo, in the western part of Venezuela."

"What have so many men done, that all the prisons are jammed?" asked the drummer, becoming interested.

It was Gumersindo who answered this question, and with passion:

"Señor Strawbridge, those prisons are full of men who are innocent and guilty. Some have attempted to assassinate the President, some to stir up revolution; some are merely suspected. A number of men are put in prison simply to force through some business deal advantageous to the governmental clique. I know one editor who has been confined in the dungeons of La Rotunda for ten years. His offense was that in his paper he proposed a man as a candidate for the presidency."

Strawbridge was shocked.

"Why, that's outrageous! What do the people stand for it for? Why don't they raise hell and stop any such crooked deals? Why, in America, do you know how long we would stand for that kind of stuff? Just one minute—" he reached forward and tapped Gumersindo two angry taps on the shoulder—"just one minute; that's all."

Lubito laughed gaily.

"Yes, La Rotunda to-day is full of men who stood that sort of thing for one minute—and then raised hell."

Strawbridge looked around at the bull-fighter.

"But, my dear man, if everybody, everybody would go in, who could stop them?"

Gumersindo made a gesture.

"Señor Strawbridge, there is no 'everybody' in Venezuela. When you say 'everybody' you are speaking as an American, of your American middle class. That is the controlling power in America because it is sufficiently educated and compact to make its majority felt. We have no such class in Venezuela. We have an aristocratic class struggling for power, and a great peon population too ignorant for any political action whatsoever. The only hope for Venezuela is a beneficent dictator, and you, señor, on this journey, are about to instate such a man and bring all these atrocities to a close."

A touch of the missionary spirit kindled in Strawbridge at the thought that he might really bring a change in such leprous conditions, but almost immediately his mind turned back to the order he was about to receive, how large it would be, how many rifles, how much ammunition, and he fell into a lovely day-dream as the tropical landscape slipped past him.

At thirty- or forty-mile intervals the travelers found villages, and at each one they were forced to report to the police department their arrival and departure. Such is the law in Venezuela. It is an effort to keep watch on any considerable movements among the population and so forestall the chronic revolutions which harass the country. However, the presence of Strawbridge prevented any suspicion on the part of these rural police. Americans travel far and wide over Venezuela as oil-prospectors, rubber-buyers, and commercial salesmen. The police never interfere with their activities.

The villages through which the travelers passed were all just alike—a main street, composed of adobe huts, which widened into a central plaza where a few flamboyants and palms grew through holes in a hard pavement. Always at the end of the plaza stood a charming old Spanish church, looking centuries old, with its stuccoed front, its solid brick campanile pierced by three apertures in which, silhouetted against the sky, hung the bells. In each village the church was the focus of life. And the only sign of animation here was the ringing of the carillon for the different offices. The bell-ringings occurred endlessly, and were quite different from the tolling which Strawbridge was accustomed to hear in North America. The priests rang their bells with the clangor of a fire-alarm. They began softly but swiftly, increased in intensity until the bells roared like the wrath of God over roof and *calle*, and then came to a close with a few slow, solemn strokes.

As is the custom of traveling Americans, Strawbridge compared, for the benefit of his companions, these dirty Latin villages with clean American towns. He pointed out how American towns had an underground sewage system instead of allowing their slops to trickle among the cobblestones down the middle of the street; how American towns had waterworks and electric lights and wide streets; and how if they had a church at all it was certainly not in the public square, raising an uproar on week-days. American churches were kept out of the way, up back streets, and the business part of town was devoted to business.

Here the negro editor interjected the remark that perhaps each people worshiped its own God.

"Sure we do, on Sundays," agreed Strawbridge; "or, at least, the women do; but on week-days we are out for business."

When the motor left the mountains and entered the semi-arid level of the Orinoco basin, the scenery changed to an endless stretch of sand broken by sparse savannah grass and a scattering of dwarf gray trees such as chaparro, alcornoque, manteco. The only industry here was cattle-raising, and this was uncertain because the cattle died by the thousands for lack of water during the dry season. Now and then the motor would come in sight, or scent, of a dead cow, and this led Strawbridge to compare such shiftless cattle-raising with the windmills and irrigation ditches in the American West.

On the fifth day of their drive, the drummer was on this theme, and the bull-fighter—who, after all, was in the car on sufferance—sat nodding his head politely and agreeing with him, when Gumersindo interrupted to point ahead over the llano.

"Speaking of irrigation ditches, señor, yonder is a Venezuelan canal now."

The motor was on one of those long, almost imperceptible slopes which break the level of the llanos. From this point of vantage the motorists could see an enormous distance over the flat country. About half-way to the horizon the drummer descried a great raw yellow gash cut through the landscape from the south. He stared at it in the utmost amazement. Such a cyclopean work in this lethargic country was unbelievable. On the nearer section of the great cut Strawbridge could make out a movement of what seemed to be little red flecks. The negro editor, who was watching the American's face, gave one of his rare laughs.

"Ah, you are surprised, señor."

"Surprised! I'm knocked cold! I didn't know anything this big was being done in Venezuela."

"Well, this isn't exactly in Venezuela, señor."

"No! How's that?"

"We are now in the free and independent territory of Rio Negro, señor. We are now under the jurisdiction of General Adriano Fombombo. You observe the difference at once."

By this time the motor was again below the level of the alcornoque growth and the men began discussing what they had seen.

"What's the object of it?" asked Strawbridge.

"The general is going to canalize at least one half of this entire Orinoco valley. This sandy stretch you see around you, señor, will be as fat as the valley of the Nile."

The idea seized on the drummer's American imagination.

"Why!" he exclaimed, "this is amazing! it's splendid! Why haven't I heard of this? Why haven't the American capitalists got wind of this?"

Gumersindo shrugged.

"The federal authorities are not advertising an insurgent general, señor."

After a moment the drummer ejaculated:

"He will be one of the richest men in the world!"

Gumersindo loosed a hand from the steering-wheel a moment, to hold it up in protest.

"Don't say that! General Fombombo is an idealist, señor. It is his dream to create a super-civilization here in the Orinoco Valley. He will be wealthy; the whole nation will be wealthy,—yes, enormously wealthy,—but what lies beyond wealth? When a people become wealthy, what lies beyond that?"

This was evidently a question which the drummer was to answer, so he said:

"Why, ... they invest that and make still more money." The editor smiled.

"A very American answer! That is the difference, señor, between the middle-class mind and the aristocratic mind. The bourgeois cannot conceive of anything beyond a mere extension of wealth. But wealth is only an instrument. It must be used to some end. Mere brute riches cannot avail a man or a people."

The car rattled ahead as Strawbridge considered the editor's implications that wealth was not the end of existence. It was a mere step, and something lay beyond. Well, what was it, outside of a good time? He thought of some of the famous fortunes in America. Some of their owners made art collections, some gave to charity, some bought divorces. But even to the drummer's casual thinking, there became apparent the rather trivial uses of these fortunes, compared with the fundamental exertion it required to obtain them. Even to Strawbridge it became clear that the use was a step down from the earning.

"What's Fombombo going to do with his?" he asked out of his reverie.

"His what?"

"Fortune—when he makes it?"

"*Pues*, he will found a government where men can forget material care and devote their lives to the arts, the sciences, and pure philosophy. Great cities will gem these llanos, in which poverty is banished; and a brotherhood of intellectuals will be formed—a mental aristocracy, based not on force but on kindliness and good-will."

"I see-e-e," dragged out the drummer. "That's when everybody gets enough wealth—"

"When all devote themselves to altruistic ends," finished the editor.

The drummer was trying to imagine such a system, when Gumersindo clamped on the brakes and brought the car to a sudden standstill. Strawbridge looked up and saw a stocky soldier in the middle of their road, with a carbine leveled at the travelers.

Strawbridge gasped and sat upright. The soldier in the sunshine, with his carbine making a little circle under his right eye, focused the drummer's attention so rigidly that for several moments he could not see anything else. Then he became aware that they had come out upon the canal construction, and that a most extraordinary army of shocking red figures were trailing up and down the sides of the big cut in the sand, like an army of ants. Every worker bore a basket on his head, and his legs were chained together so he could take a step of only medium length.

The guard, a smiling, well-equipped soldier, began an apology for having stopped the car. He had been taking his siesta, he said; the popping of the engine had awakened him, and he had thought some one was trying to rescue some of the workers. He had been half asleep, and he was very sorry.

The cadaverous, unshaven faces of the hobbled men, their ragged red clothes gave Strawbridge a nightmarish impression. They might have been fantasms produced by the heat of the sun.

"What have these fellows done?" asked the American, looking at them in amazement.

The guard paused in his conversation with Gumersindo to look at the American. He shrugged.

"How do I know, señor? I am the guard, not the judge."

Out of the rim of the ditch crept one of the creatures, with scabs about his legs where the chains worked. He advanced toward the automobile.

"Señors," he said in a ghastly whisper, "a little bread! a little piece of meat!"

The guard turned and was about to drive the wretch back into the ditch, when Strawbridge cried out, "Don't! Let him alone!" and began groping hurriedly under the seat for a box where they carried their provisions.

When the other prisoners learned that the motorists were about to give away food, a score of living cadavers came dragging their chains out of the pit, holding out hands that were claws and babbling in all keys, flattened, hoarsened, edged by starvation. "A little here, señor!" "A bit for Christ's sake, señor!" "Give me a bit of bread and take a dying man's blessing, señor!" They stunk, their red rags crawled. Such odors, such lazar faces tickled Strawbridge's throat with nausea. Saliva pooled under his tongue. He spat, gripped his nerves, and asked one of the creatures:

"For God's sake, what brought you here?"

The prisoners were mumbling their *gracias* for each bit of food. One poor devil even refrained, for a moment, from chewing, to answer, "Señor, I had a cow, and the *jefe civil* took my cow and sent me to the 'reds.'" "Señor," shivered another voice, "I ... I fished in the Orinoco. I was never very fortunate. When the *jefe civil* was forced to make up his tally to the 'reds,' he chose me. I was never very fortunate."

An old man whose face was all eyes and long gray hair had got around on the side of the car opposite to the guard. He leaned toward Strawbridge, wafting a revolting odor.

"Señor," he whispered, "I had a pretty daughter. I meant to give her to a strong lad called Esteban, for a wife, but the *jefe civil* suddenly broke up my home and sent me to the 'reds.' She was a pretty girl, my little Madruja. Señor, can it be, by chance, that you are traveling toward Canalejos?"

The American nodded slightly into the sunken eyes.

"Then, for our Lady's sake, señor, if she is not already lost, be kind to my little Madruja! Give her a word from me, señor. Tell her ... tell her—" he looked about him with his ghastly hollow eyes—"tell her that her old father is ... well, and kindly treated on ... on account of his age."

Just then the bull-fighter leaned past the American.

"You say this girl is in Canalejos, señor?" he broke in.

"*Sí*, señor."

"Then the Holy Virgin has directed you to the right person, señor. I am Lubito, the bull-fighter, a man of heart." He touched his athletic chest. "I will find your little Madruja, señor, and care for her as if she were my own."

The convict reached out a shaking claw.

"*Gracias á Madre in cielo! Gracias á San Pedro! Gracias á la Vírgen Inmaculada!*" Somehow a tear had managed to form in the wretch's dried and sunken eye.

"You give her to me, señor?"

"*O sí, sí! un millón gracias!*"

"You hear that, Señor Strawbridge: the poor little bride Madruja, in Canalejos, is now under my protection."

The drummer felt a qualm, but said nothing, because, after all, nothing was likely to come from so shadowy a trust. The red-garbed skeleton tried to give more thanks.

"Come, come, don't oppress me with your gratitude, *viejo*. It is nothing for me. I am all heart. Step away from in front of the car so we may start at once. *Vamose*, señors! Let us fly to Canalejos!"

Gumersindo let in his clutch, there was a shriek of cogs, and the motor plowed through the sand. The bull-fighter turned and waved good-by to the guard and smiled gaily at the ancient prisoner. The motor crossed the head of the dry canal, and the party looked down into its cavernous depths. As the great work dropped into the distance behind them, the dull-red convicts and their awful faces followed Strawbridge with the persistence of a bad dream. At last he broke out:

"Gumersindo, is it possible that those men back there have committed no crime?"

The negro looked around at him.

"Some have and some have not, señor."

"Was the fisherman innocent? Was the old man with the daughter innocent?"

"It is like this, Señor Strawbridge," said Gumersindo, watching his course ahead. "The *jefes civiles* of the different districts must make up their quota of men to work on the canal. They select all the idlers and bad characters they can, but they need more. Then they select for different reasons. All the *jefes civiles* are not angels. Sometimes they send a man to the 'reds' because they want his cow, or his wife or his daughter—"

"Is this the beginning of Fombombo's brotherhood devoted to altruistic ends!" cried Strawbridge.

"*Mi caro amigo*," argued the editor, with the amiability of a man explaining a well-thought-out premise, "why not? There must be a beginning made. The peons will not work except under compulsion. Shall the whole progress of Rio Negro be stopped while some one tries to convince a stupid peon population of the advisability of laboring? They would never be convinced."

"But that is such an outrageous thing—to take an innocent man from his work, take a father from his daughter!"

The editor made a suave gesture.

"Certainly, that is simply applying a military measure to civil life, drafted labor. The sacrifice of a part for the whole. That has always been the Spanish idea, señor. The first conquistadors drafted labor among the Indians. The Spanish Inquisition drafted saints from a world of sinners. If one is striving for an ultimate good, señor, one cannot haggle about the price."

"But that isn't doing those fellows right!" cried Strawbridge, pointing vehemently toward the canal they had left behind. "It isn't doing those particular individuals right!"

"A great many Americans did not want to join the army during the war. Was it right to draft them?" Gumersindo paused a moment, and then added: "No, Señor Strawbridge; back of every aristocracy stands a group of workers represented by the 'reds.' It is the price of leisure for the superior man, and without leisure there is no superiority. Where one man thinks and feels and flowers into genius, señor, ten must slave. Weeds must die that fruit may grow. And that is the whole content of humanity, señor, its fruit."

Two hours later the negro pointed out a distant town purpling the horizon. It was Canalejos.

Strawbridge rode forward, looking at General Fombombo's capital city. The houses were built so closely together that they resembled a walled town. As the buildings were constructed of sun-dried brick, the metropolis was a warm yellow in common with the savannahs. It was as if the city were a part of the soil, as if the winds and sunshine somehow had fashioned these architectural shapes as they had the mesas of New Mexico and Arizona.

The whole scene was suffused with the saffron light of deep afternoon. It reminded the drummer of a play he had seen just before leaving New York. He could not recall the name of the play, but it opened with a desert scene, and a beggar sitting in front of a temple. There was just such a solemn yellow sunset as this.

As the drummer thought of these things the motor had drawn close enough to Canalejos for him to make out some of the details of the picture. Now he could see a procession of people moving along the yellow walls of the city. Presently, above the putter of the automobile, he heard snatches of a melancholy singing. The bull-fighter leaned forward in his seat and watched and listened. Presently he said with a certain note of concern in his voice:

"Gumersindo, that's a wedding!"

"I believe it is," agreed the editor.

Lubito hesitated, then said:

"Would you mind putting on a little more speed, señor? It ... it would be interesting to find out whose wedding it is."

Without comment the negro fed more gasolene. As the motor whirled cityward, the bull-fighter sat with both hands gripping the front seat, staring intently as the wedding music of the peons came to them, with its long-drawn, melancholy burden.

Strawbridge leaned back, listening and looking. He was still thinking about the play in New York and regretting the fact that in real life one never saw any such dramatic openings. In real life it was always just work, work, work—going after an order, or collecting a bill—never any drama or romance, just dull, prosy, commonplace business ... such as this.

CHAPTER VI

Canalejos was no exception to the general rule that all Venezuelan cities function upon a war basis. At the entrance of a *calle*, just outside the city wall, stood a faded green sentry-box. As the motor drove up, a sentry popped out of the box, with a briskness and precision unusual in Venezuela. He stood chin up, heels together, quite as if he were under some German martinet. With a snap he handed the motorists the police register and jerked out, from somewhere down in his thorax, military fashion:

"Hup ... your names ... point of departure ... destination ... profession...."

It amused Strawbridge to see a South American performing such military antics. It was like a child playing soldier. He was moved to mimic the little fellow by grunting back in the same tones, "Hup ... Strawbridge ... Caracas ... Canalejos ... sell guns and ammunition...." Then he wrote those answers in the book.

An anxious look flitted across the face of the sentry at this jocularity. His stiff "eyes front" flickered an instant toward the sentry-box. While the negro and the bull-fighter were filling in the register, a peon came riding up on a black horse. He stopped just behind the motor and with the immense patience of his kind awaited his turn.

While his two companions were signing, Strawbridge yielded to that impulse for horse-play which so often attacks Americans who are young and full-blooded. He leaned out of the motor very solemnly, lifted the cap of the sentry, turned the visor behind, and replaced it on his head. The effect was faintly but undeniably comic. The little soldier's face went beet-colored. At the same moment came a movement inside the sentry-box and out of the door stepped a somewhat corpulent man wearing the epaulettes, gold braid, and stars of a general. He was the most dignified man and had the most penetrating eyes that Strawbridge had ever seen in his life. He had that peculiar possessive air about him which Strawbridge had felt when once, at a New York banquet, he saw J. P. Morgan. By merely stepping out of the sentry-box this man seemed to appropriate the *calle*, the motor and men, and the llanos beyond the town. Strawbridge instantly knew that he was in the presence of General Adriano Fombombo, and the gaucherie of having turned around the little sentry's cap set up a sharp sinking feeling in the drummer's chest. For this one stupid bit of foolery he might very well forfeit his whole order for munitions.

Gumersindo leaped out of the car and, with a deep bow, removed his hat.

"Your Excellency, I have the pleasure to report that I accomplished your mission without difficulty, that I have procured an American gentleman whom, if you will allow me the privilege, I will present. General Fombombo, this is Señor Tomas Strawbridge of New York city."

By this time Strawbridge had scrambled out of the motor and extended his hand.

The general, although he was not so tall as the American, nor, really, so large, drew Strawbridge to him, somehow as if the drummer were a small boy.

"I see your long journey from Caracas has not quite exhausted you," he said, with a faint gleam of amusement in his eyes.

Strawbridge felt a deep relief. He glanced at the soldier's cap and began to laugh.

"Thank you," he said; "I manage to travel very well."

The general turned to the negro.

"Gumersindo, telephone my *casa* that Señor Strawbridge will occupy the chamber overlooking the river."

The drummer put up a hand in protest.

"Now, General, I'll go on to the hotel."

The general erased the objection:

"There are no hotels in Canalejos, Señor Strawbridge; a few little eating-houses which the peons use when they come in from the llanos, that is all."

By this time Strawbridge's embarrassment had vanished. The general somehow magnified him, set him up on a plane the salesman had never occupied before.

"Well, General," he began cheerfully, using the American formula, "how's business here in Canalejos?"

"Business?" repeated the soldier, suavely. "Let me see, ... business. You refer, I presume, to commercial products?"

"Why, yes," agreed the drummer, rather surprised.

"*Pues*, the peons, I believe, are gathering balata. The cocoa estancias will be sending in their yield at the end of this month; tonka-beans—"

"Are prices holding up well?" interrupted Strawbridge, with the affable discourtesy of an American who never quite waits till his question is answered.

"I believe so, Señor Strawbridge; or, rather, I assume so; I have not seen a market quotation in...." He turned to the editor: "Señor Gumersindo, you are a journalist; are you *au courant* with the market reports?"

The negro made a slight bow.

"On what commodity, your Excellency?"

"What commodity are you particularly interested in, Señor Strawbridge?" inquired the soldier.

"Why ... er ... just the general trend of the market," said Strawbridge, with a feeling that his little excursion into that peculiar mechanical talk of business, markets, prices, which was so dear to his heart, had not come off very well.

"There has been, I believe, an advance in some prices and a decline in others," generalized Gumersindo; "the usual seasonal fluctuations."

"*Sí, gracias,*" acknowledged the general. "Señor Gumersindo, during Señor Strawbridge's residence in Canalejos, you will kindly furnish him the daily market quotations."

"*Sí,* señor."

The matter of business was settled and disposed of. Came that slight hiatus in which hosts wait for a guest to decide what shall be the next topic. The drummer thought rapidly over his repertoire; he thought of baseball, of Teilman's race in the batting column; one or two smoking-car jokes popped into his head but were discarded. He considered discussing the probable Republican majority Ohio would show in the next presidential election. He had a little book in his vest pocket which gave the vote by states for the past decade. In Pullman smoking-compartments the drummer had found it to be an arsenal of debate. He could make terrific political forecasts and prove them by this little book. But, with his very fingers on it, he decided against talking Ohio politics to an insurgent general in Rio Negro. His thoughts boggled at business again, at the prices of things, when he glanced about and saw Lubito, who had been entirely neglected during this colloquy. The drummer at once seized on his companion to bridge the hiatus. He drew the *espada* to him with a gesture.

"General Fombombo," he said with a salesman's ebullience, "meet Señor Lubito. Señor Lubito is a bull-fighter, General, and they tell me he pulls a nasty sword."

The general nodded pleasantly to the torero.

"I am very glad you have come to Canalejos, Señor Lubito. I think I shall order in some bulls and have an exhibition of your art. If you care to look at our bull-ring in Canalejos, you will find it in the eastern part of our city." He pointed in the direction and apparently brushed the bull-fighter away, for Lubito bowed with the muscular suppleness of his calling and took himself off in the direction indicated.

At that moment the general observed the peon on the black horse, who as yet had not dared to present himself at the sentry-box before the *caballeros*.

"What are you doing on that horse, *bribon?*" asked the general.

"I was waiting to enter, your Excellency," explained the fellow, hurriedly.

"Your name?"

"Guillermo Fando, your Excellency."

"Is that your horse?"

"*Sí*, your Excellency."

"Take it to my cavalry barracks and deliver it to Coronel Saturnino. A donkey will serve your purpose."

Fando's mouth dropped open. He stared at the President.

"T-take my *caballo* to the ... the cavalry...."

A little flicker came into the black eyes of the dictator. He said in a somewhat lower tone:

"Is it possible, Fando, that you do not understand Spanish? Perhaps a little season in La Fortuna...."

The peon's face went mud-colored. "*P-pardon, su excellencia!*" he stuttered, and the next moment thrust his heels into the black's side and went clattering up the narrow *calle*, filling the drowsy afternoon with clamor.

The general watched him disappear, and then turned to Strawbridge.

"*Caramba!* the devil himself must be getting into these peons! Speaking to me after I had instructed him!"

The completely proprietary air of the general camouflaged under a semblance of military discipline the taking of the horse from the peon. It was only after the three men were in Gumersindo's car and on their way to the President's palace that the implications of the incident developed in the drummer's mind. The peon was not in the army; the horse belonged to the peon, and yet Fombombo had taken it with a mere glance and word.

Evening was gathering now. The motor rolled through a street of dark little shops. Here and there a candle-flame pricked a black interior. Above the level line of roofs the east gushed with a wide orange light.

The dictator and the editor had respected the musing mood of their guest and were now talking to each other in low tones. They were discussing Pio Barajo's novels.

In the course of their trip the drummer had that characteristic American feeling that he was wasting time, that here in the car he might get some idea of the general's needs in the way of guns and ammunition. In a pause of the talk about Barajo, he made a tentative effort to speak of the business which had brought him to Canalejos, but the general smoothed this wrinkle out of the conversation, and the talk veered around to Zamacois.

The drummer had dropped back into his original thoughts about the injustice and inequalities of life here in Rio Negro, and what the American people would do in such circumstances, when the motor turned into Plaza Mayor and the motorists saw a procession of torches marching beneath the trees on the other side of the square. Then the drummer observed that the automobile in which he rode and the moving line of torches were converging on the dark front of a massive building. He watched the flames without interest until his own conveyance and the marchers came to a halt in front of the great spread of ornamental stairs that flowed out of the entrance of the palace. A priest in a cassock stood at the head of the procession, and immediately behind him were two peons, a young man and a girl, both in wedding finery. They evidently had come for the legal ceremony which in Venezuela must follow the religious ceremony, for as the car stopped a number of voices became audible: "There is his Excellency!" "In the motor, not in the *palacio*!" The priest lifted his voice:

"Your Excellency, here are a man and a woman who desire—"

While the priest was speaking, a graceful figure ran up the ornamental steps and stood out strongly against the white marble.

"Your Excellency," he called, "I must object to this wedding! I require time. I represent the father of the bride. It is my paternal duty, your Excellency, to investigate this suitor."

Every one in the line stared at the figure on the steps. The priest began in an astonished voice:

"How is this, my son?"

"I represent the father of this girl," asserted the man on the steps, warmly. "I must look into the character of this bridegroom. A father, your Excellency, is a tender relation."

A sudden outbreak came from the party:

"Who is this man?" "What does he mean by 'father'? Madruja's father is with the 'reds.'"

General Fombombo, who had been watching the little scene passively, from the motor, now scrutinized the girl herself. It drew Strawbridge's attention to her. She was a tall pantheress of a girl, and the wavering torchlight at one moment displayed and the next concealed her rather wild black eyes, full lips, and a certain untamed beauty of face. Her husband-elect was a hard, weather-worn youth. The coupling together of two such creatures did seem rather incongruous.

General Fombombo asked a few questions as he stepped out of the car: Who was she? What claim had the man on the steps? He received a chorus of answers none of which were intelligible. All the while he kept scrutinizing the girl, appraising the contours visible through the bridal veil. At last he waggled a finger and said:

"*Cá! Cá!* I will decide this later. The señorita may occupy the west room of the palace to-night, and later I will go into this matter more carefully. I have guests now." He clapped his hands. "Ho, guards!" he called, "conduct the señorita to the west room for the night."

Two soldiers in uniform came running down the steps. The line of marchers shrank from the armed men. The girl stared large-eyed at this swift turn in her affairs. Suddenly she clutched her betrothed's arm.

"Esteban!" she cried. "Esteban!"

The groom stood staring, apparently unable to move as the soldiers hurried down the steps.

By this time General Fombombo was escorting the drummer courteously up the stairs into the deeply recessed entrance of the palace. Strawbridge could not resist looking back to see the outcome of this singular wedding. But now the torchbearers were scattering and all the drummer could see was a confused movement in the gloom, and now and then he heard the sharp, broken shrieks of a woman.

His observations were cut short by General Fombombo who, at the top of the stairs, made a deep bow:

"My house and all that it contains are yours, señor."

Strawbridge bowed as to this stereotype he made the formal response, "And yours also."

CHAPTER VII

As the general led the way into the palace, through a broad entrance hall, the cry of the peon girl still clung to the fringe of Thomas Strawbridge's mind. He put it resolutely aside, and assumed his professional business attitude. That is to say, a manner of complimentary intimacy such as an American drummer always assumes toward a prospective buyer. He laid a warm hand on the general's arm, and indicated some large oil paintings hung along the hallway. He said they were "nifty." He suggested that the general was pretty well fixed, and asked how long he had lived here, in the palace.

"Ever since I seized control of the government in Rio Negro," answered the dictator, simply.

For some reason the reply disconcerted Strawbridge. He had not expected so bald a statement. At that moment came the ripple of a piano from one of the rooms off the hallway. The notes rose and fell, massed by some skilful performer into a continuous tone. Strawbridge listened to it and complimented it.

"Pretty music," he said.

"That is my wife playing—the Señora Fombombo."

"*Is* it!" The drummer's accent congratulated the general on having a wife who could play so well. He tilted his head so the general could see that he was listening and admiring.

"Do you like that sort of music, General?" he asked breezily.

"What sort?"

"That that your wife's playing. It's classic music, isn't it?"

The general was really at a loss. He also began listening, trying to determine whether the music was of the formal classic school of Bach and Handel, or whether it belonged to the later romantic or to the modern. He was unaware that Americans of Strawbridge's type divided all music into two kinds, classic and jazz, and that anything which they do not like falls into the category of classic, and anything they do is jazz.

"I really can't distinguish," admitted the general.

"You bet I can!" declared Strawbridge, briskly. "That's classic. It hasn't got the jump to it, General, the rump-ty, dump-ty, boom! I can feel the lack, you know, the something that's missing. I play a little myself."

The general murmured an acknowledgment of the salesman's virtuosity, and almost at the same moment sounds from the piano ceased. A little later the door of the salon opened and into the hall stepped a slight figure dressed in the bonnet and black robe of a nun.

For such a woman to come out of the music-room gave the drummer a faint surprise; then he surmised that this was one of the sisters from some near-by convent who had come to give piano lessons to Señora Fombombo. The idea was immediately upset by the general:

"Dolores," and, as the nun turned, "Señora Fombombo, allow me to present my friend, Señor Strawbridge."

The strangeness of being presented to a nun who was also the general's wife disconcerted Strawbridge. The girl in the robe was bowing and placing their home at his disposal. The drummer was saying vague things in response: "Very grateful.... The general had insisted.... He hoped that she would feel better soon...." Where under heaven Strawbridge had fished up this last sentiment, he did not know. His face flushed red at so foolish a remark. Señora Fombombo smiled briefly and kindly and went her way down the passage, a somber, religious figure. Presently she opened one of the dull mahogany doors and disappeared.

The general stood looking after his wife thoughtfully and then answered the question which he knew was in his guest's mind:

"My wife wears that costume on account of a vow. Her sister was ill in Madrid, and my wife vowed to the Virgin that if her sister were restored she would wear a Carmelitish habit."

"And she's doing it?" ejaculated Strawbridge, in an amazed voice.

The general made a gesture.

"Her sister was restored."

The American began impulsively:

"Well, I must say that's rather rough on.... Why, her vow had nothing to do with.... You know her sister would have...." It seemed that none of the sentences which the American began could be concluded with courtesy. Finally he was left suspended in air, with a slight perspiration on his face. He drew out a silk handkerchief, dabbed his face, and wiped his wrists.

"General," he floundered on to solider ground, "now, about how many rifles are you going to want?"

The dictator looked at him, almost as much at loss as the drummer had been.

"Rifles?"

"Yes," proceeded the drummer, becoming quite his enthusiastic self again at this veering back to business. "You see, it will depend upon what you are going to do with 'em, how many you will need. If you are just going to hold this state which you have ... er ... seized, why, you won't need so many, but if you are going out and try to grab some more towns, you'll need a lot more."

With a penetrating scrutiny the dictator considered his guest.

"Why do you ask such a question, Señor Strawbridge?" he inquired in a changed tone.

"Because it's your business."

"My business!"

"Why, yes," declared Strawbridge, amiably and with gathering aplomb. "You see, General, when my firm sends out a salesman, the very first rule they teach him is, 'Study your customer's business.' 'Study his business,' said my boss, 'just the same as if it was your own business. Don't oversell him, don't undersell him. Sell him just exactly what he needs. You want your customer to rely on you,' says my old man, 'so you must be reliable. When you sell a man, you have really gone into partnership with him. His gain is your gain.'" By this time Strawbridge was emphasizing his points by thumping earnestly on the dictator's shoulder. "A hundred times I've had my old man say to me, 'Strawbridge, if you don't make your customer's business your own, if his problems are not your problems, if you can't give him expert advice on his difficulties, then you are no salesman; you are simply a mut with a sample case.'"

This eruption of American business philosophy came from Strawbridge as naturally and bubblingly as champagne released from a bottle. He had at last got his prospect's ear and had launched his sales talk. With rather a blank face the general listened to the outburst.

"So you were inquiring through considerations of business?" he asked.

"Exactly; I want to know your probable market. Perhaps I can think up a way to extend it."

"I see." The general was beginning to smile faintly now. "Because I am going to buy some rifles from you, you ask me what cities I am going to attack next."

A slight disconcert played through Strawbridge at this bald statement, but he continued determinedly:

"That's the idea. If you are going to use my guns, I'm partners with you in your ... er ... expansion. That's American methods, General; that's straightforward and honest."

General Fombombo drew in his lips, bit them thoughtfully, and considered Strawbridge. No man with a rudimentary knowledge of human nature could have doubted the drummer's complete sincerity. The general seemed to be repressing a smile.

"Suppose we step into my study, here, a moment, Señor Strawbridge. We might discuss my ... my business, as you put it, if you will excuse its prematurity."

"That's what I'm here for—business," said Strawbridge, earnestly, as he passed in at a door which the dictator opened.

A wall map was the most conspicuous feature of General Fombombo's library, a huge wall map of Venezuela which covered the entire west wall of the room. As the two men entered, only the lower third of this cartograph was revealed by reading-lamps ranged along tables, but the general switched on a frieze of ceiling lights and swept the whole projection into high illumination.

The general stood looking at it meditatively, glanced at his watch as if timing some other engagement, then pointed out to Strawbridge that the greater part of the chart was outlined in blue, while the extreme western end of the Orinoco Valley was in red.

"That is my life work, Señor Strawbridge—extending this red outline of the free and independent state of Rio Negro to include the whole Orinoco Valley. I want to consolidate an empire from the Andes to the Atlantic."

Strawbridge stood nodding, looking at the blue-and-red map, and began his characteristic probing for detail:

"How many square miles you got now, General?"

To Strawbridge's surprise, the dictator repeated this question in a somewhat louder tone:

"How many square miles does the state of Rio Negro now contain, Coronel Saturnino?" and a voice from the north end of the study answered:

"Seventeen thousand five hundred and eighty-two, General."

The general repeated these figures to Strawbridge.

At the first words uttered by the voice, Strawbridge turned, to see a third person in the library, a young man behind a reading-lamp at the other end of the room, busy at some clerical work. Strawbridge turned his thoughts back to the figures and fixed them in his mind, then set out after more details.

"How much more is there to be consolidated?"

This question in turn was relayed to the clerk, who said:

"Two hundred and thirty-two thousand four hundred and eighteen."

The American compared the two figures, looked at the map.

"Then it will take you a long time, a number of years to finish," he observed.

"Oh, no!" objected the general, becoming absorbed in his subject. "Our progress will be in geometrical, not in arithmetical ratio. You see, every new town we absorb gives us so much human material for our next step."

"I see that," assented the drummer, looking at the map; "and your idea is to absorb the whole Orinoco Valley?"

The general's answer to this was filled with genuine ardor. The Orinoco Valley was one of the largest geographical units in the world, a great natural empire. It was variously estimated at from two hundred and fifty thousand to six hundred and fifty thousand square miles in area. It was drained by four hundred and thirty-six rivers and upward of two thousand streams. These innumerable waters would convert the whole region into a seaport. With such cheap transportation the Orinoco country could supply the world with cocoa, tonka-beans, cotton, sugar, rubber, tropical cabinet-woods, cattle, hides, gold, diamonds.

"But what I have just traveled over is almost a desert," objected Strawbridge. "The cattle were dying of thirst."

"*Precisamente!*" interjected the general, with a sharp gesture; "but right at this moment I am driving a canal from here to here." He took a long ruler and began to point eagerly on the map.

"Yes, I saw your ... your men at work." The drummer stuttered as the ghastly "reds" recurred to his mind.

"That canal will furnish water in the dry season. In the wet season it will form a conduit to impound the waters in this great natural depression here." The dictator pointed dynamically at the configuration showed on the map. "Young man, can you imagine such a development? Can you fancy the Nile Valley magnified thirty times?" He waved at the brilliantly lighted map. "Can you imagine league after league lush with harvest, decked with noble cities, and peopled by the aristocrats of the earth? I refer to the Spanish race. You must realize, señor, there have been but two dominant races in modern history—the English and the Spanish. We two divided the New World between us. You will agree with me when I say that the English North Americans have cultivated the material side of civilization to a degree that has never been approached in the sweep of human history. Is it unreasonable to suppose that the other great segment of humanity, the Spanish South Americans, will cultivate the immaterial side, will establish a great artistic, intellectual, and spiritual hegemony in the world? By such a division our imperial races will supplement each other. One will show the world how to produce, the other how to live. We shall be the halves of a whole."

Strawbridge followed this dithyramb keenly in regard to the irrigation and development project; the artistic end sounded rather nebulous to him.

"And you've got this far with it," he particularized, pointing at the red boundary; "what's the next step?"

The dictator was riding his own hobby now, and he answered without reservation:

"This town, San Geronimo."

"When are you going to do it?"

"We will absorb San Geronimo…. Let me see, … Coronel Saturnino, on what date do we attack San Geronimo?"

"On the twenty-third of this month," came the voice from the back of the study.

"Exactly. We want to incorporate that town with the state of Rio Negro before our flotilla returns up the Amazon from Rio Janeiro."

"When do you expect them back?"

"Inside of two months."

"Are they the boats Gumersindo was talking about? He spoke of my going up the Orinoco, crossing to the Amazon, and then going down to Rio Janeiro."

"Those were the instructions I gave Señor Gumersindo."

Strawbridge stood looking up at the map. A sudden plan popped into his head.

"Since I'll be here," he said, "it wouldn't be a bad plan for me to run along with your army to San Geronimo and see how the trick of absorbing it is done. Give me some notion of the working end of this business."

"Do you mean you desire to accompany my army to San Geronimo?"

"Wouldn't be a bad idea."

"You would be running a certain risk, señor."

"Is it dangerous?" The salesman was surprised. The general had talked so comfortably about "absorbing" San Geronimo that it sounded a very peaceable operation. "Anyway," he persisted with a certain characteristic stubbornness, "this will be a good opportunity to learn about actual conditions down here, and if you can make a place for me, I believe I'll go."

The dictator became grave.

"It is my duty to advise you against it."

Strawbridge considered his host.

"Your objections are not to me personally, are they, señor?" he asked bluntly.

"No, not at all. My resources are entirely at your disposal."

"Then I think I ought to go," decided the American. "You see, when my old man started me out, he said to me, 'Study conditions first-hand, Strawbridge. Find out what your customer has to meet. Make his problems your problems, his interest your interest.' So, you see, I am very glad of the chance to see just how this absorption business works."

All this was given in a very enthusiastic tone. The dictator smiled faintly.

"You are personally welcome to go. You may speak to Coronel Saturnino. He will arrange your billet."

"Good! Good!" Strawbridge was gratified. Then he dropped automatically into the follow-up methods taught him by the sales manager of the Orion Arms Corporation.

"And now, General," he continued intimately, "about how many rifles do we want shipped here?" As he asked this question he used his left hand to draw a leather-covered book from his hip pocket, while with his right he plucked a fountain-pen from his vest pocket. With a practised flirt he flung open his order-book at a rubber-band marker. Thus mobilized, he looked with bright expectation at his prospect.

The general seemed a little at loss.

"Do you mean how many rifles *I* want?"

Strawbridge nodded, and repeated in an intimate, confident tone, "Yes; how many do we want?" The pronoun followed up the impression of how thoroughly he had identified himself with the interest of his customer.

Fombombo hesitated a moment, then asked aloud:

"Coronel Saturnino, how many rifles do we want?"

The young colonel did not pause in his work.

"Twenty-five thousand, General." His brain seemed to be a card-index.

"Twenty-five thousand," repeated Fombombo.

A jubilant sensation went through the drummer at the hugeness of the order. He jotted something in his book.

"When do you want them delivered?"

"As soon as I can get them."

Strawbridge made soft, blurry noises of approval, nodding as he wrote.

"And how shipped?"

All through this little colloquy the general seemed rather at sea. At last he said:

"We can arrange these details later, Señor Strawbridge."

The drummer suddenly turned his full-power selling-talk on his prospect. This was the pinch, this was where he either "put it across" or failed. For just this crisis his sales manager had drilled him day after day. He turned on the dictator and began in an earnest, almost a religious tone:

"Now, General, I can make you satisfactory terms and prices. Every article that leaves our shop is guaranteed; the Orion Arms brands are to-day the standards by which all other firearms are judged. You can't make a mistake by ordering now." He pushed the pen and the book closer to the general's hand. All the general had to do now was simply to close his fingers.

"Señor, we can hardly go into such details to-night." The dictator moved back a trifle from the drummer, with a South American's distaste of touching another human being of the same sex. "There is no necessity. You will be here for weeks, waiting for my canoes from Rio. They will bring drafts, some gold, some barter. When all this is arranged I will send you down the Amazon to embark at Rio for New York, but we have a long wait until my flotilla arrives."

The salesman made a flank attack, almost without thinking. He gently insinuated the book and pen into the general's fingers.

"Now, your Excellency," he murmured, raising his brows, "you sign the dotted line, just here; see?" He pointed at it absorbedly. "I want you to do it to protect yourself. If the prices happen to advance, you get the benefit of to-day's quotations; see? If they fall—why, countermand and order again; see? I'm trying to protect your interests just the same as if they were mine, General."

The dictator returned pen and book.

"We will discuss these details later, señor." He again drew out his watch and seemed struck with the hour. "I am sure you are weary after your long ride, Señor Strawbridge. I myself, unfortunately, have another engagement. Allow me to introduce to you Coronel Saturnino." He moved with the salesman toward the man at the desk, a moment later presented the colonel, and bowed himself away.

The drummer was discomfited at his prospect's escape; nevertheless he shook hands warmly with Coronel Saturnino. The colonel was a handsome young officer, in uniform, and his sword leaned against the desk at which he sat writing. Saturnino's face tended toward squareness, and he had a low forehead. His thick black hair was glossy with youth. His square-cut face was marked with a faintly superior smile, as though he perceived all the weaknesses of the person who was before him and was slightly amused by them. He was of middle height. Strawbridge would have called him heavy-set except for a remarkably slender waist. When the colonel stood up and shook hands with the drummer, Strawbridge discovered that he was in the presence of an athlete.

The salesman put himself on a friendly footing with this officer at once, just as he always did with the clerks in American stores. He seated himself on the edge of Coronel Saturnino's desk, very much at ease.

"Well, I thought I was going to land the old general right off the bat!" he confided, laughing.

"Yes?" inquired Saturnino, politely, still standing. "Why your haste?"

"Oh, well—" Strawbridge wagged his head—"push your business or your business will push you. Never put off till to-morrow what you can do to-day. Why, there might be a German salesman in here to-morrow with another line of goods!"

"Is a German salesman coming?" asked the colonel, quickly.

"Oh, no, no, no! I said there might be." Strawbridge reached into an inner pocket, drew out and flipped open a silver case. "Have a cigar."

"No, thank you." The colonel hesitated, and added, "I don't smoke after twelve o'clock at night."

Strawbridge jumped up.

"Good Lord! is it as late as that?"

The colonel thought it was.

"By the way," interrupted the drummer, "I'm to go with you to San Geronimo. The old man said so. I'll get the hang of things down there. I suppose it pays—this revolting—or the old man wouldn't stay in the business."

As the colonel simply stood, Strawbridge continued his desultory remarks:

"The old man's got a grand scheme—hasn't he?—canalizing the Orinoco Valley. Say, this goes: when you fellows put that across, this beautiful little city of Canalejos will just have a shade on any damn burg in this wide world. Now you can take that flat; it goes." He made a gesture with his palm down.

Coronel Saturnino did not appear particularly gratified by this encomium heaped upon his home town. He picked up a paper-weight and looked at it with a faint smile.

"Did the general tell you about that?"

"Oh, yes," declared Strawbridge, heartily, "we buddied up from the jump. Why, I never meet a stranger. I'm just Tom Strawbridge wherever you find me."

The colonel passed over Mr. Strawbridge's declaration of his identity.

"Did the general's plan for canalization strike you as economically sound?" he asked, with a certain quizzical expression.

"Why, sure! That's the most progressive scheme I've heard of since I struck South America. I'm for it. I tell you it's a big idea."

The colonel laid down the paper-weight, and asked with a flavor of satire:

"Why should a colony of men canalize a semi-arid country when they can go to other parts of South America and obtain just as fertile, well-watered land without effort?"

With a vague sense of sacrilege the drummer looked at the young officer.

"Why—good Lord, man!—you're not knocking your home town, are you?"

Coronel Saturnino was unaware that this was the cardinal crime in an American's calendar.

"I am stating the most elementary analysis of an economic situation," he defended, rather surprised at his guest's heat.

The drummer laughed in brief amazement at a man who would decry his place of residence for any reason under the sun.

"You certainly must never have read Edgar Z. Best's celebrated poem, 'The Trouble Is Not with Your Town; It's You.'"

"No," said the officer. "I've never read it."

"Well, I'll try to get it for you," said the drummer, in a tone which told Coronel Saturnino that until he had read "The Trouble Is Not with Your Town: It's You," he could never hope to stand among literate men.

Having thus, one might say, laid the foundation of the American spirit in Canalejos, Strawbridge yawned frankly and said:

"If you'll be good enough to show me my bunk, I believe I'll hit the hay."

Coronel Saturnino pressed a button on his desk and a moment later a little palace guard in uniform entered the library, carrying a rifle. The colonel gave a brief order, then walked to the door with his guest and bowed him out of the study.

CHAPTER VIII

Next morning the cathedral bells roused Strawbridge with dreams of fire-alarms. He thought he was in a burning house and he struggled terrifically to move a leg, to twitch an inert arm. Somewhere in the sleeping bulk of the drummer a strange, insubstantial entity sent out desperate alarms. At last a finger flexed, an eyelid trembled, then suddenly something in the sleeper's brain expanded, flowed out through and identified itself with the whole body. It was reinstated as a traveling salesman with trade ambitions who pursued devious ends through ways and means imposed on him by custom and training. The drummer opened his eyes and sat up. He wiped the sweat from his face and damned the bells for waking him. The fact that by some strange means he had been cut off a moment or two from his body, that he had engaged in a terrific struggle to regain its control, did not suggest a mystery or provoke a question in his mind. He had had a nightmare. That explained everything. He often had nightmares. To Thomas Strawbridge's type of mind anything that happens often cannot possibly contain a mystery.

Nevertheless his experience left him in a dour mood. He turned out of bed, shoved his feet into some native alpargatas, and shuffled to the bath which adjoined his chamber.

The bath-tub was a basin of white marble, rather dirty, and built into the tiled floor. It was a miniature swimming-pool. Overhead was a clumsy silver nozzle on a water-pipe. The drummer turned it on, and the water which sprayed over him was neither cool nor very clean. The roaring and banging of the cathedral bells continued as if they would never leave off.

As Strawbridge soaped and rubbed he recalled somewhat moodily his engagement to go with General Fombombo's force to San Geronimo. At this hour of the morning the adventure did not appeal to him. It was rather a wild-goose chase, and he decided he would tell the general he had changed his mind, and have Saturnino remove his name from the lists.

The bells continued their uproar. They did not stop until the drummer had finished his bath and was back in his room. Then their silence brought into notice a distant, watery note. This came from the cataracts in the Rio Negro somewhere below Canalejos. The disquietude of the water was rumored through the room, over the city, and it spread across the llanos for miles and miles. It held a certain disagreeableness for Strawbridge. He liked a quiet morning. Somewhere on the street a native donkey-cart rattled. The cathedral bells started again, but this time not for long—merely to gather in the faithful their previous tumult had awakened. But it all struck Strawbridge on raw nerves.

In fact, every morning Strawbridge was subject to what he called his grouch. He got up with a grouch on. It was a short daily reaction from his American heartiness, his American optimism, his tendency to convert every moment into a fanfare and a balloon ascension. This early morning depression continued until he had had his coffee and the fife-and-drum corps of his spirit started up their stridor again. It is just possible that the American flag, instead of stars, should bear forty-eight coffee beans rampant.

A woman in black passed the barred windows of Strawbridge's room. The drummer, after the manner of men, moved slowly about his window to keep her in sight as long as possible. He fussed with his tie as he did so. He watched her cross the plaza. She passed under a row of ornamental evergreen trees which looked as if they had dark-green tassels hung at regular intervals on perfectly symmetrical limbs. The grace of the trees somehow lent itself to the girl who passed beneath them. At the same moment an odor of frangipani drifted in through the bars, out of the morning.

When any man is looking at a woman, any odor that comes to his nostrils automatically associates itself with her—a relic, no doubt, of our animal forebears, during their mating seasons.

Strawbridge watched the girl intently until at last he had his face pressed against the bars to get a final glimpse of her at a difficult angle.

When he straightened from this rather awkward posture and returned to his tie, he became aware that the maid had entered his room with his morning coffee. She was a short girl, of dusky yellow color, and was evidently half Indian and half negro, or what the Venezuelans call a *griffe*. She also had moved about the window to its last angular possibility, and when Strawbridge saw her she was peering with very bright black eyes to see who had been the gentleman's quarry.

At this the drummer became acutely aware of every movement he had made. He frowned at the *griffe* girl.

"Here, give me the coffee! Don't stand all day staring like that!"

The girl started and nervously handed her salver to him.

"Whyn't you knock when you came in?" demanded Strawbridge.

"I did, señor, but I thought you were asleep," she said, a little frightened.

It was the maid's custom to find her master's guests asleep, to steal in noiselessly, awaken them, and administer in a tiny cup two tablespoonfuls of Venezuelan coffee, black as the pit and strong as death.

The incident of the servant-girl counteracted, to a certain extent, the heartening effect of the coffee. Strawbridge looked out on the brightening morning and wondered if by any chance her gossip might affect his landing General Fombombo's order for rifles, because he knew that the girl in black he had been watching at such inconvenience was the Señora Fombombo. He felt sure the *griffe* girl knew it also. But he decided optimistically that she would say nothing about it, or, if she did, it would have no influence on his sale.

The big, somber bedroom to which General Fombombo had assigned his guest was a good observation point, and no doubt the dictator had chosen it for this very reason. The scene at which Strawbridge was looking might have aroused enthusiasm in a more susceptible man. At an angle it gave a view of the Plaza Mayor and a glimpse of the cathedral seen through the trees. Straight east a bit of paved street showed, and beyond that a garden with a side gate facing Strawbridge's window. A heavy hedge divided the garden from the plaza. Beyond the garden rose the walls and buttresses of the rear of the cathedral, and this was a handsome thing. In the soft morning light it was an aspiration toward God.

Beyond the cathedral, the wide river stretched eastward. Two hundred yards down the river bank rose another low, massive building, more heavily built and gloomier even than the palace. In the uncertain light Strawbridge thought he discerned two or three figures on the flat roof of this building.

A little later the sun's limb cut the far eastern reach of the river. Distant quivering reflections marked the rapids whose subdued turmoil brooded over the city and the llanos. The light increased momentarily. Against its widening flame blinked tiny black native boats, like familiar demons traversing the fires of some wide and splendid hell.

None of this interested Strawbridge. He stared at it through the same mechanical compulsion that causes a moth to head toward light, but he did not see it. The first thing that really caught his attention was a bugle blowing reveille; the next breath, from the top of the low building came the flash of a cannon, faintly seen against the brilliant east. After an interval came a brief, hard report.

The concussion not only startled Strawbridge but did some obscure violence to his sensibilities. It did not roar and rumble and so suggest the pomp and panoply of war. The flatness of the llanos lent no echo. The shot was just a hard, abrupt blow, a smash, then silence. There was something dismaying about it. Then Strawbridge could see the figures on the flat roof leaving their cannon and descending.

Like all good Americans who observe a foreign military demonstration, Strawbridge thought:

"That's nothing. An American army with big American guns could blow that little toy right out of existence." Nevertheless he continued to be depressed and somehow dismayed by the hard and savage suddenness of the sunrise gun, and in his heart he determined firmly that he would not go with the army to San Geronimo. In his mind Strawbridge uttered these thoughts resolutely, and he felt himself to be one of those strong-willed men who, having once settled on a program, never vary from it, no matter what chance befalls.

A gong announcing *almuerzo* brought the drummer out of his reverie and moved him toward the breakfast table. As he went he shook off his mood, and resumed, as if he were putting on a suit of clothes, his quick American walk, his optimism, and his dashing business manner. As he moved briskly down the great hallway, a guard with a rifle directed him to the *comidor*.

The palace was divided into an east and a west wing, by a series of patios, and the breakfast-room proved to be a little place latticed off from one of the smaller patios. The lattice was overgrown with vines. In this retreat Strawbridge found a small basketry table laid with snowy linen, on which were oranges, sweet lemons, rolls, and coffee.

Thanks to Strawbridge's quick movements, he was the first person here. He sat down at the table and enjoyed the sunshine glinting at him through the vines. Through an end door of the breakfast-room he could see the kitchen. Its principal furnishing was a Venezuelan cooking-range. This was a great stone table punctured with little iron grates each holding a handful of charcoal fire. Above the table spread a big sheet-iron canopy, to convey away the gases and fumes. Ranged on the little fires were pots and pans and saucepans. At the farther end of the kitchen a wrinkled old negress was on her knees on the earthen floor, pouring boiling water into an old stocking leg filled with ground coffee. The beverage dripped out into a silver pot which sat on the ground in front of the crone. Beyond the negress, in the sunshine, stood a meat block with a machete stuck in it and a joint of meat lying on it. Around the meat the flies were so thick that they appeared to Strawbridge as a kind of wavering shadow over the block.

A sound behind the drummer caused him to turn, and he saw the Señora Fombombo, in her religious black, evidently just returned from early mass. The sight of her gave Strawbridge a certain faint satisfaction, but at the same time it brought back the vague embarrassment he had felt on the previous evening. He returned her salutation of "*Buenos dias*," and was pondering something else to say, when she expressed a fear that the sight of a Venezuelan *cocina* (kitchen) would be disagreeable to him. She had heard how spotless were American kitchens.

The salesman began a hasty assurance that the kitchen was very interesting, but the señora called to a servant to close the shutter. The same *griffe* girl whom Strawbridge had seen that morning answered the call, and before she retired she gave the señora and the salesman a certain understanding look, which linked up in Strawbridge's mind with what the girl had seen an hour or two earlier.

The señora herself was proceeding with her table talk.

"We can get only native servants here in Canalejos," she was saying in the faintly mechanical manner of a hostess who has an uninteresting guest, "and they prepare everything in the native way."

Strawbridge said he liked Venezuelan cooking.

"It is monotonous," criticized the señora. "The chicken is always cooked with rice, and the plantains are always fried."

Strawbridge started to say that he loved chicken and rice and fried plantains, but even his imperfect sense of rhetoric warned him that he had already overworked those particular phrases. So he checked that sentiment, cast about for a substitute, and finally fished up:

"I saw you going to early mass this morning, señora."

The girl glanced at him, agreed to this, and continued peeling her orange with a knife and fork, in the Venezuelan fashion.

The drummer wanted strongly to follow this opening with something brisk and lively to compel her attention and interest, but his head seemed oddly empty. His embarrassment persisted and made him a little uncomfortable. He wondered why. It was irritating. Why didn't he tell her a joke, one of his parlor jokes? Strawbridge knew scores and scores of obscene jokes, and perhaps half a dozen parlor jokes which he kept for women. Now, to his discomfiture, he could not recall a single one of his parlor jokes. For some reason or other, he told himself, the señora crabbed his style.

She was a smallish woman with a rather slender, melancholy face, and her eyes had that slightly unfocused look which is characteristic of all pure-black eyes. Her eyebrows and lips were engraved in black and red against a colorless face. Her nun's bonnet and the white cloth that passed beneath it across her forehead concealed the least trace of hair. And Strawbridge speculated with a sort of apprehension whether or no she really had shaved her head nun fashion. If so, the Virgin had exacted a bitter price for her sister's recovery.

During these meditations, however, the salesman was not dumb. He automatically started one of those typically American conversations which consist in a long string of disconnected questions asked without any object whatever. Strawbridge himself regretted these questions. He had hoped to do something amusing and rather brilliant.

"Have you lived here long, señora?"

"About two years. I came here immediately after I was married to General Fombombo."

"Then you were not married here?"

"No, in Spain."

"Then you are a Spanish girl?"

"Yes, I lived in Barcelona."

"How do you like it here?"

"Very well."

"I suppose you miss the stir. I hear Barcelona is the livest town in Spain."

"I believe it is," she agreed a little uncertainly.

"What do they export? Anything besides olive-oil? I understand they export a lot of olive-oil."

Señora Fombombo touched her slender fingers to her lips a moment and then said she believed they exported olive-oil.

"I suppose the girls go in for business over there, too—bookkeepers, you know; stenogs, clerks, cash girls ...?"

"Ye-e-es."

"What was your line before you married?"

The señora came awake and looked at the drummer.

"My *line*?"

"Yes," said Strawbridge, becoming a little less of an automaton and a little more of a human. "What was your job before you hooked up with the general?"

- 55 -

The señora almost stared at the American. Then she drew in her under lip and seemed to compress it rigorously, thoughtfully, perhaps to assist her in recalling what her line was before she hooked up with the general. Then she said:

"I ... I did a little music."

"Teach?" probed the American.

"Well ... no.... Really, I'm afraid I didn't do anything."

Strawbridge nodded as if some puzzle had been solved for him.

"Now, that's where you made your mistake," he explained paternally. "A woman ought to have a job just the same as a man. She ought to be able to hold over her goods until the market is right. Now take me: suppose I had to sell my rifles right now because I didn't have the overhead to keep them ninety days longer; I'd be in a bad way. It's the same way with you girls. With no overhead, it's no wonder you married Ge—" He caught himself up abruptly, aghast at the implication to which his monologue had led him. He floundered mentally in an effort to turn it off, but all he could do was simply to moisten his lips and stop talking. He wondered chillily if the señora had caught it.

Apparently she had not. A spray of flowers swung near her from the vine. She drew a raceme to her face and began smoothly:

"I know feminism is very modern and up to date, but somehow we Spanish women don't care for it. We are as idle as these flowers." She turned and looked at the blossoms. "This variety of wistaria grew in my garden in Barcelona; that's why I had it planted here. It reminds me of home." She looked up at the American, smiled faintly, and added rather disconnectedly:

"It may seem strange to you, Señor Strawbridge, but once I very nearly entered a convent in Barcelona."

By this time Strawbridge was convinced that she had not observed his false step. He was still warm, and a little shivery, but he was recovering. He said very simply and truthfully:

"Well, I'm glad you didn't. If I have to stay in Canalejos, I'm glad there is an agreeable woman in it to talk to."

The señora expressed her pleasure if she could enliven his stay at Canalejos, and as they talked Coronel Saturnino entered the breakfast-room. He bowed to the señora and inquired of Strawbridge, in his somewhat amused voice, if he had slept well after his enlistment.

Oh, yes, he had slept like a top.

"Enlistment?" echoed the señora.

"*Seguramente*," smiled the colonel. "Señor Strawbridge has enlisted in the cavalry to march against San Geronimo."

Señora Fombombo seemed utterly astonished. She stared at the colonel, then at the drummer.

"You don't mean Señor Strawbridge will be in the cavalry attack on San Geronimo?"

"Yes, señora; I arranged his billet last night." The colonel made a smiling bow.

The girl turned to the American.

"But why are you going to fight at San Geronimo, señor?" she asked.

Strawbridge hesitated, cleared his throat, glanced through the vine-grown lattice into the sunshine, then apparently came to some inward decision.

"Now, it's like this, señora," he began, getting back the ring and confidence in his voice which had heretofore been missing: "It's like this. In order to meet your clients' needs you've got to get first-hand information." He patted his right fingers against his left palm and looked the señora squarely in the eye for the first time. "Before you can grasp your patrons' problems, you've got to make 'em yours. Why, the first thing my old man said to me, he said: 'Strawbridge, an expert salesman is first aid to the financially injured; he's the star of Bethlehem to the sinners of commerce.' He's a cutter, my old man is. I wish you could know him, señora."

"You mean your father?" hazarded the President's wife.

"Holy mackerel, lady! no!" cried the drummer, with a touch of Keokuk gusto in his voice. "I mean my boss, the head knocker of my firm. Great old chap, and rich as Limburger cheese. Say, he owns fifty-one per cent. of the Orion Arms stock, and he started in as a water boy. How do you like that?" Mr. Strawbridge gave his auditors a little triumphant smile.

"*Caramba!* Very American, I say," laughed the colonel.

The señora interposed quickly:

"And very good and very fine, I say, Señor Strawbridge!" She looked at the colonel with a certain little light in her eye, then added emphatically, "I am sure I should like him."

She was rising to leave the table.

Coronel Saturnino, who was about to seat himself, said:

"If I concede his admirable qualities, I wonder if you would stay and eat another orange, señora?"

But the girl pleaded that she must practise some music in the cathedral.

Strawbridge hesitated, half-way out of his chair. He was undecided whether to stay with Coronel Saturnino or to go with the señora. He decided for the latter and walked out of the breakfast-room with her, but he was vaguely embarrassed for fear he had done the wrong thing.

CHAPTER IX

His talk at the breakfast table, with Señora Fombombo, braced the spirits of Thomas Strawbridge. The girl seemed to bring a kind of comfort to the drummer. Now as he walked down the long marble steps of the *presidencia*, the tropical sunshine slanting into the plaza, the cries of gathering street venders, the rattle of carts, the stir of pigeons in the cathedral tower all conspired to speed his thoughts and energy along their customary channel—that is to say, toward the selling of merchandise. He was in fettle, and he wanted to sell hardware. He felt so full of power he believed he could sell anything to anybody.

And the Señora Fombombo was in some degree responsible for his exaltation. A pleasant woman always grooms a man for a fine deed. So it was the Spanish girl who sent the big blond American striding through the plaza, smiling to himself and seeking whom he might sell.

It was Strawbridge's plan to go to the general merchandise stores in Canalejos and stock them up on hardware, by the mere élan and warmth of his approach. It is conceivable that enough Thomas Strawbridges, a whole army of them, could bankrupt the manufacturing interests of all foreign nations, could wither them right out of existence in the overpowering sunshine of their good-fellowship and love for humanity.

As Strawbridge hurried through the plaza, filled, one might say, with this destructive amiability, he was accosted by a voice asking him if he did not desire a fortune of ten million pesetas.

The drummer looked around and saw a lottery-vender holding out his sheaf of tickets. He was offering coupons on the National Spanish Lottery, an institution which circulates its chances all over South America, including even insurgent Rio Negro.

The good fairy who was offering this chance of fortune was a ragged man whose lean ribs and belly could be seen through the rents in his clothes. The American paused, took the sheaf, and looked at the tickets curiously. Each ticket was a long strip of small coupons which could be torn into ten pieces and divided among indigent buyers. They were vilely printed on the cheapest of paper.

Strawbridge stood looking at the tickets and shaking his head. Life, he told the ticket-seller, was what a man made it, and he could not afford to mix up his solid success with lottery chances and such like. What he wanted was certainties, and not moonshine. Here he handed back the sheaf and moved on briskly through the plaza, a big, well-tailored American, the ensample of a man who had taken his life in his own hands and molded it into a warm and shining success. The vender stared emptily after the drummer. Never before had his hope of a sale inflated so suddenly, or collapsed so completely.

Strawbridge had gone only a little way when a man came running out of a bodega that was down a side street. He was waving his sombrero and calling Strawbridge's name. The American stood in doubt whether he had heard aright, for no one in Canalejos knew his name, and then he saw a wad of hair on the shouter's head and recognized the bull-fighter. Lubito came up quickly and somewhat unsteadily. His face was flushed, his black eyes glistened with alcohol, and his bull-fighter's pigtail was somewhat awry.

"I was just starting to the *palacio* to see you, señor," he began a little thickly. "I was just starting when my *compadre* in the bodega says,'There goes the *Americano* now,' so out I came."

"What can I do for you?" asked the drummer, with brief patience.

The torero grinned laxly.

"You were my *comarado* coming here from Caracas, señor. You remember, we rode all the way together."

"Sure! Get to your point."

Lubito straightened.

"Well, would you see your *comarado* wronged? Are you going to see him turned into a laughing-stock?"

"You've turned yourself into a laughing-stock; you're drunk."

"*Caramba!* Whose fault is it?"

"Why, yours, of course!"

The bull-fighter spread the fingers of both hands on his chest.

"I! It is no fault of mine. The President did this!"

"Aw, you're talking nonsense."

"No, it is true, the fault is with General Fombombo. I am no tippler. I am a bull-fighter. That's what I wanted to see you about. You are a *caballero*, and a friend of the President. You can stand up and talk to him, but he sends me off to see the bull-ring. You know, you heard him yesterday, sending me off to see the bull-ring, the moment he clapped eyes on me."

Strawbridge was faintly amused.

"Is that what you want me to see him about—because he dismissed you yesterday?"

Lubito was only slightly intoxicated, and now his anger sobered him completely:

"No! No! What do I care for his contempt? I, too, am a Venezuelan, but, señor, when any man interferes with my paternal rights—" he tapped himself threateningly on his powerful chest—"I am a bull-fighter."

"What in the world are you talking about?"

"*Cá!* Madruja!"

"But your paternal rights!"

Lubito flung out exasperated hands.

"Didn't you hear her father, the old man in the 'reds,' place her in my care?"

"Yes. Well, what has happened?"

"Enough! I saw Madruja carried, by the guards, to one of the rooms in the west wing of the *palacio*. Very good. I followed, and marked the room. The windows seemed rather old; perhaps the bars could be bent. I did not know. I was in her father's place. It was my duty to see."

Strawbridge's interest picked up, as a man's always does when a woman is introduced into the narrative:

"Yes, I guess you would be very strict about your daughter. Then what?"

"Well, last night I slept in the dressing-room at the bull-ring. That is, I tried to sleep, but I could not. I kept thinking of my daughter Madruja, pining for Esteban. I got up and walked out into the bull-ring, thinking of the lonely little bride. Ah, señor, there were stars! I can never look at stars without thinking of the eyes of brides...." Lubito shivered, reached up and straightened his hair a trifle, then went on: "I said to myself, '*Cá!* A man who stumbles goes all the faster if he does not fall.' So I made up my mind. I went back to the dressing-room, in the dark found my guitar, and started for the *presidencia*. Señor, you will believe it when I tell you I was trembling all the way, like a mimosa leaf. I slipped very quietly around the plaza, past the department of *fomento*, and so to the window where my little daughter slept. I came up softly and tried the bars with all my strength, but although I am a bull-fighter, señor, they did not budge."

The drummer stood looking at the veins in the bull-fighter's forehead. The fellow went on:

"There was nothing to do, señor, but to sing, to sing a love-song to my little Madruja, and perhaps she would come to the window, or open the door if she could. I touched the chords and began singing 'La Encantadora,' softly, into the window, just for her.

"For minutes nothing stirred, but I have a tender voice, señor. You know; you have heard me sing. It will melt any woman's heart. I began, '*Mi alma, mi amor perdida.*'

"Oh, señor, it was a sobbing, plaintive song, and when I had finished and stood holding my breath, something moved in the darkness. There came a little clinking on the windowsill, and I saw the faint gleam of metal. It was a gold coin, señor. Then the voice of General Fombombo said: 'That is Lubito, is it not? Sing to us all night long, Lubito.'"

Strawbridge opened his eyes and thrust his head forward.

"What!" he cried.

"By five thousand devils on horseback, it's true!" Lubito flung up his arms. "And me there—her father! My head grew hot. I went insane! I told General Fombombo I was in her father's place, that I, Lubito, was in her father's place, but the general only laughed and said: 'Sing, sing to us, Lubito. As to your paternal duties, your ideas went out of date with the Neanderthal man, five hundred thousand years ago." The torero came to a pause, breathing heavily; then, after a moment, he asked more rationally, "Now, what did he mean by that?"

The dictator's quip, jest, or philosophy, whatever it was, had not registered at all with Strawbridge. He stood staring at Lubito and suddenly began laughing. The bull-fighter at once looked offended, and Strawbridge began gasping an apology in the midst of his mirth. He got out his handkerchief and wiped his eyes.

"Ex-excuse me, Lubito, b-but wh-what did he say? 'S-s-sing all night! S-s-s...." His effort at the "s" rippled into laughter again.

Lubito flung up his hands in disgust.

"*Canastos!* what a man! To see a young girl deflowered—and laugh!" The bull-fighter turned on his heel, perfectly sober, and walked away.

Strawbridge also became sober; he even frowned.

"Hell! putting it like that!" Then he shrugged, and continued his unspoken soliloquy: "Well, what better could you expect from a bunch of Venezuelans ... just natives...." His good-natured face began to form another smile; then he thought of Señora Fombombo. At that he became serious enough. The Spanish girl seemed to raise some obscure question in his mind. He made a hazy effort to clarify that question, but nothing came of it.

With this, Strawbridge removed his thoughts from the incident and proceeded to canvass the town in the interest of the Orion Arms Corporation. He walked out of Plaza Mayor into a narrow, dirty *calle* which was the principal street of the city. It was lined with the usual ill-lighted, inconvenient business houses which characterize Venezuelan towns; a roulette establishment, a charcoal and kindling store with a box of half-decayed mangos as a side line, a gloomy book-store with the works of Vargas Vila lying, back up, on a table outside. The first general merchandise store he found had a single bolt of calico on display. Above the bolt swung the name of the store in faded letters, "Sol y Sombra."

Such complete absence of attractive displays was a real pain to the American. It spurred his commercial missionary spirit. He entered the dark "Sol y Sombra." It had once been an ancient dwelling. Its use had been changed from domestic to mercantile ends by the simple expedients of knocking out some partitions and roofing an old patio. In fact, when a Venezuelan merchant covers an old patio and thereby adds to his floor space, he has just about uttered the last word in Venezuelan progressiveness.

Strawbridge turned into the shop and asked for the proprietor. The proprietor had not arrived, but one of the clerks offered his services. The American introduced himself and vigorously grasped the young man's limp hand.

"I'm a hardware man," he began briskly; "and now, if you'll just carry me back to your hardware department, we'll check through and see what you're short on; then I can hand your boss the lists and prices of the very things he needs and save him a lot of time."

The clerk was a small, withered youth with sad brown eyes that resembled a monkey's. He looked at Strawbridge and said:

"My employer will have all the time there is when he gets here, señor."

"Um ... well, ... we can shove the deal through quicker, anyway."

The little clerk turned and started doubtfully toward the hardware department. It was clear that he did not want to go, but he could not hold his ground against the dynamic force of Strawbridge's enthusiasm. As he moved along he said:

"You are an American, aren't you?"

"Travel out of New York, but my home's in Keokuk. Great little burg; thirty thousand population and thirty-five hundred automobiles, not to mention flivvers...." Here Strawbridge laughed heartily, sharing the widespread American conviction that to make a distinction between an automobile and a flivver is the most amusing flight of human wit. "And, say," he added, when he had finished his lonely laugh, "I wish you could see the Keokuk window displays; give you some pointers, young man."

The young man was smiling agreeably, so the drummer turned to business.

"Well," he began optimistically, "trade picking up here as everywhere, I suppose?"

The monkey-eyed youth agreed without enthusiasm.

"Your export trade showing any strength?"

"I am only a clerk, señor; I have no export trade."

"Yes, I know; I meant...." It became clear that it was not worth while to pursue this topic. They had reached the hardware department. The clerk stood silent while Strawbridge looked around him. The stock was fuller than the American had expected.

A sudden idea occurred to Strawbridge:

"Look here, why don't you get out a big display of this stuff? You could push out a lot of it."

"I have no interest here at all, señor," repeated the little man, concealing a yawn with his fingers. "I'm just a clerk."

Strawbridge broke into cheerful irritation:

"Why, damn it, man! if you'll make this business your own, some day it will be your own. Right here is your chance to use your initiative, throw some pep into this establishment. Get this thing moving and you'll be the headliner around here." Strawbridge gave the prospective headliner a cheerful blow on the shoulder, designed to knock energy into him. A constructive impulse seized the American: "Say, I'm quite a lad when it comes to window-dressing. Let's bundle a lot of this stuff out front and fix up something of a scream by the time the old man arrives!" Like a benevolent giant Strawbridge beamed down on the little clerk. Next moment he had caught up an armful of ropes, plow points, hoes, and door hinges and was lugging them toward the front of the store.

The feather of a clerk tried to resist the American whirlwind.

"But, señor, wait one minute! *Nombre de Dios!* Señor, for God's sake stop! What you are doing is mad!"

Strawbridge was annoyed.

"Mad the devil! It's the only sensible thing in Canalejos; give your joint a prosperous, up-to-date look."

"But, señor, we don't want to look prosperous and up to date."

"What!" The American was scandalized. "Don't want to look up to date! What's eating you?"

"Nothing. We don't want to, because it will raise our taxes. We shall be forced to pay larger contributions to the governor. *Caramba!* Señor, you do not know this country!"

Strawbridge came to a halt at last.

"Your taxes will be raised if you look prosperous!"

"*Seguramente!*" affirmed the clerk, excitedly. "To look prosperous is a sort of crime in Venezuela. If we seem *too* well off, perhaps the dictator will take over our whole business. We dare not risk it. So we keep everything out of sight. That is best."

Thomas Strawbridge stood confounded. He doubted his ears.

"Look here: is that straight goods?"

"It is true, señor," asseverated the little man, solemnly, "if that is what you mean."

"But take your business from you? Take it *from* you!"

The clerk evidently thought the American did not understand his Spanish, for he elucidated:

"I mean occupy it—receive the money—have the key to the door."

Strawbridge stood staring at the little fellow, wondering if such a fantastic situation could really exist.

"Did you ever know of such a case?" he asked slowly.

"*Sin embargo.* A friend of mine had a ranch near the President's. It was a good ranch, with water so well placed that it stayed green each summer, much longer than the President's own. So suddenly, one day of a very dry summer, soldiers came to my friend's estancia and carried him away, and all his peons. It lay vacant a week or two. No one dared go on it. Then the President ran his fences around it and claimed it as waste land."

"That really happened?"

"*Sí*, señor."

"What became of the poor devil of a rancher and his peons?"

"Oh, the peons were put into the army and the man...." The clerk shrugged, and nodded his head in a certain direction. Strawbridge did not know to what he referred.

The American replaced the goods he had chosen for display, and stood in the wareroom rather stunned. A sort of horripilation ran over him as he pondered the clerk's story. Under such a government, all business was in jeopardy.

"Why, that's awful!" he said aloud. "That'll *ruin* business! If a fellow's investments are not protected, then—" he made a hopeless gesture—"then what in God's name do they hold sacred here?"

The clerk gave a Latin shrug of despondency.

"*Cá*, señor, they hold nothing sacred here. Why, even our sisters and betrothed are violated—"

Strawbridge lifted a hand and waggled a finger for silence.

"Yes, I know that old stuff, but business—not to respect a man's investment—God! but these people are savages!"

CHAPTER X

Thomas Strawbridge left "Sol y Sombra" and started back up the street, hurrying out of habit but with no objective. His conversation with the little monkey-eyed clerk had suddenly explained to the drummer the squalor and filth of Canalejos. It was an intentional filth, deliberately chosen to escape governmental mulcting. In short, Venezuelan cities were especially designed to do business in the worst possible way and with the greatest amount of friction and inconvenience. Strawbridge was bewildered. He had come from a country where the whole machinery of government is built for the especial purpose of expediting business. Now this sudden reversal of motif seemed to him a mad thing.

What was the object of it? If men did not organize a government to promote business, why did any exist? Why did the shop-keepers persist in running their dirty little shops? Why did the peons go and come, the fishermen labor up and down the rapids? If business was strangled, what reason was there for life to go on?

The drummer's steps had led him back to Plaza Mayor, and by this time the square was full of people. Most of them were loiterers, sitting on the park benches gazing listlessly at the palms and ornamental evergreens, or watching the drip of a fountain too clogged to play. In the center of the plaza was a statue, and the drummer was somewhat surprised to observe that it was a full-length figure of General Fombombo. The statue was of heroic size and held out in its hands a scroll bearing the words, "Liberty, Equality, Fraternity."

There was a slow movement, among the idlers, toward the cathedral. Señoritas came by with their missals, beggars with their cups. Youths and well-dressed men took a last puff at their eternal cigarettes, tossed away the stubs, and wandered toward the gloomy temple.

Strawbridge had never been in a Roman Catholic church in his life. In fact, since his boyhood he had scarcely been in any sort of church. Now his desire for silence and a place to think out the riddle he had found, drew him through the deeply recessed archway of the cathedral. On one of the columns he saw the holy water, in a shell of a size that amazed him in a superficial way. He passed on in and immediately forgot the shell.

The interior of the church was a semi-darkness punctuated here and there with groups of candles flickering before the different altars. To the right hand of the entrance he saw a life-size effigy of the crucifixion. The head of the figure drooped to one side, and the whole body was painted the pallor of death.

With the impersonal and faintly interested eyes of an American tourist the drummer stood looking at this figure. As he stood, an old man with an aura of white hair shuffled up before the crucifix, laid down a bundle on the stone floor, spread a filthy handkerchief, and knelt stiffly on it. Then he stared fixedly at the effigy, and spread out his old arms to it, and his lips began moving beneath his tobacco-stained beard. In his earnestness his old head shook and nodded; he reached up his scrawny arms farther and farther, as if to pull down from the figure the good he was seeking. He arose and went; other men took his place—young men, well-dressed men. They went through their devotions openly and unashamed.

But Strawbridge was somehow shamed before them. It seemed to him a rather improper thing for a man to be seen praying in public. In North America, to pray in public is a sort of test of audacity, not to say brazenness. In North America one who prays in public seldom thinks about God; he thinks about how he looks and what the people are thinking about his prayer. Now, for these Venezuelans to pray to God earnestly and unaffectedly in the open made Strawbridge feel uncomfortable, as if they were appearing in public wearing too few clothes.

The women, on the other hand, somehow pleased him. As each señorita and señora came in with a white handkerchief spread over her black hair, touched the holy water to her forehead, lips, and breast, and then knelt to pray, it gave the drummer a queer sense of intimacy and pleasure.

Presently reading and responses began in one of the chapels hidden from the American. The voice of the priest would rise in a muffled swell and then taper into silence again; a moment later this would be followed by a hushed babble of women's voices. There was something sad in the reading and responses. The same words were repeated over and over and filled the cathedral with a monotonous and melancholy music.

As Strawbridge stood musing among these frail and unaccustomed pleasures, his mind moved vaguely about the question which had brought him there: what could the Venezuelans find in life to take the place of business? Upon what other cord could any man string the rosary of his days? As the women came and went, as the responses filled the church with a many-tongued music, as the odor of incense flattered the gloom, he pondered his question, but could find no answer.

The drummer found a seat near a column of the nave and relaxed, American fashion, with his legs spread out and his arms lying along the back of the bench. He stopped thinking toward any point and allowed his fancies to drift idly. The life of the cathedral slowly developed itself around him. A woman was on her knees just inside the altar-rail, scrubbing the tiled floor. Several acolytes in lace robes were gathered in the transept, perhaps waiting to take part in some later mass. A priest in his cassock loitered near a confessional, evidently expecting a penitent. Presently a little girl did come and step into the double stall of the confessional. The father moved into the other side with the slowness of a heavy man and with a mechanical movement lifted the little shutter in the partition. The child placed her face in the aperture and began to whisper.

Strawbridge sat and looked with a dreamy emptiness at the priest and the little girl. He could feel the bench pressing his body and catch the queer fragrance of incense. Presently the child stepped out of the confessional and began a round of the stations, kneeling and telling her beads before each one. A beggar entered the booth and presently went away. A few moments later, to the drummer's surprise, Coronel Saturnino came down the aisle and stepped into the confessional. The officer put his mouth to the orifice and whispered steadily for five or ten minutes. Strawbridge could see his profile against the darkness of the booth—a handsome, almost flawless profile, with a slight sardonic molding about the nose and the corners of the mouth even in this moment of confession.

Strawbridge wondered what he was confessing; what kind of sins Saturnino committed.

Just then a hand touched the American's outstretched arm. The drummer looked around and saw Gumersindo standing at the back of his seat. The negro bowed slightly, with his thick lips smiling. Strawbridge aroused himself, really glad to see Gumersindo. He got up and joined the colored man.

"Lots of folks in church to-day," he whispered.

Gumersindo nodded.

"The cavalry expect to go to San Geronimo soon. There is always a crowding in for confession before such an expedition."

"Oh! I see." Strawbridge was rather taken aback. He looked across at the opposite aisle, where two or three soldiers were standing near another confessional, awaiting their turn. "Do they really believe anything is going to happen to them?"

"Why, they know it!" Gumersindo considered Strawbridge, faintly surprised at such a question; then he evidently decided it was one of those thoughtless queries such as every one makes at times, for he passed to another subject: "Would you like to go down into the crypt?"

Strawbridge agreed, with his mind still hovering about San Geronimo. The negro led the way, tiptoeing through the big, murmuring cathedral:

"There's a great painting in that chapel," he said, pointing into one as they passed, but not stopping to enter it; "you must see it some day." Strawbridge said he would, and immediately forgot it.

They passed through the transept and round behind the high altar. In the passage they found another priest, walking slowly back and forth, reading some religious book. Gumersindo introduced Strawbridge to Father Benicio. The priest's face held the worn, ascetic look of a celibate who endures the ardors of the tropics.

"Señor Strawbridge is the American gentleman whom I brought back from Caracas," proceeded the editor; "perhaps you noticed my article about him in the 'Correo'?"

"I have not seen to-day's 'Correo,'" said the father, looking, with the shrewd eyes of his calling, at the American.

Gumersindo was already drawing from his pocket a damp copy of his paper. He opened the limp sheet and handed it to the priest, with his finger at the article. Then he turned away and pretended to inspect the carving on the reredos, glancing repeatedly toward the readers to see what effect his article was producing.

The article itself was typical Spanish-American rhetoric. It referred to the drummer as a merchant prince, a distinguished manufacturer, a world-famous exporter, and once it called him the illustrious Vulcan of the Liberal Arts, a flourish based on the fact that Strawbridge sold hardware.

When they had finished reading, the black man turned with his face beaming in anticipation of praise.

"Elegantly done, Gumersindo," pæaned the priest. "You have a very rich style."

The editor lifted his brows.

"I never hope to command a style, Father. I always write simply. It is all I can do."

Father Benicio patted the black man's arm and smiled the rather bloodless smile of the repressed.

"He is a fountain of eloquence and doesn't know it; don't you think so, Señor Strawbridge?"

"I was never called so many fine names in all my life," murmured Strawbridge, in the subdued tones all three men were using. "I must have a bundle of these papers to send home."

Gumersindo beamed, and said all Strawbridge needed to do was to give him the names and he would mail out copies direct. Then he again proposed going down into the crypt.

The father agreed. He gathered his cassock about him for convenience in descending the steps, produced a key, opened a small door in the back wall of the cathedral, then, apologizing for preceding his guests, stepped into the opening.

The American followed the editor and groped down a flight of clammy steps into a cellar about ten feet deep. The priest presently found a match and a candle and lighted the cold, unventilated crypt. In the dim light Father Benicio pointed out some old stone slabs set in the sides of the crypt, with half-obliterated names carved upon them. Then he began a recountal of the doings of the first Benedictines who had come into the Orinoco country in 1573. They had formed a flourishing colony, but the evil deeds of the Guipuzcoana Company had provoked the Indians to attack the religious colony, and many of the monks were massacred. The gravestones marked those early martyrs.

With a certain fire the priest told the tale. These early fathers were links in a chain to which he, himself, belonged. Their constancy, their devotion to duty, their faithfulness unto death were ensamples often in his heart, which warmed his monastic life.

Strawbridge did not feel the faintest interest in Father Benicio's recital. He looked at the stone slabs without any widening of his vision of the past. Indeed, anything that antedated 1890 was without interest to him. To the drummer, history had no connection with the present. If he had analyzed his impressions he would have found that he believed that all the acts of mankind prior to the nineties formed history and were completely cut asunder from the press and importance of to-day. The world in which Mr. Thomas Strawbridge lived and had his being was absolutely new and up to date. It was like a new steam-heated apartment house with all the elevators running and the water connections going, and it was utterly cut off from all the past efforts and struggles of mankind. History, to him, was not even the blue-prints from which this house was built, the brick and mortar of which it was constructed. It was simply a kind of confusion that went on in the world until men settled down and produced something worth while—that is to say, the American nation and the New York skyscrapers.

He yawned under his fingers.

"I wonder what they did for a living, back there." He touched one of the stones with his foot.

Father Benicio glanced around at him.

"They raised maize, bananas, and a few chickens," he said drily.

"Ship 'em back to ... Spain?" hazarded the drummer.

"No, they simply lived on what they cultivated, and what the Indians gave them."

The salesman's interest flickered out completely. He glanced at the gravestones of the unenterprising monks and moved a step toward the stairs.

Gumersindo attempted to stir up human interest by pointing out a slab of stone in the bottom of the crypt.

"This is not a gravestone; it conceals the entrance of a tunnel. The early Spanish settlers were great troglodytes, Señor Strawbridge. It is impossible to find an old castle or an old church without a tunnel or two leading into it."

"It was necessary in those unsettled times when a man's house was likely to be burned with the man in it unless he could slip out," put in the priest.

"Where does it lead to?" asked Strawbridge, taking rather more interest in this purely mechanical arrangement than in the human background which caused the tunnels to be dug.

"One branch leads down to the river, another to the *palacio*, and another to the prison, La Fortuna."

Strawbridge suppressed another yawn and dismissed the tunnels from his mind. His thoughts came back to the original problem which had brought him to the cathedral. He broke out rather abruptly:

"Say, I suppose both you fellows know about the general and his ... er ... business methods?"

Editor and priest looked at their guest quite blankly.

"I mean his method of ... well, ... of confiscating ranches and horses and stores, provisions, and such like. Now, that's a rotten way to do. I was wondering whether a good, straightforward talk with him wouldn't help some."

By now the two men were staring at Strawbridge as if one of the old monks had risen out of his tomb.

"Señor," said the priest, in a queer voice, "would you have the goodness to explain yourself?"

"Sure! A chap told me while ago that the general arrested a rancher and took his ranch. I've been thinking about it all morning."

"The ranch to which your informant alludes," said Gumersindo, in a cold voice, "was deserted, and General Fombombo occupied it as waste land."

The drummer laughed friendlily.

"Yes, I know about that, but just how the general hunched the man off his ranch has nothing to do with it. I say any kind of hunching is bad business." The drummer became very earnest: "Now look here, both you fellows know the only way to make a country pay is through business. Now, look at these old monks—" he nodded at the stones. "Fizzled out because they didn't develop their holdings. I don't know just what they did do, but it's clear they built this church instead of building a factory. No returns; see? All overhead and no production. Not that I'm against praying," he added, with a placating gesture toward the priest. "I'm for it. I think it peps one up, but, as my old man says, 'Get in your prayers when there is no customer in sight'; see? Just to come down to facts: these old boys didn't run on business principles.

"Now, here's what I'm driving at: The general's idea of grabbing things balls up the market. Your market has got to be open and it's got to be protected before you get any real big volume of trade. Any man in General Fombombo's shoes can get better returns in the way of legitimate taxes on legitimate business than he can by grabbing what's in sight and scaring off business men. For, let me tell you, the eagle on the dollar is just about the timidest bird you ever tried to get to roost in your hen-house, and that's straight."

Strawbridge came to an earnest and apparently a questioning pause. The editor and the priest stood looking at him in the candle-light, quite as silent as the ancient and unbusinesslike monks beneath their feet. After a while the editor asked in a strange voice:

"Why have you ... said these things to us, Señor Strawbridge?"

"I'm asking your advice."

"About what?"

"About talking this over with the general. I believe he is making a business mistake. He would realize more if he would boost business instead of knocking it. Perhaps you've read that little poem,

"It's better to boost than to knock;

   It's better to help than to shove,

We're brothers all, on the road of Life,

   And the law of the road is Love."

The editor said he had never read it.

"The thing I'm driving at," proceeded the drummer, "is, would it be good business for me to spring this on the general? You see, I might queer a two-hundred-and-fifty-thousand-dollar order for rifles. Still, if he could see the real business side of the situation, I might establish a market for millions of dollars' worth of hardware. What do you think about it? Would you run the risk?"

The priest chose to answer:

"Our President is rather a man of impulse, Señor Strawbridge."

The big American nodded.

"I see what you mean." He looked at Gumersindo.

"The future is always uncertain, Señor Strawbridge," observed the editor.

Strawbridge nodded.

"Uh huh; I see you agree with Father Benicio." He paused, thinking.

"Well, ... I don't know...." He continued to ponder the problem before him, and presently quoted, perhaps subconsciously:

"Did you speak that word of warning?

   Did you act the part of friend?

Do your duty resolutely;

   It means dollars in the end."

CHAPTER XI

Notwithstanding Strawbridge's apt and well-timed quotation from one of the best of the American business poets, still, he left the cathedral on his way to the *presidencia* in a shilly-shally mood. He went out at the side entrance, as the most direct route. The glare of sunshine struck his eyes rather uncomfortably after the gloom of the church. Just outside the door a dense flowering hedge delimited the plaza from the garden on the other side.

The drummer felt for his case and drew out a cigar to settle his thoughts on his proposed interview with the dictator. He stopped to scratch a match, when he heard voices talking just inside the garden. They were low voices, a man's and a woman's, but their passionate undertones caught the salesman's attention. He could understand little of what they were saying, but occasionally the woman lost her poise, or her caution, and he would get a phrase or two; then he could hear the man mumbling. Once the woman whipped out, "You are mad, you are insane, Pancho!" The voice of the man seemed to admit this. Later she gasped: "But you can't do that. He's alive!" and after another interval, she cried: "What a monster! I despise you as I do him. You are a *bribon*!"

This speech was stopped abruptly, as if a hand were laid over the woman's mouth. Came sounds of some guarded physical struggle, then a slap, a little cry, and the sound of running. The woman's restrained cry went through Strawbridge with a queer effect. He tried to peer through the dense hedge, but could make out nothing more than the fact of movement on the other side. A moment's reflection told him the man and the woman had separated.

The incident gripped the salesman in a strange way. He reasoned that if the two had separated one must have gone back into the church and the other toward the small postern at the end of the garden. So he walked briskly in the direction of the latter. Just as he stepped into the thoroughfare between garden and palace, he saw a woman in a nun's costume hurry out at the little gate, cross the road, and pass in at the side entrance of the big state house. With a breath of surprise, Strawbridge recognized Señora Fombombo. He found it difficult to attribute such an adventure to this small, quiet woman in her severe religious garb. And yet she had almost run from the garden gate to the palace. The American pondered this, but at last decided that the señora had been coming from her music practice in the cathedral and some quarreling, fighting couple in the garden had frightened her. The drummer walked quickly to the little postern and looked into the garden for the disturbing couple, but, of course, they had had time to escape.

Strawbridge loitered outside the palace for a few minutes, finishing his cigar and thinking over the incident. Then he walked up to the side door. His intention to ask for the señora at once was somewhat disturbed by the fact that the *griffe* girl admitted him when he rang the bell.

As the American stepped into the entrance, a little leather-colored soldier in uniform came briskly forward, with his rifle at attention. A word from the girl established Strawbridge's right to enter.

"The señora," she said, giving Strawbridge her knowing look, "is in the music-room." She paused a moment and added, "That's her, now."

The thing which she called the señora was the chromatic scale, played with great velocity.

The maid was so insinuating that Strawbridge thought of denying he had meant to see the chatelaine at all, but he changed this to something about believing he would go and hear the music. Instead of producing the casual effect he had hoped for, this statement lit a brightly intelligent smile on the *griffe* girl's copper-colored face. As Strawbridge walked down the transverse passage to the main corridor, to turn up toward the music-room, he could feel the eyes of both maid and guard watching his back.

The drummer passed two more guards in the main corridor, and presently paused before the door whence issued the runs and cadenzas. As he was about to tap, he was again seized with the inexplicable hesitancy which afflicted him whenever he came near the señora. It was an odd thing. He knew that she was just inside the dull mahogany panels, but somehow the door seemed to shut him out completely. He felt he would not get in. He tapped uncertainly, with a conviction that it would accomplish nothing. But it did accomplish something: it stopped the music so suddenly that it startled him. Then he waited in a profound silence.

Strawbridge imagined that the señora knew that it was he, and that by the long silence she was showing him that she did not want him in the music-room. A painful humility came over him. After all, he thought, she had a right to dislike him. Every time she saw him he was dull and embarrassed. Queer how she crabbed his style. Now, at home, back in Keokuk, he was rather popular with the ladies, but here.... The drummer's good-natured face sagged in a mirthless quirk. Well, ... he might as well go away. The señora would never know what a jolly friend she was missing, for he was jolly when one took him right; he simply was jolly. And he would never know her, either. It was the fault of neither of them; he saw that. He couldn't help it, she couldn't help it. A faint sense of pathos floated through the drummer's mind, and he turned away from the door.

At that moment it opened and the señora stood before him. Since he tapped she had just had time to walk across the room.

The man and the woman looked at each other in utter surprise, but in an instant this expression vanished from the señora's face and she asked him if he would like to come in and hear her play.

The drummer moistened his lips with his tongue and explained vaguely that he had just been passing and had heard the piano....

He was so painfully ill at ease that the girl said she too had been lonely that forenoon and was wishing some one would come in. She indicated a chair near a barred window, then, wearing the faint, unamused smile of a hostess, she went back to the piano and asked what he would have her play. Mr. Strawbridge said, "Just anything lively."

The señora pondered and began a mazurka. It was a trifle of thematic runs. She began rather indifferently, but presently her fingers or her mood warmed and she did it with dash and brilliancy.

At first Strawbridge's mental state prevented him from listening at all, but gradually the richly furnished room, the murals on the ceiling, the black ebony piano, and the slender nun-like player all re-formed themselves out of original confusion. Then he became aware of the music.

He did not care much for it. The señora did not jazz the piano as Strawbridge craved that it should be jazzed. It should be explained, perhaps, that the drummer's contact with music had been confined almost exclusively to the Keokuk dance-halls. He was, one might say, a musical bottle baby, who had waxed fat on the electric piano. Now he missed that roaring double shuffle in the bass and that grotesque yelping in the treble which he knew and admired and was moved by. He at once classified the señora as a performer who lacked pep.

The girl continued to fill the stately room full of dancing fairies; presently these exquisite little creatures rippled away into the distance; the last faraway fairy gave a last faraway pirouette, and the music ceased. The señora turned with a faint smile and waited a moment for her guest to say he liked the mazurka, but finally was forced to ask if he did.

"Well, y-e-s," he agreed dubiously, he liked it; then, with animation, "Señora, do you play 'Shuffle Along'?"

She repeated the title after him, evidently trying to translate it into intelligible Spanish.

"Who wrote it, señor?" She turned to a big music-rack which apparently held the music of the world.

"I don't know," said the drummer, naïvely. "Maybe you've got 'My Ding-Dong Baby'?"

Señora Fombombo began going through the huge music-cabinet uncertainly.

"You don't know the composer of that, either?"

"No. How about 'Ten Little Fingers and Ten Little Toes'? Or have you got the 'Haw-Hee Haw-Hee Toddle'?"

The señora, who was a methodical woman, began alphabetically with Brahms and looked for the "Haw-Hee Haw-Hee Toddle." Strawbridge got up from his chair and came to assist.

"Let me help you," he volunteered. "I know the backs of those pieces just as well as I do my own face."

The señora glanced at him.

"Do you play?"

"A little," admitted the drummer. "I have been known to ripple my fingers over the elephants' tusks." Strawbridge laughed pleasantly at this tiny jest. It was the first time he had been able to speak a single sentence in a natural way, to the señora. Now this small success pleased him.

"Play me the kind of music you like," invited the señora, at once. "I don't recognize the English titles. Perhaps I have them, after all."

"Oh, all right." He smiled and sat down on the old-fashioned piano stool. With a pleased expression on his handsome, good-natured face he looked at the señora. Then he popped his left fist into his right palm and his right fist into his left palm, to warm up his finger action.

"Now, this is the rage," he explained with a faint patronage in his voice; "this is what runs 'em ragged in New York," and, lifting his hands high, he boomed into the "Haw-Hee Haw-Hee Toddle."

Strawbridge did not see the señora's face during the opening bars of his jazz, and therefore had no means of determining her mood. When, presently, he looked about at her, she was much as usual; her black eyes a trifle wider, perhaps, her smile a little less mechanical.

"I've seen a thousand people on the floor at one time, toddling to this," he called to her loudly above his demonstration.

The señora pressed her lips together, her eyes seemed fairly to dance, and she nodded at this bit of information.

Strawbridge realized that he was entertaining the señora highly. He had never seen her look so amused. He had not thought her especially pretty, before, but just at this moment she gave him the impression of a ruby with the dust suddenly polished off and held in the sunshine.

The drummer was very proud of the fact that he could play the piano and talk at the same time, and he always did this.

"Say, I like the tone of this machine," he called out in a complimentary way; "she's hitting on all six cylinders now."

The señora laughed outright, in little gusts, with attempts at suppression. It was as if she had not laughed in a long, long time.

Strawbridge wagged his blond head to the clangor and syncopation of his own making.

"Coming down the home stretch!" he yelled, pounding louder and faster. "Giving her more gas and running up her timer!" He threw his big shoulders into the uproar. "Going to win the all-comers' sweepstakes! Go on, you little old taxi! Go to it! Wow! Bang! You're it, kid! The fifty-thousand-dollar purse is yours!"

He stopped as suddenly as he had begun, reached into his vest pocket, fished out a cigar band, and, with a burlesque curtsy, offered it to the señora as the sweepstakes prize he had just captured.

The señora produced a handkerchief and wiped her eyes, then drew a long breath. With her face dimpled and ready to laugh again, she looked at the drummer.

"I knew you'd like me if we ever got acquainted," confided Strawbridge; "nothing like music to get folks together."

"Yes," acquiesced the señora, smiling, "it is one of the shibboleths of culture."

"Why, ... yes, I suppose so," agreed Strawbridge. The phrase "shibboleths of culture" sobered him somewhat. It was not the sort of phrase an American girl would have flung into a gay conversation, at least not without making some sort of face, or saying it in a burlesque tone to show it was meant to be humorous. It plunked into the drummer's careless mood like a stone through a window. "By the way," he said, on this somewhat soberer plane, "let me tell you why I followed you here into this music-room."

"Did you follow me?"

"Yes."

"Where from?" she asked in a different voice.

"From the garden."

The mirth vanished from the señora's face as if some one had turned down a lamp. It left her pale, delicately engraved, and not very pretty.

"May I ask why you followed me?" she questioned.

"Sure!" said Strawbridge with a protective impulse stirring in him. "I was coming out of the cathedral and I heard some rough-neck couple raising a row over in the garden. I came on to the *palacio* and saw you running out of the gate. I knew they had frightened you with their yelping, and it made me mad. So when you go to the cathedral again, just tip me off, please, and I'll go along with you."

The señora stood leaning over the end of the piano, studying him intently.

"That is very kind, and ... and it's a very unexpected kindness, Señor Strawbridge. I am grateful."

"Don't thank me at all.... Do the same for any woman. And, say, that reminds me what I was balled up about."

"'Balled up'? What do you mean—'balled up'?"

"Oh!—" with little gesture—"I don't know what to do. It's a matter of business."

"Are you bringing me a matter of business?"

"Sure! Why not? You've got your ideas."

She continued to look at him curiously.

"Well, what is it?"

"It's about your husband. I consider that he runs this country on the most unbusinesslike basis I ever heard of."

The Spanish girl opened her eyes still wider at this astonishing turn.

"Unbusinesslike?"

"Sure, it's like this," and Strawbridge proceeded to explain what he knew of the dictator's methods; who had told him, and that he thought the general was losing money.

During the recital he was surprised to see the señora's pale face grow paler still. Finally she gasped:

"And does he take property, too?"

"Why, good God!" cried the drummer, in amazement, "didn't you know that?"

After a long pause the Spanish girl said almost inaudibly, "No, I didn't know ... that."

"Huh!" ejaculated Strawbridge, growing very much embarrassed. "I'm sorry I mentioned it, I ... I...." He looked at her, moistening his lips, and broke out with a desperate note of remorse, "Well, I swear I hate mentioning that!"

The señora shrugged wearily.

"Oh, ... *that* doesn't matter."

She kept accenting her "thats" as if other things preyed more deeply on her thoughts.

At this moment a big French motor-car murmured past the window of the music-room. It happened that both the drummer and the señora saw it, were looking straight at it. The car contained General Fombombo, and in the seat beside him Strawbridge recognized the peon girl Madruja, the little bride whom the dictator continued to detain in the palace until he could come to some judicial decision as to what to do with her.

CHAPTER XII

The passing of General Fombombo with the peon girl, Madruja, will call to the philosophical mind one of the sharpest distinctions between North American chastity and Venezuelan laxity. In America, no man, not even the most degraded specimen of our race, would think of parading his mistress before his wife. Such a thing is not done in America. Where the Latin flaunts his dalliances openly, the puritanical North American invariably makes an effort to conceal his shortcomings and to present to the world an innocuous and inoffensive front.

Spanish-American moralists are prone to ascribe this flowering of the great Anglo-Saxon cult of concealment to hypocrisy. Nothing could be shorter of the truth. Hypocrisy is an effort to deceive, but the best English and American types deceive no one. Their intention is not to deceive but to keep life clean, pure, and enjoyable for their fellow-men. For here is the peculiar thing about vice: A man's own shortcomings never appear censure-worthy, whereas the sins of other men are hideous. To be seen openly sinning is to make of oneself a public nuisance.

The genius of the Anglo-Saxon realizes this, and he avoids paining and distressing others by performing his dalliances as privately as possible. This secrecy is each man's private contribution to the comfort and reassurance of his fellow-citizens. Taking us all in all, perhaps America's greatest gift to the world is the peccadillo of low visibility.

As an instance of the deplorable effect of being seen, observe how the passing of General Fombombo and Madruja completely destroyed Mr. Thomas Strawbridge's pleasure in the society of Señora Fombombo. Yet all the time he had known from Lubito the actual state of the case. It had seemed humorous when Lubito told the story, but the sight of the dictator and the peon girl passing in the car was not humorous at all. On the contrary, it was oppressive and painful. It ended abruptly his tête-à-tête with the señora. Indeed, it hung about him for days, popping up every little while with disagreeable iteration.

The incident upset Strawbridge's own code. It caused him to doubt the rightness of any husband deceiving any wife. He had never before thought even of questioning such a situation. He had known many drummers, married men, who when they got to a city would take a little flyer. It had seemed perfectly all right, a sort of joke. Now, abruptly, it all seemed wrong, and he was vaguely angry and ill at ease.

And the personal end of the affair puzzled him. He could not understand how any sane man would run away from so delightful a girl as Dolores Fombombo, to the over-accented and uncultivated charms of a Madruja.

He tried to put himself in the general's place, to fancy himself the husband of Dolores. Would he betray her? Would he deceive the confidence of so dainty a creature? Indeed no! The very thought filled him with a most unusual and tremulous tenderness. Why, before he would break faith with Dolores ... before he would do that.... He got out a cigar, bit off the nib with a snap, and lighted it in vague anger. He continued pacing up and down his room from one barred window to another, looking out at the river, at the gloomy prison called "La Fortuna," at the back of the cathedral.

Then his thoughts veered away from the general's infidelity, and he began thinking about a strange thing which had happened to him a day or two before, when he called on the proprietor of "Sol y Sombra." He decided he would mention it to Dolores; perhaps she could explain it.

The decision to see Dolores and tell her this thing comforted Strawbridge somewhat. He drew an eased breath, went over to the window, reached through the bars, and tapped off the ash of his cigar, then walked out into the corridor, turned toward the rear of the palace, and passed out through a back entrance onto a sort of piazza—a roofless paved space about forty feet wide, which extended from the building quite to the edge of the take-off that led down a long, steep slope to the yellow river.

On the western end of this piazza projected the kitchen, and it was littered on that side with unsightly bags of charcoal, chicken feathers, bundles of kindling, bones, and other rejectæ from the cooking-department of the palace. This litter increased or decreased according to the spasmodic energy of the *griffe* girl, the wrinkled old hag, and three or four other familiars of the kitchen. When these caretakers were induced to purge their premises, they simply shoved the refuse over the edge of the piazza and allowed it to distribute itself as it would down the long slope.

Strawbridge dragged out a chair on the east side of the piazza and sat down to his cigar and the sunset. This had grown to be his custom every late afternoon. Until the señora joined him he was more attentive to his cigar than to the sunset. But when she came, her arrival, oddly enough, seemed to open his eyes to the fact that sunsets in the Orinoco Valley are famous for their brilliant coloring and dramatic effects.

He had finished perhaps a third of his cigar when he heard a servant come dragging the señora's chair behind her. This ended a faint suspense in

Strawbridge. He looked around, and the two of them smiled at each other the satisfied smiles of friends who had been anticipating just this pleasure of watching the sunset together.

For the first evening or two they had talked dutifully all the time. Strawbridge had exerted himself to amuse the señora, but of late they had found long silences mutually pleasant. So now, as the señora came up, he simply remarked that he thought they were going to have a nice sunset.

The drummer himself was immeasurably content. He sat watching the change and play of that huge and airy mansionry of vapors. Somehow it reduced him and Dolores to two human midges seated behind a little palace, on a tiny piazza, in microscopic wicker chairs. It sent a shudder of pleasure through him: they were so very, very small, and so very, very comforting each to the other.

As they sat staring at the vast chromatic architecture, a faint breeze brought him the malodor of the kitchen at the other end of the piazza and stirred him out of his reverie. He looked around.

"By the way, señora, a queer thing happened to me the other morning. I've been meaning to tell you about it, but I never can think to when I'm with you."

"Yes?"

"About that clerk at 'Sol y Sombra.' That little chap who put me wise to business conditions in this country. You remember what a row he raised because I wanted to make a hardware display."

"Yes, that's Josefa."

"Well, he's gone."

The señora moved lazily in the gloom, to face her companion.

"You wanted to tell me Josefa was gone?" He could tell by her voice that she was smiling.

"Not so much that as the way I heard it. Day or two ago I called on the proprietor. He was as polite as pie, but he didn't warm up to my selling talk. Finally I offered him my leader—some shovels at a price that'd make him think he stole 'em. I was pushing the goods pretty hard when finally he looked at me with a sort of whitish face and says, 'Señor Strawbridge, I am not in the market for your goods at any price.'

"'That lets me down,' I says, 'if low prices and high quality don't interest you. That's all I got—the lowest prices and the highest quality."

"I saw he was going to bow me out regardless, so I thought I would be polite up to the limit and inquire after the health of the little clerk I had met in the store several mornings before that.

"When I asked after him, the proprietor jumped from his chair. 'Señor!' he cried, 'you shall not mock at my distress! You may have the leading hand now, but as sure as there is a God in heaven, He will punish you!' He shook a finger at me. 'He will punish you! He will punish you!'

"I stared at him. I never came so near hitting a man in all my life, but I remembered something my old man told me when I first went to work with him. 'Strawbridge,' he'd say, 'keep your temper; nobody else wants it.' So I thought to myself, 'Here's where I keep her,' and I said, 'Señor, you've got the advantage of me. If I've done you or yours any harm, I'm sorry, but how have I done it?'

"He looked at me as keen as all you black-eyed folks can look. 'Don't you know where Josefa is?' he asked.

"'Certainly I don't, or I wouldn't have asked where he was.'

"'Well—he's not here any longer.'

"'Did you discharge him?' I asked.

"The merchant looked at me, and I be damned if there wasn't tears in his eyes. 'Señor Strawbridge,' he said, 'Josefa is gone. He is simply gone. He was a good boy; that is all I can say to you about it.'"

Here Strawbridge's narration was interrupted by a little sound from the girl in the darkness. He stopped short.

"Why, what's the matter, señora?" he asked in surprise.

"Oh, nothing ... nothing...." Her voice quavered. "Poor Josefa!"

The salesman tried to peer into her face.

"What are you saying, 'Poor Josefa,' about? I thought you didn't know him particularly well."

"I didn't. Oh, Señor Strawbridge, everything is so horrible here!... so terrible!... Oh.... Oh ..." and suddenly the señora began to weep, a pathetic little figure in her nun's costume.

Something clutched the drummer's diaphragm. He leaned toward her.

"Señora!" he remonstrated. "What's the matter? Have I done anything?"

One arm was crumpled about her face, she stretched the other toward him.

"Oh, no, no! you've done nothing to me. I ... I thought I was getting used to it. I used to cry all the time when I first came here. I thought I was growing hard, but I suppose I'm not."

The drummer was tingling at the appeal in her attitude and of her hand which had caught two of his fingers. A faint pulse began murmuring in his ears. He wanted to pick the whole of her daintiness up in his arms and comfort her.

"For God's sake, what do you mean?" he begged.

The girl collected herself.

"I will tell you," she said in a low tone. "There, sit closer, please, so I can talk in a low tone. Don't make any noise, señor."

Strawbridge adjusted his chair silently and sat staring at the slight figure, in mute speculation. His head was full of the wildest conjectures: Josefa was her brother ... her lover. Josefa had followed her over from Spain....

"You say you never heard of Josefa before you came here?" he asked aloud.

"No, I'd never heard of him."

"Then why in the world—"

She made a weary gesture.

"Oh, Señor Strawbridge, because life is all terrifying here; every part has the same horrible quality!"

"But you don't know where Josefa is?"

"*Sí, sí,* señor; indeed I do!"

"Then where is he?" asked Strawbridge, more bewildered than ever.

The girl pointed silently through the gloom.

"Yonder," she whispered.

Strawbridge turned, half expecting to see the little monkey-eyed clerk behind him. But the piazza was deserted, and he saw nothing more than the low, heavy walls of the fort against the last umber light in the east.

"What do you mean?" he asked.

"I mean ... the prison, señor."

A cold trickle went over the drummer.

"You don't mean that little clerk's in prison?"

"*Sí*, señor."

The drummer stared at her.

"For God's sake, why? What did he do?"

"Nothing señor, except...."

"Except what?"

"Except talk to you, señor."

She whispered this last in a rush which ended in a gasp, and this told Strawbridge she was weeping again.

The big drummer miserably watched her distress.

"Talked to me!"

"Because he told you about President Fombombo's methods."

With a queer sensation the American turned to look at the prison again.

"O-o-oh ... I see. Well, I'll be ... damned!" he uttered in slow stupefaction.

"And that is nothing ... nothing!" accented the girl passionately. "There are scores, *scores* in there—the maimed, the tortured, the sick, the dying. They have filthy crusts to eat. Never a physician or a priest. When they die, the guards throw them into the river, to the crocodiles. Oh, Señor Strawbridge, somehow God will punish this terrible place! Listen!" she whispered. "At night, Father Benicio sleeps in the cathedral, where he overlooks the river and the prison. When any noise awakens him and he sees the guards throwing something into the water, the priests go to the altar and say the mass for departing souls."

The American shook his head as he stared at the prison.

"Merciful God!" he said in a whisper.

Presently she began telling Strawbridge her sensations when she came from Spain as General Fombombo's bride and found herself amid such a reign of terror.

"It was like stepping into hell, Señor Strawbridge. There never was a woman so miserable as I. I was afraid to confess such awful things, even to Father Benicio, but at last I did. He was the only human soul to whom I could turn. Good, kind Father Benicio! He saved me from going mad."

As she finished her story the American's optimism returned. "Maybe I can do something about this," he said thoughtfully. "I never have talked to

General Fombombo about his business policy, but I really must now. I'll start in about Josefa. I'll show the general how the boy meant no harm. I'll get him taken out; then I'll show the general how his policy as a whole is bad for business—"

"Oh, no, no, no!" interrupted the señora in alarm. "It won't help at all."

"Not if I show him it's bad business?"

"Señor, the general doesn't care that about business!" She snapped her fingers.

Thomas Strawbridge smiled in the darkness.

"That's where you don't know men, señora," he assured her from his wider knowledge. "Every man cares about business. There is no man on earth that isn't wrapped up in some sort of business. Well, I think I'll step inside and see what I can do." He patted her hand where it lay on the arm of her chair. There was something about its softness and littleness that sent a strange, sweet sensation up Strawbridge's arm and suffused his body. The next moment he moved into the palace, with his usual quick, rangy strides.

CHAPTER XIII

When Strawbridge entered the library of the palace he found only Coronel Saturnino, who was working at his desk. Near the entrance stood one of the palace guards. The silence was almost complete; Strawbridge could hear the faint scratch of the colonel's pen as he toiled at his endless preparations to seize San Geronimo.

The drummer was on the verge of calling out to ask the whereabouts of General Fombombo, when it occurred to him that this Coronel Saturnino was at that moment devising plans upon which, quite possibly, his own safety depended.

It was rather an extraordinary thought for the salesman. There was something dramatic about it—a man working silently in the great, still library, determining whether Strawbridge should live or die. And there stood Strawbridge, near the door, unable to assist in the slightest degree in this determination of his fate. It was a queer, almost a ghostly feeling. Somehow it clothed Coronel Saturnino with a kind of awesome superiority. A sort of premonition of the raid on San Geronimo came to the drummer, a charging of horsemen, sword thrusts, the flash of small arms.... His visualization was based largely upon a cheap chromo called "The Fall of the Alamo" which had hung in the parlor of his home in Keokuk. In this picture the artist had been very liberal with blood and dead men. Strawbridge decided not to call to Coronel Saturnino, but to allow him to work undisturbed.

The drummer nodded the guard to him. The little brown man glanced around at the colonel, then moved silently toward the American, evidently with scruples. When he was close enough, Strawbridge whispered:

"Where is the general?"

The man was amazed at such a question.

"Señor, I am a guard, not a spy."

The salesman was faintly amused.

"Aw, come now! What's the big idea? You know me. You see me every day around this joint. So spit it out, man: where did the general go?"

The little fellow shrugged, pulled down the corners of his mouth, and moved silently back to his post.

This irritated the American. He told the guard, under his breath, to go to hell, and that faint explosion sufficed to wipe the incident from his mind. He turned out into the corridor again and walked toward the front of the building, in an aimless search for the dictator, while his thoughts returned to the señora and the misfortunes of little Josefa.

He began composing a speech against the time he found the general, a kind of sales talk designed to set Josefa free. He would say the little clerk had not volunteered the information about General Fombombo's business methods. That had been wrung from him by the fact that he, Strawbridge, was about to arrange a hardware display. From this point of departure the drummer hoped to proceed into a constructive criticism of the general's whole dictatorial policy. It might do a lot of good, probably would. He was making the general's problems his problems, and now he rather thought he had solved one. He could fancy the general looking him straight in the eye and saying, "Strawbridge—by God!—I believe you've hit the nail on the head!" As a matter of fact, the drummer knew the general never used profanity, but somehow he placed this blasphemy in the general's mouth because it sounded strong and admiring, as one frank, manly American curses at another when his admiration reaches a certain low boiling-point.

The drummer walked slowly down the corridor, listening at each door as he passed, but he reached the entrance of the palace without hearing the general's voice.

Strawbridge came to a halt near the guard at the entrance, and stood wondering what he should do. The injustice of Josefa's imprisonment spurred him to do something. He stood looking into the plaza below him, which was illy lighted. A rather large audience was collecting, for it was concert night. The semi-weekly concert of the firemen's band would begin in about half an hour. A thought that he might find General Fombombo in the audience sent the drummer down the long flight of ornamental stairs into the plaza.

In the park was a typical Wednesday-evening crowd such as were gathering in all the larger towns in South America. Near the band stand was a high stack of folding chairs, and peon boys hurried among the audience, renting these chairs at two cents each for the evening. Dark-eyed señoritas in mantillas and fashionable short skirts chose seats under the electric lights, where they could cross their legs and best display their well-turned calves and tiny Spanish feet. The greater part of the crowd preferred to walk. They moved in a procession around the plaza, the men clockwise, the women anticlockwise, so the men were continually passing a line of women, and vice versa. There was an endless tipping of hats, tossing of flowers, and brief exchange of phrases. Here and there an engaged couple strolled about the square together. To be seen thus was equivalent to an announcement.

The drummer was walking among this crowd, glancing about for the President, when a hand touched his shoulder. He looked around and saw Lubito the bull-fighter with a peon companion. This peon was a youth who wore alpargatas, but the rest of his costume had the cheap smartness of the poorer class of Venezuelans who trig themselves out for the Wednesday-night concerts. In contrast to his finery, there was something severe, almost tragic in the youth's pale-olive face.

"This is Esteban, señor," introduced the torero, reaching back and settling his wad of hair. "You remember him—Madruja's lover, who is half married to her. That makes him the demi-husband of a demi-monde."

Strawbridge extended his hand, rather amused at the oddity of the introduction.

"*Caramba!*" ejaculated Lubito. "Do you smile at a man in distress, señor?"

The drummer straightened his face.

"Oh, no, not at all! I am glad to meet Señor Esteban. By the way, I was just out hunting General Fom—"

Esteban lifted a quick hand.

"Señor," he cautioned in an undertone, "it is not wise to speak that name in a public place, such as this."

Strawbridge glanced around, rather surprised.

"I was saying no harm. Besides, he's a friend of mine. In fact, I was looking for him, to ask a little favor."

"Yes?" interrogated Lubito.

"It's about a youngster named Josefa. The general put him in prison—"

"*Diablo*, señor!" gasped Esteban. "I beg of you not to speak of these things in the plaza!"

The drummer was impressed with the peon's alarm. His feeling was reinforced by the knowledge that Josefa was in prison on account of just such a casual conversation as this. So he said:

"Well, now you know what I had to tell you, and who I am hunting."

The bull-fighter nodded gravely.

"I see you are going to do a certain friend of yours a little favor."

"Yes, get him out of trouble."

The torero turned to his companion.

"You see, Esteban, he is *un hombre muy simpatico* but very indiscreet. Do you know what he did to me in Caracas? *Caramba!* I was standing on the street corner watching some domino-players. Every one knows that the domino-players are the police's own stool-pigeons. *Cá!* I was standing there watching them when this *hombre* comes along and roars in my ears, 'Where is the *casa* where the great revolutionist, General Adriano Fombombo lives!' *Madre de Jesu!* I almost fainted. I could see myself rotting in La Rotunda!"

"He has a lion's heart," declared Esteban.

"And a donkey's brain," retorted the bull-fighter.

Strawbridge had heard enough of this.

"With your permission, señors, I will continue my search."

"But don't you want to watch the crowd, señor?" suggested Lubito. "There, look at that little officer with the swagger-stick; perhaps you know him?"

The drummer saw a sharp-featured young officer with dark circles of dissipation under his eyes.

"No, I don't know him."

"You don't know the Teniente Rosales?"

"No, I never heard of him."

Lubito gave the drummer a side glance.

"It is not a bad idea to say you don't know him, at any rate."

"Why, I don't!" repeated the drummer, emphatically, looking around at the bull-fighter in surprise.

Esteban interrupted:

"You see, Lubito, he is far more discreet than you gave him credit for. Perhaps he recognized *you* on the street corner of Caracas."

The bull-fighter looked at Esteban and then at Strawbridge.

"*Caramba!* I never thought of that!"

This conversation was getting too cryptic for Strawbridge.

"I don't know what you're talking about," he said, "so, once more with your permission, I'll go." He turned to leave his companions.

Lubito interrupted:

"Wait; we're going in your direction ourselves. Come on, Esteban, we might as well have pleasant company."

"Oh, ... all right," agreed the drummer, rather surprised at this.

The three men drew away from the crowd, and for some distance walked in silence. They directed their course along the shadowy parts of the plaza and then to the adjoining streets. At last Lubito said with a casual air:

"We hear you have joined the cavalry, señor."

"For the expedition against San Geronimo," qualified the drummer.

"You are a military man, no doubt?"

"No, not at all."

The bull-fighter seemed surprised.

"Are you going as a simple private?"

"Well, y-es," hesitated Strawbridge, with the complete reason of his going floating unsaid in his mind.

"No doubt you wish to make friends with the common people—the peons, the *griffes*, the mestizos, who make up this God-forsaken country, señor, and who are not of the pure Castilian blood as Esteban and I."

Strawbridge could not see whither this conversation was leading. He said, very honestly:

"Naturally; I want to make friends with every one."

"We thought so," nodded the torero; "we observed how you speak to all persons, great and small, how you stop on the street to give moral advice even to the lottery-ticket venders, how you sympathize with the unfortunate Josefa, and say conditions should be changed. Yes, you certainly are very careful to make friends with every one."

Strawbridge was surprised that the bull-fighter had so complete a digest of his most trivial acts. Also, here and there in Lubito's tones flickered an insinuation of some hidden meaning which annoyed the drummer.

"Look here," he said frankly. "What are you driving at? You know I rode from Caracas with you. You know I'm selling firearms to the general, and hardware to anybody else."

"*Sí*, señor," agreed Lubito, politely, "but why should you seek to make friends with this fellow and that fellow—the lowest and the meanest?"

The drummer was a little irritated.

"I want to make friends with everybody; in the long run it will be of advantage to my house."

"Your house?" from Esteban.

"I mean the commercial firm I work for."

The two peons nodded thoughtfully. Esteban observed:

"A lottery-ticket vender, who cannot afford clothes for his nakedness, will hardly buy guns and hardware...."

The salesman was growing weary of these innuendoes.

"Look here," he said in the perfectly friendly voice with a disagreeable content that is sometimes used by Americans in these circumstances, "I don't give a damn what you fellows think. I can't explain every look and word by my business. I'm friendly because I ... I'm just naturally friendly. I call a man who isn't friendly a damn fool. Here I am walking with you two guys. I don't expect to sell *you* guns and hardware, either, but I'm walking with you, just the same."

He looked at both of them after this little speech. Both were obviously and entirely unconvinced. They shrugged slightly.

"*Pues, pues! Bien! Cá! Seguramente!*" They walked slowly on, evidently in deep thought. Presently Lubito broke the silence:

"Señor, you will pardon me. We knew all the time you were telling us the precise truth. What I said was by way of jest. Esteban, there, misunderstood, because he is a little dull. There is just one other point Esteban does not understand, and I confess it puzzled me a bit, too. But I will not ask it if you are angry, señor. Perhaps, after all, we would better talk of other things. I think you have lost patience with your two poor stupid friends."

"No," denied the drummer, rather ashamed of his little outbreak, "I haven't lost patience, but you don't seem to believe what I tell you."

"Oh, *sí*, señor! yes we do!" chorused the two, earnestly. "*Caramba!* We would not think of doubting a *caballero's* word!"

"Well, then, what's your question?"

"Exactly this: you are not a military man?"

"No."

"You are going to fight at San Geronimo as a trooper?"

"Yes."

"You came here to sell hardware?"

"Yes."

"Then ... I am very stupid ... but why do you fight?"

"Can you sell hardware to dead men on a battle-field?" added Esteban.

Strawbridge looked at his questioners, with a misgiving that he would never make them understand the true situation. They would never realize the necessity of learning the complete details of a customer's business. He began talking very carefully, as if he were explaining a lesson to a child:

"I am joining the raid on San Geronimo to get a working idea of my patron's business conditions."

Lubito nodded.

"Before I sell a market, I like to know it thoroughly."

"*Precisamente.*"

"Before I sell a man a tool, I want practical, first-hand knowledge of just how he is going to use it, what he needs, why he needs it. That's the American method." Launched on his favorite theme, Strawbridge spoke with a certain fervor.

"But why is that, señor?" puzzled Esteban. "If you sell a man anything, it is his. He has it. You have sold it."

"Sh! let him explain!"

"No, that's a good question," declared Strawbridge, with enthusiasm. "I sell you something. Why am I concerned about how you use it? The use of that article is your problem. But perhaps with my expert knowledge I can show you how to use it better, or perhaps I can devise a way to make you a better tool. Then you will be a satisfied customer, and a satisfied customer is the best advertisement in the world." Strawbridge shook his fist. "When you buy anything from me, gentlemen, you are not buying just my goods, you are buying human service!" He popped his fist into his palm. "You are buying the best in me to coöperate with the best in you, and between us we'll make this world a better world to live in." He nodded sharply. "See?"

The drummer paused. The bull-fighter and the peon looked at each other. After several seconds had passed, Esteban said:

"For example, señor, if I wanted to buy a dirk to cut Lubito's throat, you would come and cut it first to see what kind of knife I should use?"

Strawbridge was a little cooled.

"Well, ... that is just about the size of my San Geronimo trip; isn't it? You seem to have hit the nail on the head."

Esteban became thoughtful.

"So you are going to aid—" his voice sank—"General Fombombo."

"Yes, sure I am."

"And it makes no difference whether *he* is right or wrong. You will help him steal my Madruja, steal Señor Fando's horse, steal Señor Rosario's ranch, put Josefa in irons, do this, that, and the other, break our bodies, destroy our souls, cut us down, and grind us like corn in his mill. It makes no difference to you; you are going to help him in all that!"

Strawbridge was shocked at this sudden attack on the moral end of his business, by the peon who had lost his sweetheart. He became more carefully logical and less rhetorical. In fact, he was exploring new ground, a territory over which his old man had not coached him, so he was not so sure of himself.

"It's like this: I'm doing my part of this thing in a business way. If everybody would work in a business way, there wouldn't be any of this rough stuff you're talking about, because that's bad business. In fact, I was just on my way around to see the general. I'm going to get Josefa out of prison, and I think I can stop all this other sort of thing. I believe I can put this whole country on a business basis."

"But you, yourself, are going to San Geronimo to help kill men, just to show him how to work his guns!"

Here Lubito interrupted in a disgusted tone:

"Esteban, you fool, just because you've lost your Madruja, your head is hot and you see nothing in the light of reason. This tale Señor Strawbridge told us is the tale he tells the general, and makes *him* believe it. By this means he goes to San Geronimo with the cavalry. *Caramba!* I am amazed that even a stupid peon should not see so simple a thing!"

Esteban stared, and grinned faintly.

"*Cá!* He told it so cleverly that even I believed it, too!"

Strawbridge looked at his companions.

"What'n hell are you talking about?" he demanded.

Lubito held up a finger.

"Everything is well, señor." He nodded confidentially. "You are a much deeper man that I thought. Everything is as you would wish it. In only one way would I caution you."

"Damned if I know where you are heading in, but what do you want to caution me about?"

"It is this, señor—you will take it as a friend; we are brothers now—it is this: When our country became so bad under General Dimancho that it could go no farther, we appealed to General Miedo for aid, and he promised us if he won power we should have justice, that every peon should possess his wife and daughters and property in peace, señor, precisely as you say."

In the greatest astonishment Strawbridge stared at the bull-fighter.

"What's that got to do with me?"

"Nothing, nothing at all, señor, but General Miedo forgot his pledges when he reached power. He forgot his pledges as men are prone to do, and our country became even worse than when it was under General Dimancho. So we went to General—" Lubito dropped to a whisper—"to General Fombombo, who had a ranch down on the Orinoco near Ciudad Bolívar. And *he* promised our deputation if we raised him to the highest seat our wives and daughters and property should be our own. Señor Strawbridge, the monument to General Fombombo that stands back there in the plaza marks the spot where he stood General Miedo up before his soldiers and shot him through the heart."

A goose-flesh feeling brushed over the drummer.

"Lubito," he said, "what in hell has this got to do with me?"

"Nothing, señor, nothing at all. I merely mention this by way of information. You want information. All Americans want information. They want that the most badly of all the things they need. Also, there is a saying in Rio Negro, señor, that a gray-eyed man shall free us. And we have tried our own people so many times, señor, and so sorrowfully, that we are weary of trying Venezuelans, and would fain try a man of another nation."

Strawbridge was dumbfounded. He could do nothing but stand and stare at his companions. At last he made an effort and said in a queer voice:

"Men, you've got me wrong; you've got me completely wrong."

"*Seguramente!* You are a salesman of hardware, who goes to war to show the dictator what knife cuts a throat best." Lubito laughed briefly. "We do not know what throat you mean to cut first, señor—you are a deep man—but here we part for the night. This building on your left is the west wing of the *palacio*. In those lighted windows you will find the general with Madruja. You said you wished to find him. There he is. I do not know what you wish to say or do to the general. I will not ask. You say, yourself, that you are a *maestro* in the cutting of throats. No one knows when or where you may see fit to give a lesson." Lubito laughed. "Remember, Lubito and Esteban are your friends. *Adio' hasta mañana.*"

"*Adios,*" returned Strawbridge.

His two companions turned and moved away toward the plaza. In the distance the firemen's band had struck up a sensuous Spanish waltz. The drummer stood meditating on the amazing thing Lubito had told him. Such a usurpation was as remote from Strawbridge's temperament as the stars, but nevertheless he was profoundly moved. For some reason the Señora Fombombo came into his mind. He saw her as clearly as if she stood before him in bright day. He put her vision from him, and stared resolutely at the brightly lighted windows across the dark street. In an effort to bring his mind back to his own affairs, he drew out his silver cigar-case and lighted up. He tipped up his face in order that his eyes might escape the smoke. Out of the heavens a thousand brilliant stars offered him counsel. Presently Lubito and Lubito's insurgency faded from his mind. He finally sifted down the exact problem which he had to meet. Should he go over and ask for Josefa's release and extend to the general his views on the proper business methods to be used in Rio Negro?

Should he go now? That was his problem. An American caught in the presence of his mistress would probably be in a dour mood. On the other hand, the thought of the little monkey-eyed Josefa, lingering out another night in the filthy dungeons of La Fortuna, filled Strawbridge with pity and remorse. The youth was entirely innocent, and he, Strawbridge, had put him in his cell. On the other hand, a badly timed interview could very well be of no service to Josefa, and might lose the drummer a two-hundred-and-fifty thousand-dollar order for rifles.

He wondered what his old man would advise him to do in this emergency. The drummer looked up at the stars and sought advice just as earnestly as any religious martyr would have prayed to these same heavens. If he had known what his old man would suggest, he would have done it.

The coal on Strawbridge's cigar glowed and faded at long intervals, and presently there struggled up out of the drummer's subconscious a memory of a little framed motto which his employer had hung over his desk. It read:

> The greatest assets of any firm are the honor and courage of its salesmen; next comes the quality of its goods.

Religious martyrs, in their extremity, have been known to receive answers from the heavens they interrogated. Thomas Strawbridge, also, had received his. He drew a deep puff of smoke, thumped away his cigar, which made a dull spiral of fire as it fell through the darkness; then he started briskly across the street.

CHAPTER XIV

One of the palace guards delayed Strawbridge for a few moments at the entrance of the west wing of the palace, to ask his master if the American might be admitted. A little later the soldier returned and opened a door into a brightly lighted sitting-room which evidently corresponded to the music-room in the east wing. Some rugs made of Indian blankets, chairs, and a couch of colored native wickerwork gave a look of richness and rather intemperate color to the room. The high light of this ensemble, that which held it all together and subordinated it, was the peon girl Madruja. Strawbridge obtained rather a bewildered impression of her. In fact, no man ever gets the details of an unusually comely woman at first glance.

General Fombombo, rising from the wicker couch where he had been sitting beside the girl, begged permission to leave her for a moment, to which Madruja assented with a mute gesture. The President came forward to Strawbridge, with both hands outstretched, radiating welcome.

"*Mi caro amigo*," he greeted, "I am charmed to have you see my little ménage. What do you think of my color scheme?" He stood gripping the drummer's hand and looking about at the room with that detachment which the arrival of a third person always gives an artist toward his work. The general picked out a doubtful point: "What do you think of the clasp that holds down the drapery between her breasts?"

Strawbridge barely managed to see the clasp against the glow of the girl. He said he thought it was a very nice clasp.

"No, I mean would you prefer garnet or ruby just there? I tried garnet at first, but I found that her eyes would endure the fire of a ruby. Ah, Señor Strawbridge, you are doubtless aware that not one woman in fifty can wear a ruby in her bosom."

Strawbridge cleared his throat and said he knew rubies were very expensive.

This introduced a little gap in the conversation. The dictator changed his manner from the enthusiasm of an artist to the courtesy of a host:

"I believe you have not as yet had the pleasure of meeting Señorita Rosamel." Here he led Strawbridge nearer Madruja. "Señorita, may I present my dear friend Señor Tomas Strawbridge of Nueva York?"

The girl remained seated and simply extended a hand. Whether she did this out of timidity, or out of pride in her new silks and jewels, the drummer could not guess. The hand she placed in his was small and not badly shaped, but hard and rough from the work of a peon woman. She said nothing at all, but sat looking at Strawbridge out of black eyes which could endure the fire of a ruby. They were the shining, surfacy eyes one sees in wild animals and in entirely illiterate persons. Of what thoughts, if any, lay behind those surfaces, the drummer could not get the slightest inkling.

However, she seemed tractable enough. With a little sinuous movement she made room on the couch for the general. With perfect inertness she allowed him to possess her hand. He picked it up, spread it in his palm, and began patting and stroking it while his conversation returned to Strawbridge.

"You may light a cigar in here and be comfortable," he invited. "Madruja is no obstacle to relaxation; rather, an assistance. Have you never observed that your thoughts flow more smoothly when your arm is about a pretty woman?"

None of the scene was agreeable to Strawbridge, but this peculiar turn caused him to ejaculate:

"You can *think* better with your arm around a woman?"

"*Seguramente*, señor," agreed the dictator. "Have you not observed that some men twiddle a pencil when they think, others smoke, some walk up and down with their hands behind their backs? All of these are mere bachelorish makeshifts. Your true thinker meditates with a woman's head on his shoulder. It is, you might say, señor, the only connection between a woman's head and thought."

As the general's thought had become more involved, he had drawn Madruja to him and now sat caressing her, his fingers playing abstractedly with the ruby and along the faint indentures of her clavicles.

Strawbridge disapproved of this almost beyond patience. He resented this establishment in the west wing of the palace, on account of the señora. It seemed to him that it would have been much more decent and respectful if the dictator had taken away this second ménage, had hidden it out of sight and denied it as Americans do in such cases.

"I don't know about a woman giving a man ideas," he blurted out, with disapproval tingeing his tones.

"Read the life of Simon Bolivar," returned the general, easily, still caressing the source of his own inspiration. "In the 'Diario de Bucaramanga,' by de la Croix, we learn that Bolivar was unable to plan any of the great battles which freed the South American continent except when he was dancing with a woman. Every night, during his military campaigns, he danced till one or two o'clock, planning his next great stroke at Spain. That is what genius is, Señor Strawbridge—the ability to draw on outside sources of power. The women with whom Bolivar danced—what were they? Batteries. Bolivar was the motor. They furnished him the energy to lift this whole continent from tyranny to the untrammeled freedom enjoyed in Rio Negro to-day."

The general paused a moment and continued:

"Take me and Madruja. Out of the wealth of this woman's muliebrity, I will extend the state of Rio Negro from the Andes to the sea. She and I will build up great cities; gardenize the llanos; develop a people with the finesse of the French, the energy of the Americans, and the immensitude of the Spanish!" He pressed the girl to him passionately, moved with the magnificence of his vision, then put her beside him again and came down to a more normal mood by taking her hand once more and spreading it in his own.

This last ebullition was more than Strawbridge could tolerate. If all this had been expounded over Dolores Fombombo, had Dolores been alternately crushed and caressed, the drummer would have thought the relations between the President and his wife the most beautiful he had ever known. But the fact that Fombombo had shifted women rendered it outrageous. Strawbridge had to speak for the wife.

"Look here," he criticized. "That's all right. You seem to get a lot of pep out of this young lady, but look here—" at this point Mr. Strawbridge made one of those moral pauses which Americans inherit from their Sunday-school teachers—"had you thought of your wife?"

"Had I thought of my wife?"

"Yes; had you?"

"What is there to think of my wife?"

For some reason the drummer blushed slightly.

"It looks to me like she ought to come in there somewhere. Doesn't look like another woman should step in and ... er ... uh...." He waved his hand.

The general was enlightened.

"I see what you mean." He smiled. "That is a quaint American idea of yours."

"It's American," defended Strawbridge stoutly, "but I don't see that it's quaint."

"Perhaps 'quaint' is not the word, but if I may speak impersonally and in no way appear to criticize the American point of view, I should say it is very disrespectful in a man to think of a wife in such a way as this. I feel safe in saying that no Spanish *caballero* would consider it for a moment."

The drummer stared at this extraordinary statement.

"Disrespectful! Do you think it would be more disrespectful to plan your empire under your wife's inspiration than to set up an establishment like this?"

"*Caramba*, Señor Strawbridge! certainly! When I enter my wife's presence I am a Spanish gentleman." Here the dictator made a bow to a space which represented his wife. "I think of nothing but her. For example, if Dolores were in this room would our conversation have wandered about like this? Certainly not. Could we have smoked, or talked on risqué topics? Certainly not. The Spaniard keeps his mistresses, Señor Strawbridge, out of sincere respect and devotion to—" he made another slight bow toward the empty space—"to his wife."

It was an extraordinary attitude, and as far as the drummer could analyze it, seemed informed with a fine chivalry. He sat looking rather numbly at the dictator with the gorgeous peon girl in his arms. He gave up that point of attack, and shifted the topic of conversation, American fashion, by saying suddenly and rather loudly:

"Well, not to change the subject, General, I dropped around to-night to set right a little mistake we made the other day."

The President abandoned South America's favorite topic, Woman, with evident reluctance.

"Yes?" he questioned.

"Yes, it's about Josefa."

The President repeated the name emptily.

"The little clerk you put in prison the other day; don't you remember? You jailed him because he told me how you ran your government."

Even the diplomatic general showed surprise.

"Josefa? How do you know I imprisoned a man named Josefa?"

Strawbridge burst out laughing.

"You can't expect me to tell who told me. You might jug that person, too."

"Hardly that," said the dictator, drily. "Then will you tell me why this unmentioned person said I imprisoned a man named Josefa?"

"I'll tell you about Josefa. He's already in trouble. The other day I was down at the 'Sol y Sombra,' and I wanted to make a hardware display to boost trade in my line. Josefa was dead against it. I was about to put up the display anyway, when Josefa said if I did it would certainly cause the government tax on the store to advance, and maybe lead to its confiscation. I didn't believe it, but he went ahead to tell me how the Government had grabbed one man's ranch because it stood the dry season better than—"

"Señor Strawbridge," interrupted the general, with a little line coming around the lobe of his nose, "you have been made the victim of the usual calumnious gossip which circulates too freely in Canalejos. The ranch to which you probably refer was a deserted hacienda, and, rather than allow its lands to go to waste, the Government occupied it."

Strawbridge saw by the general's face that he would help no one by pursuing that course, so he said, "Oh, was that the way?" as if he had heard the explanation for the first time. He then shifted about to his next topic.

"General," he began, "I've been thinking about Canalejos and Rio Negro, and the way you run things down here. Don't you believe you would get more out of it if you would make all investments perfectly safe in your country?"

"I shall have to ask you to explain that, too."

"For example, Fando, that peon whose horse you took for your cavalry. No doubt the loss of his horse stopped the cultivation of his hacienda, and yet to some extent the wealth of Rio Negro depends upon Fando's land being cultivated."

"That is true," admitted the dictator, stiffly, "but it is more important that the liberty and independence of Rio Negro be maintained than that Fando have a horse. You must be aware, Señor Strawbridge, that the prime necessity of any government is its governmental existence. You are an American. Everything you possess, down to your body, is liable to conscription in time of military necessity, is it not?"

"Yes, that's true, but I get paid for what my Government seizes."

"What would it pay you?"

"Money, of course."

"There you are," smiled the general, getting back on comfortable abstractions again. "Money is a medium of exchange, a promise of goods in the future. The value of American money depends upon America's winning her wars. Unfortunately I have no Rio Negran money yet, though I think I shall print some. If I had it, of course I would pay Fando. Why not? It wouldn't cost me anything. On the other hand, if I finally win against the State of Venezuela, Fando will not be forgotten. In short, my dear Señor Strawbridge, I seize the goods of the people for the good of the people—just as every other government does."

Thomas Strawbridge nodded his agreement and, with a sense of frustration, arose to make his devoirs. He wished he could have got Josefa out. The poor little monkey-eyed clerk was at that moment lying in some loathsome dungeon of La Fortuna. Well, it could not be helped.

Strawbridge gave a little sigh, smiled mechanically, and advanced to the couch with outstretched hand.

"Well, I hope my talk has done no harm, General. I'm really keen to help you in a business way."

The dictator arose, and suggested that his guest remain. He said Madruja would be charmed if Strawbridge would stay. With the girl thrust on his attention like that, the salesman bent over her hand to make his adieus to her.

Her hand rested limply in his, and she remained mute while he expressed his pleasure at meeting her.

As she stood thus, looking at him over their clasped hands, with her black surfaced eyes, there came the sound of a door opening behind the men. The black eyes of the girl shifted a little from Strawbridge's face and stared over his shoulder. A change came over her features as if she had seen a ghost. Even her scarlet lips paled. With her lips she formed, rather than said the name, "Esteban!"

Both Fombombo and Strawbridge whirled. In the doorway stood a peon boy with a knife in his hand. He wore the cheap finery which peons don for concert night. Esteban's face was drawn and clay-colored, and he stood blinking in the bright light which bewildered his eyes.

The dictator evidently did not know who Esteban was. He rapped out sternly:

"*Bribon*, what do you mean entering this room without permission?"

The youth replied with a sudden lunge at the President. Strawbridge saw the flash of the knife, and, with a remnant of his old football interference, shot his body, shoulder down, straight into the midriff of the leaping figure.

The American's two hundred and ten pounds hit the boy like a catapult. It smashed him backward and down. His knife snapped out of his hands, his hat flew off, his head struck heavily on the tiled floor. The general was calling angrily for the guards. A moment later three of these little men entered the door, with their rifles.

The President pointed at the youth on the floor.

"Take that *bribon*. He made an attack on me. You rascals will have to explain how he got in!"

The three guards, rather panic-struck, pounced on the peon. They got him up and held his arms behind him. Strawbridge's blow in the stomach had made Esteban sick, and now he bent over as far as his captors would permit, retching and slobbering, with anguished eyes looking at the girl.

"Madruja!" he gasped between his convulsions. "Eh, Madruja, *mi vida*, I would give my last breath for—"

"What are you saying to Madruja?" demanded the President.

"She is my wife," gasped Esteban, painfully. "You locked her up in this room and then ... took her!"

The dictator stared at the fellow.

"Locked her up and took her! Do you imagine I would take any woman? She came to me of her own will!" He turned to the girl and his voice changed: "Here, Madruja, my darling, my little heaven, deny this empty-headed rascal's charge!"

The girl stood staring at the two men.

"What, *Señor el Presidente*?" She trembled.

"Deny this charge. Or, rather, here is a villain who calls himself your husband; choose between us. You are free, you have always been free. And you, *bribon*, you too are free. I mean it.—Loose him men!—Choose between me and this wretch!"

The three guards released Esteban's arms. The peon looked about, then advanced a step toward the girl, with a bewildered joy coming into his sick face.

"Madruja!" he wavered, holding out his arms. "Madruja, did you hear what the *Presidente* said? Did you hear what the good *Presidente* said, little

Madruja?" He was approaching her, shuddering with his sickness and his sudden rapture.

The girl looked at him fixedly. She withdrew a step.

"*Caramba*, Esteban!" she shrugged, "you smell of donkeys. You have done a mad thing coming here. I am not a peon girl any more. I am the mistress of *Señor el Presidente*. Look at me! See this silk, this ruby! Do you imagine I would grind cassava for a peon who smells like a donkey?" She shrugged, and turned away to a window.

In the silence that followed, one of the little guards saluted.

"What shall we do with him, your Excellency?"

"Kick him out of the *palacio* and let him go!"

The three soldiers obeyed literally and promptly. They seized Esteban from behind and trundled him toward the door, with hard kicks of their knees against his buttocks. The wretch moved, half falling, half held up, in a series of jounces which kept his head bobbing and his mop of shining youthful hair whipping from side to side. After the quartet passed through the door Strawbridge could still hear the muffled thuds of the guards' knees as they kicked Esteban down the corridor toward the entrance.

The incident left Strawbridge mute. The dictator interrupted his intellectual vacancy by saying:

"Señor Strawbridge, I have to thank you for your interference. I might have had a cut or two from that young madman before I could secure his knife." The general's arm encircled Madruja as he spoke. The girl submitted without any expression whatever on her wild, handsome face.

"It was nothing, General, nothing at all. As I have said before, any little service...." Strawbridge broke off and stood pondering a moment, then asked, "Will you tell me, General, why you imprison Josefa for merely speaking a word of criticism of your country, and then have Esteban kicked out and allowed to go free when he makes an attack on your life?"

The dictator shrugged.

"What I did to Esteban will stop Esteban; what I did to Josefa will stop Josefa." The President of Rio Negro stood faintly smiling and caressing the finely molded shoulders of his mistress.

Strawbridge was outraged.

"Why, there is no justice in that! Imprison a man for life for speaking a word; let another go free when he attempts murder!"

With amused eyes the President regarded his guest.

"Señor Strawbridge, what you say is a result of your unfortunate American commercial training. You Americans have a naïve idea that justice is a sort of balancing of an account. You try to make the severity of the punishment balance with the heinousness of the crime. It is your national instinct to keep a ledger.

"But what is justice? Is there any accountant in heaven or on earth calling for any such exactitude? Is punishment a thing that can be measured or weighed? What good does punishing a man do? Whom does it benefit? Nobody. There is only one object in punishment, and that is to stop crimes. Any effort to balance a punishment with a crime is absurd and the work of infantile intelligences. Take Esteban. He attacked my life. If I disgrace him before this lovely señorita here, if I kick him out of my palace, do you fancy he will ever have the hardihood to return? You know he won't. On the contrary, if I had imprisoned him, as I did Josefa, that would have made a hero of him, and every lover of every one of my mistresses would feel obliged to come and chop at me with his knife. If they know they will be kicked out and laughed at, they will not come. In short, the punishment cures the crime."

"But look at Josefa!" cried Strawbridge. "He did almost nothing, and you have put him in a dungeon for life!"

The dictator became stern.

"He talked too much. The only place for a man who talks too much is where there is no one to talk to. No other punishment on earth will stop an idle tongue."

Strawbridge stood thinking over this extraordinary code of law. It was not justice as the drummer knew it; it was a code of expediency. As usual, the President's reasoning appeared to be correct and unanswerable.

CHAPTER XV

To Thomas Strawbridge the expedition against San Geronimo was invested with a sense of unreality. Every detail of it cast a faint doubt on the credibility of the drummer's impressions—the rabble of peon cavalry, mounted on mules, donkeys, and a few horses; a motley of women—wives, mistresses, and sweethearts of the soldiers—some in carts, some riding donkeys, some on foot. The troops hauled a single three-pound field-gun with its snout in an old canvas bag and its breech wrapped in palm-leaves. Not less unbelievable was the priest, Father Benicio, in his black cassock and priest's round black hat. He was mounted on a mule, and at his pommel hung his crucifix, a little gourd of consecrated oil, and a vial of holy water. With these instruments of grace he would administer extreme unction to the unfortunate of the expedition.

The string of adventurers was sufficiently long so that when Strawbridge looked back from his place in the van the women and soldiers at the end of the column appeared hazy from the dust and shimmered with the heat-waves.

It was a breathless and wilting heat. When Strawbridge crossed the llanos in a motor-car the hot wind had depressed him, but now, without the speed of the automobile, the heat enveloped him with a greasy, pinching sensation. The warmth of his horse's body kept his legs sudsy. He tried to squirm his flesh away from his wet underclothes. Often he would ride five minutes at a time with his eyes shut against the glare of the sun reflected from the sand.

For ten or twelve kilometers the route of the army followed the left bank of the Rio Negro. The rapids set in just below the city of Canalejos, and for upward of a mile they filled the air with a vast watery rumble. But the river was so wide that Strawbridge could see from the shore nothing but a ripple in the broad yellow waters. The thunder of the rapids appeared to arise out of a placid expanse without cause. It was as if the river were in some mysterious travail.

The passage of the army flushed white egrets from along the bank, and once six flamingos arose and winged slowly away, making a crimson line against the sky. Along the sand-bars huge caymans slept in an ecstasy of heat. Their long whitish bellies fitted over stones and the curves in the sand with a kind of disgusting flexibility.

Some time later the line of march veered away from the river and lost itself in the endless, almost imperceptible undulations of the llanos. The monotony of these llanos somehow nibbled away the last shred of reality for Thomas Strawbridge. It seemed to him that everything in the world had ceased to exist except this shimmering furnace of sand.

The drummer rode at a post of honor, at the head of the column beside Coronel Saturnino. Behind him came the fighters, in a gradually thickening dust, until the end of the column traveled in a cloud. The colonel himself moved along impassively, apparently as little affected by the heat as the saddle he sat. He kept looking about as if he recognized landmarks in the endless repetition of the llanos. Presently he pointed through the glare and said:

"There is 'El Limon,' Señor Strawbridge."

The drummer screwed up his eyes against the shimmer, and made out what looked like a grove of trees on the horizon. Nearer, the spot developed into trees and a house of some sort. There seemed to be only one house. Strawbridge stared mechanically. The heat dulled his perceptions.

"What is it?" he asked.

"A hacienda. It belongs to an English firm, and is in federal territory. We are outside of General Fombombo's scope of influence now."

Strawbridge repeated these last words mechanically; the meaning was almost baked out of them by the heat of the sun beating on his head. "Outside of General Fombombo's scope of influence...." The drummer remembered the red line on the map in the library. So that was where he was—on that red line. The whole force of peons, officers, men, and women were crossing that red line and trying to extend it.

"How far is it to San Geronimo?" he asked.

"We're about half-way."

Strawbridge rode on for ten or fifteen minutes, with his eyes resting on the deep green of the grove. It was a eucalyptus grove. He noted this vaguely; then his mind went back to the answer to his questions. They were about half the distance ... outside the scope of General Fombombo's influence.... A red line on the map of Venezuela.... They were extending that, pushing it eastward and southward.... Somewhere the señora was playing a piano in a cool room.... The pleasant señora.... God, but it was hot!

The estate of "El Limon," in the Orinoco basin, belonged to an English meat-packing concern, and it was managed by a Trinidadian and his wife, the Tollivers. These English colonials lived in a ranch-house made of stone instead of adobe. Near the dwelling-house stood a vast wooden barn. It was this barn which Strawbridge had seen from a distance. House and barn were shaded by a magnificent eucalyptus grove, and these great trees formed the only restful spot amid the leagues of burning llanos. It was an English experiment and importation, this grove, and not another like it existed in all Venezuela.

Mr. Tolliver was a tall, rangy man wearing a native palm-fiber hat and alpargatas. He was burned browner than the natives themselves, but it was the deep reddish-brown of the Anglo-Saxon, not the yellowish-brown of a Spaniard. Out of this deep-brown face two pale English eyes looked on Venezuela, in chill condemnation.

As the seekers of liberty rode up, Mr. Tolliver stood with his back to a high barbed-wire enclosure around his barn, with his elbows and one big foot propped back against its wires. With a depth of sarcasm marking his bearded mouth and glinting out of his pale eyes, he watched the cavalcade. As the army filed into the cool glade, Mr. Tolliver remarked in the queer mouthy English of a West Indian colonial:

"Well, you bloody sons of liberty are after my stock again, I see."

Coronel Saturnino betrayed no annoyance at this reception. He bade the rancher "*Buenos tardes*," and asked if his men might eat in the shade. The big Trinidadian gave a sardonic consent. Saturnino sat on his horse, enjoying this relief from the sun, and glanced about over the barbed-wire enclosure.

"You have a fine Hereford bull, Señor Tolliver," he admired.

The rancher did not turn his head.

"At present I have," he remarked drily.

"And some excellent chickens," smiled the colonel, who seemed to be enjoying some private jest.

These very mild and complimentary observations seemed suddenly to enrage Tolliver. He put his foot down and burst out:

"What the bloody hell makes you drool along like that? Why don't you say what you're going to steal, and quit purring like a cat?"

Saturnino shrugged politely.

"You must pardon me, Señor Tolliver. I so seldom meet an Englishman, I am not yet an expert in discourtesy." The officer continued his observation of the estate: "And horses, Señor Tolliver, mounts for my men. If you could spare a few horses...."

The suggestion irritated the Trinidadian to a remarkable degree. His eyes filled with a pale fire, and with a concentration which surprised the drummer he called down the curses of God on the colonel. In the midst of this outburst, the rancher's eyes fell on Strawbridge. He stopped his profanity abruptly and stared.

"Look here," he demanded, "aren't you a white man?"

The tone and implication left Strawbridge rather uncomfortable in the presence of the Venezuelan.

"I'm an American," he said, avoiding the issue of color.

"Well, what the bloody hell are you following this gang of cut-throats and horse-thieves around for!"

The rancher's qualifications were edged with a righteous anger. Indeed, the fellow's oaths seemed to strip off a certain moral semblance which had hung over the expedition and leave it threadbare and shabby. The drummer hardly knew how to answer, when Coronel Saturnino relieved him of the necessity of answering at all. The officer very courteously introduced the rancher to the salesman and explained the latter's business.

The deep-brown Englishman stood appraising Strawbridge, and at last remarked:

"Well, you Americans certainly chase dollars in tighter places than any other decent man would. But, anyway, you're a white man. So come on in and have lunch. My wife and I get so bloody lonesome out here in this hell-hole, we're glad to see anything that's white."

Strawbridge was about to refuse this scathing hospitality, when Coronel Saturnino burst out laughing.

"Go!" he urged. "We shall be here for some time, rounding up some horses, and you need a rest and something to eat; you look exhausted."

The drummer agreed, and climbed stiffly off his horse. Notwithstanding the Englishman's brusquerie, Strawbridge rather liked the tall, brown, pale-eyed man. After the perpetual tepid courtesy of the Venezuelans his downrightness was as bracing as a cold shower.

Once Tolliver had decided to accept Thomas Strawbridge as a respectable white man in good standing, he did it wholeheartedly. He preceded his guest through a yard set with flowers in formal stone-bordered beds, a mode of flower arrangement dear to an Englishwoman's heart, no matter in what part of the world she is. The stone house had a wide wooden porch running completely around it. In front this was furnished with mats, a number of pieces of porch furniture, and a swing; around at one side were littered harness, garden tools, two or three boxes, and a number of large calabashes sawed off at the top. All the doors and windows were screened with copper gauze. Tolliver went to the door and spoke through the screen.

"Lizzie," he called, "Mr. Strawbridge, an American gentleman, will lunch with us," and a moment later a woman's pleasant voice called back, "Ask him whether he will have green or black tea, George."

While the two men were seated on the porch, looking over the grove, Tolliver, with an Englishman's pertinacity, returned to the topic of American dollar-chasing.

"I don't see how you run around with these scrapings," he criticized. "My eyes, man! you've got to be careful who you sell rifles to in this bloody country! Half these beggars can't be trusted with firearms—" He broke off, peering out into his barn lot. "Look—look yonder, at those women catching up my chickens! When an army of liberation sets out from Canalejos, about half of 'em stop at my ranch, load up with my live stock, and go back home—the damn, thieving...." Here Tolliver clapped his hands, and a native boy of about fourteen appeared in the doorway.

"Pedro," snapped the rancher, "go tell that bloody officer not to disturb any hens with chickens. I won't have it!"

The boy bobbed and darted away with the message.

The Trinidadian watched him go, and then returned sourly to the subject under discussion:

"Revolutions are always stewing in Rio Negro—one set of thieves after another. A bunch comes through every six or eight months. They are always about to do wonderful things. I remember one time I provisioned General Dimancho. He was just about to save his country. I believed him. He won, and spoiled like an egg. Then Miedo made me a very expensive visit. He really talked me over. They can all talk you over if you listen to 'em. As long as they are not in power, they're the best of patriots. Miedo was going to stabilize Venezuela. Well, he did take Rio Negro, and he squeezed it drier than the shell of that calabash yonder." The rancher made a rough gesture. "God! the rotters who have squirmed and fought their way to power and debauchery in this damnable country!" With pale, angry eyes he stared into the grove. "The trouble is in the stock ... scrub ... scum. You can't make any decent government out of this ... manure." And Tolliver dropped the subject.

Twenty minutes later a rather faded but still pretty young woman in a gingham dress came out at the door, smiled at the two men, and told them that tiffin was ready. Strawbridge was introduced to Lizzie Tolliver. Later, during the lunch, the drummer learned that his hostess was the daughter of the Bishop of St. Kitts.

The luncheon hour was occupied by George Tolliver in relating the peculiar difficulties which beset his cattle ranch. This hacienda had been established as a feeder for an English meat-packing corporation at Valencia.

To begin with, a packing-house had been established at Valencia, and a contract made with the Venezuelan President that he should furnish the house with so many first-class steers daily. This the President had failed to do, furnishing, instead, a supply of under-grade animals. Repeated protests from the English company produced no effect. At last the company had established this ranch on the Orinoco to furnish itself with meat. The venture proved a success. By importing fine bulls the company raised the grade of the llano longhorns into a very superior beef cattle. As soon as the English syndicate had demonstrated its ability to raise good beef, the Venezuelan President instructed the Venezuelan congress to place a heavy interstate tax on all cattle transported from one state to another. This tax was so onerous that the company could not afford to move a hoof from the State of Guarico to the State of Carabobo, where Valencia was situated. The result was that the company was forced to buy the President's low-grade cattle, while the meat raised on its own hacienda had no possible market and simply went to waste.

At the conclusion of this narrative, Tolliver broke into acidulous laughter.

"Now you see why I aided General Dimancho and General Miedo to start a revolution against the Venezuelan Government. In fact, I was given the hint from the London office. Well, each of these men won in his turn, and both grew so bad that they were ousted. Fombombo was the last deliverer. But of late I hear rumors that he has turned out to be a damned rascal and they are trying to overthrow him now."

Here Lizzie Tolliver, who had been giving her husband significant glances throughout this narrative, interrupted to say:

"George, you would better not speak so unreservedly of Mr. Strawbridge's friends."

"Friends! Friends!" shouted the Trinidadian. "They are not Strawbridge's friends! We Anglo-Saxons trade with these natives; we talk with 'em, live among 'em, and occasionally marry 'em, but we never really get acquainted with any of 'em, and we never make a friend."

There was a certain verity in the rancher's appraisal, and the Tollivers themselves proved it. During this brief lunch hour the drummer and his English hosts were talking intimately and understandingly in a fashion which Strawbridge perhaps would never achieve with the colonel, Lubito, Father Benicio, or even with the señora....

The drummer wondered about the señora....

A few minutes later the little party was interrupted by the appearance of the native boy in the doorway, who said that Coronel Saturnino was waiting outside. Tolliver arose, and Strawbridge followed, saying that perhaps the troops were ready to march.

On the porch they found Coronel Saturnino standing at attention, with a very affable air, holding in his hand a sheet of paper.

He made a slight bow and tendered the paper.

"Here is a receipt, Señor Tolliver, for twenty horses, three cows, fifty chickens, and eleven ducks," he explained blandly. "As we come back by here General Fombombo would greatly appreciate one of your thoroughbred Hereford bulls, to be used on his ranch for breeding-purposes, and I have just included the bull in this receipt."

The Trinidadian burst out into another paroxysm of profane anger. The officer shrugged mildly.

"You need not take it, *mi amigo*, unless you want it, but it will be valuable to you some day."

"What day? How? I've heard that before!"

"This receipt is payable on the day General Fombombo extends his estate to the sea. When that day comes, present this receipt at the capital of the future state of Rio Negro, and you will be paid in full."

Tolliver broke into sardonic laughter.

"To hell with you and your receipt! General Miedo was to pay me when he marched into Caracas as a conqueror."

Coronel Saturnino bowed and tossed the paper away.

"You English folk are childish," he philosophized. "You have no sense of the inevitable. You, señor, suffer from the same evils as all other citizens of Venezuela. I, and my men out there, are risking our lives to rectify those ills. Many of them will die to-morrow, that is ineluctable. Yet while they spend their lives to benefit you, you grudge them even the beef and a few fowls which they eat and the horses upon which they ride to their death."

Tolliver drew a disgusted mouth.

"I've heard that so many times it makes me sick."

Saturnino bowed again.

"May I pay my respects to the señora, and may I wish you *adios, pues*." He turned to Strawbridge. "Señor, the company awaits your convenience."

CHAPTER XVI

The commandeering of the horses at the English ranch shocked Strawbridge; when the cavalcade set forth on the march again, the heat and glare of the llanos aggravated his mental disturbance. As he sweltered in the center of a vast shimmering horizon, he kept repeating mentally, at unexpected intervals, the epithet "horse-thieves." Each time these words bobbed up in his mind he put them down, rather like a man who is trying to keep some buoyant object under water, "horse-thieves ... horse-thieves ... horse-thieves ..." over and over. His thinking did not progress much farther than that. What made the buoyant object so difficult to control was the fact that he himself was riding one of Tolliver's horses. The very rhythm of the fine animal between his legs was a reminder and a reproach.

Sweat trickled into the drummer's eyes and stung them. He blinked through the quivering heat, with screwed-up lids, and wondered what he could have done about the horse. When Coronel Saturnino insisted that he take one of the best of the English mounts, he could not have said, "No, I am a decent American salesman, and I won't ride a stolen horse." He could not have said such a thing as that in the face of the colonel's polite consideration.

On the other hand, the damning thought that he was riding a stolen horse gnawed at the drummer with the persistence of a rat. It gave him a faint, ghastly feeling in the pit of his stomach, where, perhaps, is located the genuine seat of conscience with us all.

Presently Strawbridge noted a surprising thing. Looking back over the cavalcade, he observed Father Benicio riding one of the confiscated horses. The good father jogged along in his dusty black cassock and his little round hat, with the sacred emblems dangling from his pommel, and he was riding a stolen horse. His questionable mount had not changed the priest's face at all. It was the same thin, ascetic face with its look of passionate spirituality burning through the repression, almost the mortification of the flesh. Strawbridge wondered what mental attitude Father Benicio assumed toward his horse in order to preserve so eremitic an expression. He felt the holy father must have some inward justification which he, himself, did not possess. Almost involuntarily he picked his way among the troopers, to the priest's side. As he came near he observed that Gumersindo was riding beside the father. The negro editor's face was covered with dust, and he looked queer because the dust settling in the furrows of his forehead made whitish lines against his black skin.

The black man waved the American a grave salute.

"Do you know, Señor Strawbridge," he called above the wide noise of the horses' feet, "that this is the same sort of expedition Bolivar led against Montillo when he freed this continent? They had beaten the *Libertador* everywhere else, but when they threw him back upon these interminable llanos, he drew fresh strength, like Antæus, and struggled on."

Strawbridge nodded wearily.

"Sure, sure...." He looked at the priest, a little doubtful how to proceed. The negro journalist continued talking, in a sort of exaltation:

"I never start on an expedition of this kind that I do not think, 'Perhaps to-day I am making history.' That is a wonderful thought, Father Benicio—history! Think! Perhaps this very moment is historic! Perhaps it will be embalmed in the memory of the future. It is just as if we should march forever through the mind of mankind! Other deedless generations will rise up and vanish as unremarked as the succeeding harvests of llano grass, but perhaps what we do to-day will be painted, carved in marble, sung in song, and told in story as long as civilization lasts! I say it is possible!"

Such a dithyramb from a negro among a band of horse-thieves moved Strawbridge with a certain disgust. He drew a handkerchief and wiped his sweaty, gritty face.

"I guess you're making history for that English ranch," he satirized; "a record of these horses will appear in their profit-and-loss column."

Gumersindo looked around at the drummer, and suddenly began to laugh.

"*Caramba!* He's thinking about the dollars and cents of this adventure!"

This was just the fillip needed to set the drummer off. He straightened in his saddle.

"Well, by God, it's not dollars and cents, either; it's just plain honesty. I don't know how you fellows feel, but I'm damned uncomfortable riding a horse we stole from Tolliver!"

Both editor and priest were staring at him.

"What a disturbance over a detail!" ejaculated the black man.

"How do you feel about your mount, Father Benicio?" asked Strawbridge.

The priest's ascetic face relaxed into a rather pleasant smile.

"I feel it is much more comfortable than the mule I rode, my son."

The drummer was amazed.

"Don't you think it's wrong?"

"Our action is directed toward a great and noble end, my son. Venezuela is sick to death. If confiscating these horses rids the country of a dictator, surely the end justifies the means!"

"But look here!" cried Strawbridge. "The English company is not in on this. They are the innocent bystander who gets the bullet through the heart."

"They are already shot through the heart, señor," answered Father Benicio, patiently; "their horses and cattle are worth nothing to them, on account of unjust legislation."

"But their property still belongs to them," cried the drummer. "That doesn't justify us in stealing it!"

"Did God create these horses simply to live and die without being of use to any one?"

"That's up to the company. It's their horses."

The priest looked at the drummer oddly. Gumersindo interposed:

"Father, let me explain Señor Strawbridge to you. I said, a while ago, he had reduced this to dollars and cents. So he has. You must remember that property is a fetish in America. Americans do not possess their property, they are possessed by it. In America the prime factor of civilization is property; in Venezuela the prime factor is Man."

Strawbridge was hot enough to grow angry instantly.

"Look here," he cried, "let me nail that lie right now, while I got my hammer out! We Americans spend our money just as free as you Venezuelans, and a damn sight freer!"

"But, Señor Strawbridge," returned the editor, politely, "that has nothing to do with my analysis. In America all your social framework is built around money. Rich men are respected, and poor men are not. It would be better to say that in America property is respected and men are not."

"That's impossible!" cried Strawbridge, steadily growing angrier.

"Not at all. When an American loses his money, he loses the friendship and respect of his fellow Americans. The man who acquires the former rich man's fortune, acquires also the respect that goes with it." Gumersindo made a gesture. "*Pues*, do you recall, Señor Strawbridge, that the first draft of the American Declaration of Independence read in this fashion: 'All men are born free, and are equally entitled to life, liberty, and the pursuit of property'? The word 'happiness,' substituted by Jefferson, was merely an American euphemism for 'property'; it means the same thing in America."

"Why—by God!—I recall nothing of the kind!" shouted Strawbridge, with the American conviction that if one denied history in a loud voice it would cease to exist. "No, that's just a damn lie some damn Venezuelan started on Americans!"

"Certainly I am no expert in American history," agreed the editor, smoothly. "You doubtless know the history of your country better than I do."

"Well, I hope I do!" grumbled Strawbridge, feeling for the moment that because he was an American he necessarily knew more of American history than Gumersindo, who was not an American.

"So, dropping the historical statement—which may be false, although I discovered it in some research work in your own Congressional Library at Washington—dropping that, pure inductive reasoning will tell you Americans do respect property, and that they do not respect human beings.

"Remember, your country is populated mainly by immigrants who came to the New World to seek their fortunes. Most of these newcomers were without culture and without any feeling for human values. They were poor, and, never having had any money, they naturally thought that money must contain all value. Therefore they transposed the value of a man's fortune to the man himself. They thought any man who became wealthy must have great value, and they called him a success. They thought any painting which commanded a high price must be a great painting; they thought any piece of jazz music which sold a million copies must be a great piece of music. They thought that any house which cost a million dollars must necessarily be finer than one that cost only five thousand dollars. Now Americans think that."

The drummer peered hard at the negro editor.

"Well, by God, that's a fact," he declared vigorously. "Nobody denies that, do they? Don't you know a million-dollar house would be finer than a five-thousand-dollar house?"

Even Father Benicio joined Gumersindo in the laughter this article of faith evoked.

"*Pues*," placated the priest, the next moment, "that is the reason, my son, why we ride our horses without compunction, and why your horse annoys you. And I must observe that your scruples honor you. I respect your frankness and your point of view."

Strawbridge rode some farther distance with the two men, but he was uncomfortable. He knew they were amused at him, and it was not pleasant. Presently he returned to the head of the column.

CHAPTER XVII

At last Strawbridge's adventure had come to a focus. He sat, galled and dusty, on his English mount and stared at the distant metallic gleam which encircled the southern and western segments of the horizon. That thin, shining arc was the junction of the Orinoco and the Rio Negro. Against its shimmer arose a single spire, so tiny and so far away that the drummer had to scrutinize it with particularity before he could make it out at all. So this was the upshot of all their riding and burning and thirsting—for these sweat-caked peons to advance against a church steeple!

Half a dozen different impressions clamored for the American's attention. Just behind him officers were barking their soldiers into two squads. A little farther to the rear, the men were pulling themselves from their wives and mistresses, to join the ranks again. There was something elemental and unashamed in the passion of their parting. They were much the same color as the sand they trod. They might have been figures sprung out of the heat and travail of the melancholy llanos, as indeed they were. They clung to each other, these earth-colored peons; they sobbed, they kissed each other with unrestraint, absorbed in their griefs. There was something wide and impersonal in this passionate outpouring of their misery. They were mummers depicting completely what every lover feels on parting with his love. Some inhibition, some reserve seemed to melt in Strawbridge's mind, and with a trembling tenderness he thought of the señora. He could see her delicate face looking at him sorrowfully. Such a sense of pathos filled him that he wondered if it did not forbode some evil to him. Perhaps he was about to be killed; else why should the señora's sad face appear to him so vividly?

Strawbridge became aware of a horseman coming up, on his left. It was Coronel Saturnino, his face a mask of dust. For once the colonel seemed keen and alive. His black eyes, in this dust mask, were full of fire, but the dusty mouth was set in its inevitable sardonic quirk.

"I rode over to suggest that you hang a carbine to your saddle." He smiled.

Strawbridge looked down at his pommel doubtfully.

"I thought perhaps if I went in as a neutral—"

"*Pues*, you are likely not to come out at all."

"Then you think I had better carry a gun?"

"It's safer." The colonel beckoned a soldier to him and gave an order that sent the man to the rear, to return presently with a carbine for Strawbridge. While the peon strapped it to the drummer's saddle, the colonel's black eyes, with their look of chronic amusement, passed over his recruits.

"These peons are going out to fight for their freedom," he observed with his tone of satire. "They are perpetually going out to fight for their freedom. Different saviors rise up—a Miedo, a Fombombo. Now it is Saturnino, and only the Holy Virgin knows who next will be leading these tatterdemalions to freedom!" With sardonic wrinkles in his dust mask he looked at the drummer.

Strawbridge tried to shift his leg so it would not touch the hard carbine. He was somehow incensed at Saturnino's tone.

"What better thing can they fight for than their freedom?"

The colonel shrugged.

"Probably nothing. It makes a very exciting game for gentlemen—these peons wanting to be free. What finer thing could a peon do than to entertain a *caballero*?"

Strawbridge stared at the dust mask.

"Good God, Saturnino! Is that all this is to you?—an entertainment, a game?"

The officer shrugged again.

"*Pues*, of course it isn't business." He paused with a quizzical look, and then went on: "But what I really rode over to tell you is, I am dividing the men into two squadrons. I will lead one in a frontal attack on the *casa fuerte*. The other, Lieutenant Rosales will lead around by the river. It will make its way through the wharves and attack the *casa fuerte* from the rear."

Strawbridge had become attentive, and nodded to these plans.

"You may go along with either of the parties," invited the colonel, "or you may stay here with the women until the fight is over."

"No, certainly not! I'll go by the river," chose Strawbridge, at once.

The colonel nodded, and smiled once again through his grime.

"As you will; and may luck wait on your courage! *Adios!*"

The two men reached across the necks of their stolen horses and shook hands.

"Same to you, colonel, and so long," said the drummer, somewhat moved.

Saturnino suddenly jerked his horse in a curvette, and saluted easily as the big English animal plunged with him back toward his line.

The drummer turned his own mount and rode toward Rosales's column. Lieutenant Rosales was a smallish, sharp-featured youth whose eyes were surrounded with such dark rings that they showed through the dust. Strawbridge remembered having seen him before, in the plaza. Now he was going to fight under this little *roué*, perhaps die under his command. He felt as if he were going to fight with a crowd of street gamins. It was a mean adventure.

The men under Rosales sat stolid and quiet on their mules and horses. Saturnino's sarcasm revisited the drummer's mind: "These peons are perpetually fighting for their freedom, under this savior and that. They've been at it upward of four centuries. Now I'm leading them," and he had laughed.

A gust of pity shivered through the American's bowels for these stolid men, arming and seeking a leader for four centuries, and led by Saturnino, a man to whom their travail was a game!

At that moment the sickly-looking officer whipped out his sword and barked an order, and the next moment the cavalry set off at a gallop through the heat and dust. The drummer fell into the ranks. He twisted in his saddle for any easement he could find. His carbine added a new pain to his riding. It banged his thigh with a strange adroitness. Within ten or fifteen minutes a dust rose up among so many galloping horses which made the air almost unbreathable. These petty tortures so harassed the drummer that he looked forward to actual fighting as a relief. To avoid the dust he swung his horse out of line and spurred him to the van of the column. By the time the American was even with Lieutenant Rosales, he had reached clean breathing, and he expanded his lungs with a sense of great relief. But the peons, the dirt-colored men who after four hundred years of rebellion were now playing Coronel Saturnino's game, these peons rode resolutely in the heat and dust without breaking line. The thin-faced officer with the black circles about his eyes stared fixedly ahead.

Presently the troopers galloped up another long swell in the desert, and when they reached its crest Strawbridge was shocked to see how close they were upon the city of San Geronimo. He could see the red roofs of the adobes, a wireless tower run up like a spider-web, and the very bells in the campanile. Around the street entrances were swarms of people in a state of excitement. Some rushed into their houses; others went flying into the llanos—straggling figures bound for no other goal than to escape the coming storm.

Strawbridge watched the scene curiously, as if he were some idle spectator. Presently Rosales drew his sword, swung his men out of line with the main entrance, and veered toward the west, toward the stretch of water which was growing more and more enormous as they approached it.

Horses and mules, on they went, faster and faster. There was a wide space between the town and the river, to give play to the overflow in the rainy season. Into this space Rosales headed. The hoofs of the cavalcade made a dull drumming in the sand. Far down the river bank, opposite the business part of town, Strawbridge could see the big freight goletas from Trinidad and Ciudad Bolívar, hastily making sail to escape the tempest.

Suddenly, from somewhere over on their right, came a hard blow in the air. The flat plains lent no resonance. It was simply a crash—a sharp, terrific impact. It was followed by another, by twos and threes, by some indeterminable number. They hammered terrifically at Strawbridge's eardrums with a sense of devastating power. The Federals in the *casa fuerte* were cannonading Coronel Saturnino.

The cannonading must have been an agreed signal between the colonel and Rosales. At its roar the lieutenant yelped at his men and flung his column headlong into the open space along the wharves of San Geronimo.

Strawbridge went with them. He rode inexpertly, swaying dangerously on his English mount. With his left hand he jerked at his carbine, trying to get it out of its holster, with his right he clung to the pommel of his saddle. He peered ahead, and the whole wharf-side seemed rushing at him, shaken by the terrific vibrations of the horse. The few stragglers left in sight skurried about to avoid the cavalry charge. Far ahead, puffs of smoke came out at barred windows in the adobes. At that moment the rumble of hoofs in the sand turned into a crashing clatter. The horses had struck the cobblestones of the wharf. An increased heat from the glare of the hot cobbles pinched the drummer. More smoke puffs blew out at the windows. It occurred to the drummer that these were peons firing on the cavalry.

A long row of palms were planted straight down the middle of the *playa*. As these palms vibrated toward him, the drummer glimpsed the head and shoulders of a man, pointing a rifle, high up in a clump of leaves. A little thrill went over him. He swung his carbine toward the figure.

"Hey, look at that scoundrel up that palm! Blow him out of there!" He pointed his gun without thinking of using it. "Blow him out, I say."

Half a dozen riders heard and looked. They swung up their carbines and fired as they galloped. Strawbridge could see the spatter of the bullets against the big leaves; next moment the head and shoulders made a limp lurch forward, and the figure of a man dropped out of the palm and turned over and over in the air. With a primitive satisfaction the drummer watched the fall. He had wiped out an enemy. He stared down the *playa*. Far down where the quay narrowed with distance, a line of men were marching through the sunshine. He could see the glitter of their bayonets and their intense shadows moving in front of them. At sight of these federal soldiers the carbines about Strawbridge began a staccato snapping. The distant line of soldiers stopped, knelt, aimed, like a little row of toys in the brilliant sunshine. Then came the faint crack of their volley.

The effect appalled Strawbridge. A peon on the drummer's right reeled from his saddle; ahead of him a horse reared and fell, flinging his rider on the cobbles, under the hoofs of the horses. The drummer saw the wretch thresh about as he was broken upon the stones.

For answer the insurgents deployed the width of the *playa*, between the houses and the palms, and charged. Horses, mules, howling peons, and chattering carbines roared down the quay. The Federals fired one more volley, then suddenly broke and fled. They scurried in every direction. Their little human speed was so puny that the horses overhauled them like giants. A feeling of tremendous strength filled Strawbridge. He was a Gulliver plunging down on Lilliputians. He selected a man to kill. The Federal sprinted desperately, but his short legs seemed barely to move in front of the English stallion.

The chase became a vertigo. A hard pulse pounded in Strawbridge's ears. Never before had he known the terrific excitement of hunting a man down and killing him. The drummer's adroitness and horsemanship sharpened to the delight of murder. He cleared his carbine and aimed at the runner. He meant to hit him in the cross of his canteen strap. He pulled the trigger....

A terrific concussion almost bowled over the drummer and his horse. It displaced the whole platoon. Strawbridge whirled, and saw the roofs of the adobes lined with federal troops, firing down on the cavalry.

Men and horses fell beneath continuous volleys. The squadron was falling back toward the river. The men acted as if they struggled in the teeth of a furious wind-storm. Suddenly some of them wheeled off toward the river. Rosales was behind his men, howling and spewing Spanish oaths. He beat the fugitives with the back of his sword. In the uproar the hatchet-faced lieutenant, leaning forward toward the enemy, pointed at the roofs.

He might have been trying to reach the crashing rifles with the tip of his saber. He was howling for his men to charge. A flame of sympathy went through Strawbridge for this indomitable knave of an officer. He headed his stallion about in the careening column. He shouted a mixture of English and Spanish:

"*Adelante!* Bore into 'em! *Pronto!* Wipe 'em out—the hellions!"

The powerful horse might have been a stanchion shoring up the column. His mere lunge turned three or four fugitives toward the enemy. This whirling movement became the focus of a renewed charge. Every man took courage from Strawbridge, from the thin-faced reprobate who led them. The column flung itself into the teeth of the fire from the roofs.

The stink and sting of powder-gas jabbed up Strawbridge's nose. The Federals on the roof shone dimly behind a mist of smokeless powder. As Strawbridge charged in, he could see the face of a man staring at him, and the circle of a rifle muzzle under his right eye. The cavalry plunged in against the mud walls. Horses smashed against them, reared, fell, or squatted trembling at this blank obstruction. What for? Strawbridge did not know. He was furiously angry. He meant to strike.

Rosales had directed his charge toward the lowest roof in the whole *playa* side. It was not more than eight feet high. The focusing of his fire on this point had cut down the defense just here and left a gap in the line of defenders. As Rosales dashed up to this building, he caught the adobe eaves and succeeded in drawing himself up to the roof. A Federal seemed to discharge a gun through his head, but the daredevil pressed on, with his automatic going. Half a dozen, a dozen other *llaneros* followed. A score gained footing on the low roof. They were amazing horsemen. The Federals were not deployed on the roofs. They could fire only from the ends of their columns. The knot of cavalry on the red tiles grew, expanded, pressed back the feeble ends of the enemy. The fight had transferred itself from the streets to the house-tops—the classic stage for South American battles.

In the midst of this extraordinary manœuver, Strawbridge found himself trying to scramble up the corner of a building. He could not take off from the saddle. From the ground he could just reach the eave. He clung to the hot adobe and pulled with all his strength, kicking and pawing at the corner with knees and feet. Now and then a bullet flicked adobe dust into his face. With a desperate kick he did succeed in hanging a toe over the cornice. Just as he was wriggling his heavy body up on the roof, something about his hold broke. He dropped broadside from where he sagged, falling about five feet and landing in the litter which collects about Spanish-American huts.

The big drummer lay inert, and cursed with every blasphemy to which he could lay his tongue. He cursed Federals, insurgents, house, sun, dust. He invoked the Deity to consign each to its particular hell. He lay in burning dust, swearing at a mud wall not six inches from his nose.

The tearing volleys of rifle shots were drawing a little away from where Strawbridge lay. The quest of the peons for liberty was withdrawing itself somewhat. Presently the American made an effort to get out of his burning bed. He stirred, and found to his discomfiture that one of his arms was numb. He wondered anxiously if he had broken it.

He used his good arm, made shift to sit up, then got to his feet. Then he was surprised to see that his numb hand was bloody. A closer examination showed that the bones in his palm had been shattered by a bullet. That was what flung him from the roof. He looked at his hand in dismay, turning it over and back. It did not seem to belong to him. He began swearing again, mentally. What a hell of an accident to happen to him! For him, Thomas Strawbridge, to get shot! What a damnable piece of luck! He continued damning his luck, with quivering earnestness. He could not realize that it was his hand, attached to his wrist. He kept looking at it. The hand did not pain him in the least. It had no sensation at all.

There had been a certain order kept by the peon cavalry, of which Strawbridge had not been aware. Now, as he looked about, he saw the insurgents' horses trotting in a dark group far down the *playa*. They were under the care of hostlers, which the hair-splitting plans of Saturnino no doubt had arranged for, for just such an emergency as this. Naturally, Strawbridge's English stallion had vanished with the herd.

Near at hand lay men and horses, dead and wounded. One mule, shot through the back, was dragging itself by its fore feet. Strawbridge picked up his carbine with his good hand and ended its struggles.

For a few minutes the drummer stood looking at this dead mule, at a dead peon some ten steps farther east, then at a sort of windrow of mules and horses and peons where the cavalry had hesitated before charging.

These were the men whom Strawbridge had seen, only an hour before, embracing and weeping over their loves; now they lay in all sorts of twisted and grotesque postures; already the green flies were buzzing about the mouths their sweethearts had kissed. Such was the outcome of their fight for liberty. This was the freedom they had found, these brown exhalations of the llanos, who rose up out of the earth, fought, struggled, plotted, murdered, and sank into the llanos again. And all their pain and fury had ever done in four centuries was to exchange one dictator for another....

A profound weariness came over Strawbridge. The crotches of his legs, which the horse had skinned, began burning again. An unlocalized throbbing set up in his wounded arm. A fly came buzzing about, and the drummer waved it away. Then he examined his wound again, and as he looked he grew sick at heart. He would be crippled for the rest of his life. Never before had a mishap befallen his big, comfortable body, and now his hand was gone and he could never have it again. This seemed to Strawbridge the most tragic thing which had happened in the battle of San Geronimo—that he, who was such a busy man, who needed his hand so much, should have lost it.

With an American's dread of germs he wanted to tie up his wound, to prevent infection. With this object in view, he looked anxiously about over the shambles.

The wharf was deserted by the living. The small *drogistas* which usually are found along Latin-American streets were all shut like blind eyes. Sounds of the fighting, a little softened, came from the direction of the *casa fuerte*. A rather wild notion came to Strawbridge to follow the soldiers and obtain his dressing from the medical corps of the insurgents; then he recalled that they had no medical corps. They had brought along with them a priest to save the dead, but they had not even a first-aid pack for the wounded.

Beyond the row of palms down the center of the *playa*, the drummer presently observed a goleta, one of those curious Orinocan schooners with preternaturally tall masts, and a little square sail swung down under her jib. She was lying close to the bank, and evidently was stuck on a sand-bar, for her owner was on deck, trying, with a long spar, to pry her off.

This sort of craft often carried passengers on the river, and the American felt sure she would possess some of the simpler surgical aids. So he picked up his carbine and set off at a painful pace to the waterside.

When the drummer had passed the row of palms and appeared moving definitely toward the schooner, the man on deck stopped poling. He peered through the glare, at the American, and next moment dashed out of sight below deck.

His action cheered Strawbridge. The drummer felt that the skipper had understood the situation and had rushed below for his surgical dressings, to have them ready by his arrival. This thoughtfulness put a little better heart into the wounded man as he moved shakily along through the glare and heat. He could not help thinking of the inherent courtesy in all

Venezuelans. It was perhaps not sincere every time, thought the American, but it was as soothing as a poultice.

As Strawbridge moved gratefully toward the goleta, the skipper reappeared on deck with a stick; no, it was an outrageously long gun. He leveled it at the drummer and fired point-blank. The bullet whistled past the American's ear, and plunked into a heap of balata balls behind him.

Strawbridge stopped and stared, bewildered. The skipper was feverishly reloading his extraordinary gun. It seemed to be some sort of single-shot arrangement. The drummer was amazed, and suddenly outraged.

"Here!" he shouted. "What the hell do you mean?"

The master of the schooner lifted his weapon again, to correct his faulty shot, when the salesman instinctively dived behind some bags of tonka-beans. He peered over the tops, still scarcely able to believe his senses, when the captain fired again and something nicked the American's hat.

At this second discharge the drummer went furious. To be fired on casually and without any provocation whatever! With his good arm, he flung his carbine along the top of the bags leveled down, and fired at the captain. At his first movement, however, the sailor had dropped down and disappeared below the garboard of the schooner.

The American fired two vicious shots at the place where the captain must have been prone. Then he glared at the vacant deck, with the bitterest sense of injury he had ever known. To be fired upon when he was seeking aid and comfort—to be shot at like a rat!

His feeling of injury became so intense he burst out cursing the invisible sailor, loading him with every obscene and profane qualification. With his carbine leveled over the bags, he swore furiously for two or three minutes. Then he began to repeat his oaths, and presently fizzled out through a mere sense of rhetoric. Then he damned his enemy for a coward, and invited him to stand up like a man and get killed.

Passed a slight interim, and a voice behind the gunwale, but considerably removed from where the fellow had disappeared, called out, "Señor!"

Through some strange reaction, this placating "Señor" added fuel to Strawbridge's wrath. He broke out again, howling, swearing, and urging the captain to get up and be shot.

But the captain conducted his end of the conversation from cover.

"Señor," he repeated without any resentment in his tone, "are you not a *revolutionista*?"

"No!" yelled Strawbridge. "I'm a decent American citizen down in this hell-fired country...." He continued this strain upward half a minute.

When he became silent again, the hidden one ejaculated mildly:

"*Caramba!* How should I know you were an *Americano*, señor?"

"Well,—by God!—you ought to look who you're shooting at!"

"Up this Orinoco valley, señor, if you look too long before you shoot, you may not get to shoot at all."

"Huh! I bet you knew I was an American all the time."

"No, really, señor! Why should I shoot at an *Americano*?"

Strawbridge could think of no reason why any one should want to shoot at an American. During the silence which followed, the sailor asked in a placating tone:

"May I stand up, *Señor Americano*? This deck is very warm indeed."

The drummer relinquished his notion of killing the man.

"All right, get up," he conceded. "We're not doing any good like this." And Strawbridge walked out from behind the tonka-beans at the same time the captain sat up and then stood.

The sailor was a brown man, dripping with sweat, and with smudges of pitch on his clothes which he had got from the seams in the deck. He had a good-humored face, rather scared just now, and he looked curiously at Strawbridge as he mopped his face and neck with a red handkerchief.

"Will you come aboard my ship, señor?" he inquired courteously, getting his spar again and running it out to where Strawbridge could by wading a little reach the end of it. The drummer walked aboard.

The moment the drummer stepped on deck, the captain began hastily:

"Now, señor, if you would be kind enough to lend me a little help ... I am trying to float the *Concepcion Inmaculada*."

"What's the rush?" asked the salesman, looking at his wounded hand.

The fellow swung his weight against the spar.

"*Caramba!* If the *revolutionistas* catch me here, they will strip my poor *Concepcion Inmaculada* to her last sheet."

"Steal your stuff!" echoed Strawbridge. "What makes you think so!"

"Lightning of God!" cried the shipmaster. "They are ladrones, bandits, cutpurses! Come, give a poor man a hand, señor!" He was shoving now with all his strength.

"You're wrong about that!" defended the drummer, warmly. "I know those fellows. Came up here with 'em." He doubled up his good fist and began making strong, convincing selling gestures with it.

"You can take this from me, señor," he said: "The revolutionists are just as high-toned a set of men as you'll find in Venezuela. I honestly believe General Fombombo has higher ideals than any public man I ever knew, and as for that Coronel Saturnino—say! you got to hand it to him for courtesy and politeness! So don't get all fussed about your boat. You're safe as a church, right here." Strawbridge paused impressively, and then asked, "Say, can you do anything for this damned hand of mine!"

The captain was convinced. Perhaps of all the men in the world the American salesman has a style of talk the most sincere in sound. The captain visibly put by his doubts of the revolutionists, and then looked at the hand.

"*Caramba!* that's a bad punch!"

"Yeh, tough luck."

A faint suspicion crossed the brown man's mind.

"You were not fighting, señor? You are not a *revolutionista* yourself?"

"Hell, no! I got this following the troops around. I wanted to see how they worked."

"*Cá!* Are you a military attaché, *Señor Americano?*"

The ship-owner was visibly impressed, but Strawbridge straightened.

"Say, do I look like a damn diplomatic lounge lizard sunning himself in some South American post! By God, I'm a man! I'm an American salesman down here investigating a point of business. I sell hardware, myself. I make this territory once a year. What's your line!"

The captain of the *Concepcion Inmaculada* opened his eyes at a man who so scorned a governmental position. His respect mounted. In fact, the captain was born into the South American cult of respect for office. He had never before met the North American's thoroughgoing contempt for politics and politicians, nor was he aware of the fact that it is barely respectable to be anything less than a senator in the United States—and often not that.

So now the sailor introduced himself with circumspection to so important a personage. He was Noe Vargas, commander of the *Concepcion Inmaculada*, sailing out of Coro. He had cruised up the Orinoco to buy tonka-beans and balata, and would carry them to Curaçao to be reshipped to Holland. In fact, a large part of the beans and balata which Strawbridge saw lying on the wharf was consigned to the *Concepcion Inmaculada*, if only Noe could succeed in lading his vessel.

All this information was delightful to Strawbridge. In fact, this was the first conversation which he had really enjoyed since coming to Venezuela. And while Captain Vargas was not particularly fond of talking of sago, copra, cassava, guarapo, and such articles of commerce, he was flattered that so great a man as Strawbridge should deign to listen to him.

As they talked, Captain Vargas made shift to bind up Strawbridge's hand. He had no surgical linen, but he thought the tail of one of his shirts would do. Strawbridge objected, on the score of germs. The captain assured him these were impossible, because only the day before he had washed this shirt, which he proposed to use, in the Orinoco, and it was a well-known fact that running water purified itself once every thousand yards.

"And think how pure the Orinoco must be, señor," added the captain, "for the Orinoco had flowed for thousands and thousands of miles!"

So Strawbridge went below, into a smelly cabin. The captain found the shirt he meant, in a bag of dunnage, pulled it out, cut off the tail, and bound up the drummer's hand.

The two men were still talking business when they returned to the deck. Strawbridge had excited himself somewhat by explaining that if the revolutionists took San Geronimo it would mean for him an order of thousands of rifles and cases of ammunition. This meant a rich commission. The skipper and the drummer stood on deck, listening to the gun-shots which would decide the American's commission. The reports came in gusts.

Strawbridge peered in the direction of the fighting. He tiptoed and moved about the deck, but all he could see was the haze of semi-smokeless powder hanging over the city in the direction of the *casa fuerte*. Presently the captain ejaculated:

"*Caramba!* To think that this fighting may put a fortune in your pocket!"

The drummer nodded.

"It may do it. Damn it! I hope Saturnino wins!"

Both men stared cityward. The volley-firing had almost died out. In its place came a desultory snapping which gave Strawbridge the impression of some person shooting the last few rats in a corn-bin. Now a rat would be found behind a plank—*bang!* Then two would start from a covert—*bang! bang!* These were the sounds which came from the city. Single reports at irregular intervals. There was something dreadful and cold-blooded about it.

Suddenly Captain Vargas pointed.

"*Mire!* Yonder they come out of the *calle!* Look!"

Sure enough, through the palms the drummer saw a line of soldiers march out of a street into the *playa*. Captain Vargas turned and ran below for a telescope. The drummer screwed up his eyes against the glare and peered without breathing. He was trying to find out whether he was thousands of dollars winner, or whether his side had lost. In the heat the soldiers and the quay danced and shimmered. It was impossible to tell whether they were Federals or rebels. However, the crowd fell into a definite arrangement. A line of men were standing up against the low adobe walls, while another line stood opposite to them in the *playa*.

A kind of crawling went over Strawbridge. His heart began to beat heavily, and he stared at the scene with fascinated eyes. At that moment Captain Vargas hurried up on deck with the telescope.

Strawbridge turned, almost jerked the instrument from the Venezuelan, and fumbled at it with his good hand and the wrist of his wounded arm. The captain helped him, and he peered through the glass. Views of palms, of blank walls, of roofs and rolling clouds swung back and forth, up and down; then abruptly appeared a line of men standing against a wall. At the very first glimpse Strawbridge's whole ventral cavity seemed to collapse. At the head of the unhappy column stood Lieutenant Rosales. The drummer could make out even his sharp, dusty features. A figure in a cassock stood in front of the lieutenant, holding up a cross. A nervous spasm swung the lense out of line. When he refocused it, Lieutenant Rosales had disappeared from the head of the column, and an ordinary peon stood next. A solitary rifle report reached the *Concepcion Inmaculada*.

Strawbridge stopped looking and with a shaking hand handed the glass to the captain. His mouth was so dry he could scarcely speak.

"That ... that ... that was ... Rosales...."

"Your friend?"

Strawbridge nodded.

"Then the insurgents have lost!"

Strawbridge nodded again. Then he went to a coil of rope in the shade of the mainsail and sat down. The slow reports came to him from the end of the *playa*—*bang!*—*bang!*—*bang!* Rosales ... Saturnino ... Gumersindo ... the peons, the indomitable peons who had ridden out with their lives in search of liberty. The banging would never, never cease.

The horror, the pathos of it shook the drummer. He leaned forward on his knees and let his head go limply in his folded arms. He did not care whether he lived or died. From the end of the *playa* the slow reports assaulted his ears. After a while they stopped. There was a singing in his ears as if he had taken quinine. Presently Captain Vargas said, "They are coming down here." Strawbridge paid no attention. All of his friends on that brave adventure were gone. Gumersindo, with his strange philosophy, was no more, nor the mocking Saturnino, nor the kindly priest. Captain Vargas was saying, "Remember, *mi amigo*, you are my first mate, if any one should ask. You have been on the *Concepcion Inmaculada* all the time. You and I did not fly as the other cowardly vessels did, because we felt that Justice, God, and the federal forces must win."

Strawbridge looked up at the captain and nodded mechanically. He could feel that his face was putty-colored. The two men ceased talking and watched the approach of the federal troops.

As Strawbridge stared at the marching men he scrutinized the officer at the head of the column, a graceful figure of medium height, with slender waist and broad shoulders. This man had just executed a whole column of insurgents, but he bore his bloody deed with a light heart. He walked jauntily, with his visor tipped up and a hand resting lightly on the hilt of his sword.

The drummer tried to make out the features of this man upon whom his own fortunes, even his own life, rested so heavily. He peered intently through the downpour of sunshine. As he looked, a queer illusion took place. The face of the strange officer seemed to melt and change into the features of Coronel Saturnino. A kind of exaltation shone through the dust on this handsome and familiar face. The drummer was shocked at such a resemblance to his executed friend. Then, in the ranks, he espied the black face of Gumersindo. Strawbridge thought he was going mad. At that moment the officer at the head of the column whipped out his sword and saluted the drummer on deck.

"*Bravo*, Señor Strawbridge!" he shouted joyfully. "I have heard how you stopped a panic and headed a cavalry charge against the ambuscade on the roofs. *Mire, mis bravos!* There stands the man who won the battle of San Geronimo!"

Under his violent revulsion, the drummer could scarcely breathe. He gaped and stared.

"What! What! Are those our troops! My God! I thought you were all dead—executed. I thought I saw poor Rosales facing a firing-squad!"

Saturnino lost his ebullience.

"You mean at the end of the *playa?*"

"Yes."

"That was Rosales. When his forces gained the *casa fuerte* by a most gallant charge from the flank, he then tried to hold the fort against my own troops." Saturnino's voice took a metallic tang: "I had to win the stronghold by fighting half my own troops. That young whelp's insurrection almost frustrated my plans."

Strawbridge was dumbfounded.

"You mean ... he deserted you in battle?... turned on you in the midst of battle?"

Saturnino waved a hand.

"For a long time there has been a plot brewing in Canalejos, against General Fombombo. It came to a head in Rosales...." He shrugged. "*Cá!* You can scarcely blame a *joven* of spirit from playing the game. If he had won...." Saturnino looked at the town and the wide river. "*Caramba!* he would have won a nucleus for a state of his own, thrust in between federal and insurgent territory. *Cá!* It was quite a stroke. I think I will give the lad a military funeral. Such souls as his have made the Latin race great." Just then the colonel's eyes fell on the drummer's bandaged hand.

"*Ola, mi amigo!* I see you are wounded!"

CHAPTER XVIII

The sheer human waste involved in the execution of Lieutenant Rosales horrified Thomas Strawbridge, and filled him with a fundamental discouragement toward all Venezuela. What fire and courage had been wantonly squandered! Could nothing have been done to reclaim so brilliant a daredevil?

However, Strawbridge was the only one who brooded over Rosales's untimely death. The captors of San Geronimo were very jovial and very busy. Saturnino began a series of confiscations which worked with machine-like efficiency. No doubt in his plans for the attack on San Geronimo the colonel had worked out the details of this confiscation. From some source he had obtained a list of the wealthy citizens in the captured town, and now he began collecting what he called "voluntary contributions to the insurgent cause." The colonel fostered the "will to give," by explaining to the prospective contributor what would occur in the event that the sum marked against his name was not forthcoming.

He was forced to carry this threat into effect in only two instances. One cocoa-broker he chained bareheaded in the plaza, and kept him there all day with a pitcher of water just out of his reach. Strawbridge got a glimpse of this wretch, but hurried away for fear he should get himself into trouble by pushing the water closer. The other man, Strawbridge simply heard about. He was shot. The plaza incident was designed purely as a publicity measure, a means of teaching cheerful and abundant donations to a worthy cause. Its value could hardly be questioned.

But the colonel's methods of suasion were not always physical. When he occupied the big wireless telegraph which the federal authorities had constructed at San Geronimo, he persuaded the federal officer to stay at his post.

The wireless plant was a little east of the city, on one of the long, gentle knolls in the llanos. It was a quiet place, barring the whine of the radio, and it was free from the scents left by the battle around the *casa fuerte*. Strawbridge often walked out there. It was operated by a dark, silent little man, an Austrian. All the wireless operators in Venezuela were foreigners, because the system itself was new and as yet there were no natives trained for the positions. The Federal Government had given this Austrian the rank of lieutenant, and he had been a regular officer in the Venezuelan Army.

There was a humanity about Strawbridge which eventually drew the operator out. One night the two were sitting outside the station, looking up at the stars and cooling off after the day's heat. As they conversed, presently the ex-lieutenant began a half-hearted defense of his desertion. He said he would not hear to it at first, that he insisted that Coronel Saturnino imprison him or stand him up before a firing-squad, but the colonel scouted such an idea. He said that really the colonel was the kindest-hearted man. He had shown the lieutenant where he was wrong.

"You are a wireless operator," said the colonel. "You should consider yourself strictly a part of your machinery, equally efficient for either side that owns the plant. It would do me no good to execute you and replace you with another man. If the Federals ever recapture this town, they will certainly feel the same way about it. You are as much a part of your plant as the aërials overhead."

The little Austrian sat staring up at the aërials swung high against the stars.

"I am just as much a part of this plant as those aërials," he repeated gloomily. "They receive messages from anywhere, and transmit them correctly—to any one."

It rather disgusted the drummer.

"Even the aërials have a static," he said, "which sometimes interferes with *their* transmission. I suppose *you* have no static."

The dark little man seemed disturbed by this, but merely repeated his formula. Heaven knows with what more casuistry Coronel Saturnino had beguiled him. To Strawbridge there was something smudged and pitiful, rather than treacherous, about the little operator.

In all these functionings of warlike ethics, Strawbridge yielded a rather shocked acquiescence to the logic of the situation. In only one instance did he become personally involved, and that was when a revolutionary squad went aboard the *Concepcion Inmaculada*.

It was a typical Latin-American scene on the schooner's deck, with the sun boiling pitch out of her strakes and a squad of short, brown, empty-faced riflemen standing in the heat, listening as Saturnino, Strawbridge, and Captain Vargas threshed out the rights of the matter.

At Captain Vargas's request, Strawbridge explained to Saturnino that he, Captain Vargas, had remained at San Geronimo during the revolutionary attack, upon the drummer's assurance that he and his schooner would receive complete justice at the hands of the insurgents.

Saturnino assented to this, with the utmost graciousness.

The captain himself then added that he did not fly with the other cowardly schooner-owners because he confided then, as he confided now, in the integrity of the *revolutionistas*, the nobility of their cause, and the spotless characters of their leaders.

Saturnino bowed deeply over the tar-streaked deck, and assured Captain Vargas that his confidence honored his heart as his judgment honored his intellect.

The captain then asked for assistance in getting his tonka-beans and balata aboard the *Concepcion Inmaculada*, that he might sail and spread abroad tidings of the justice and equity of the *revolutionistas*—which no doubt would greatly aid their cause.

The colonel agreed to this, heartily, but suggested that, since all the barter on the wharf had become insurgent property by force of capture, the insurgents now stood in the shoes of the original owners of the property, and that he, Coronel Saturnino, should be paid for the freight.

At this Vargas became thoughtful, and said that he had already paid the owner for the goods. When the colonel asked him for a receipt, the skipper made some vague excuse about the receipt not having been delivered, but he assured the colonel that payment had been made.

Saturnino said he did not doubt this; he said if he were acting for himself he would deliver the freight at once and allow Captain Vargas to sail, but he was not acting for himself. No, every transaction he performed had to be accounted for with the strictest business formality, to President Fombombo, in order that every citizen might be treated with an exact and impartial justice. Therefore *el capitan* would excuse the technicality, but he would have to pay for his tonka-beans and rubber again, in order that he, Saturnino, might have a proper record of the deal. Then the captain could file a claim, if he wished, with the insurgent government, against the man who originally took the money, and thus he would infallibly get it back.

Captain Vargas's good-humored face immediately became serious, but eventually the three men went below into the skipper's cabin, and there Vargas opened a strong-box and turned over to Saturnino a considerable quantity of American gold pieces, and several ounces of raw gold which the skipper had traded for at the mouth of the Caroni River. When the soldiers had lugged the box of money up on deck, Captain Vargas's cheerfulness returned, and he requested that soldiers be furnished to lade the schooner with the beans and rubber on the wharf.

The colonel seemed surprised.

"On the wharf?"

"*Seguramente*, señor!" exclaimed the skipper, also surprised. "That was the cargo consigned to me."

"But, señor," demurred the colonel, "you cannot expect the revolutionary government of Rio Negro to be bound and crippled by the contracts of its enemies! We should soon land in a pretty impasse."

"But you sold me the balata on the wharf, yourself!"

"*Cá!* No. Your tonka-beans and balata will be delivered in their proper turn. Here, I will give you a receipt for the money. Now, this balata, we are going to ship to Rio...."

Coronel Saturnino was drawing forth a receipt-book, to write Captain Vargas a receipt, when the injured sailor forgot caution and broke into all manner of Spanish abuse. He declared the *revolutionistas* were thieves, cut-throats, and rascals, exactly what he had heard and believed all the time. He shouted that Saturnino might keep the rubber, tonka-beans, and gold, that he was going to sail away and never cruise up the accursed Orinoco again!

Strawbridge, too, was incensed at the barefaced robbery. He declared that such methods were bad business, that Saturnino would ruin all possible commerce in Rio Negro, that the country's reputation was worth more than a cargo of balata.

"It's just like one of our great American poets says, colonel," cried Strawbridge, earnestly. "You must recall the famous poem entitled, 'Has It Ever Struck You?' Everybody knows the lines. I'll bet they are pasted up in half the offices in America. Now listen to this. The poet says:

"All of us know that Money talks throughout our glorious nation,

But Money whispers low compared to business reputation.

For men will talk this wide world o'er; take this under advisement.

To have them talking for you is the wisest advertisement.

Pull off no slick nor crooked deal, for pennies or for dollars.

God! think of all the trade you'll lose if just one sucker hollers!"

For some reason these admirable verses seemed to irritate Coronel Saturnino more than all the abuse shouted by Captain Vargas. He turned sharply on Strawbridge.

"Señor," he snapped, "there is a difference between a stupid business conducted in the midst of profound peace and a band of men struggling for life in the midst of war. In peace one can look to the future, but in war we must seize on the present. That barter on the dock represents so much available capital for our insurgent government. Do you imagine I am going to divide it with a private individual when the salvation of our whole country hangs in the balance?"

Captain Vargas reiterated his intention of sailing away without more ado, down the river, but Coronel Saturnino then informed him that the insurgent government would be forced to conscript the *Concepcion Inmaculada* for the purpose of freighting barter to Rio.

Oaths, arguments, and prayers availed nothing with the colonel. The *Concepcion Inmaculada* would be employed by the provisional government until hostilities ceased.

As Strawbridge returned up the *playa* with the colonel, that officer's good humor returned. He began smiling again, a little ironically.

"Now, this matter of the *Concepcion Inmaculada*.... If our revolution wins, Señor Strawbridge, I shall be accounted in history as a great financier; if we lose, I shall be known as a thief and a murderer. In your own country, señor, have you ever discovered any difference between thieves and financiers, except that the one loses and the one succeeds?"

On the third day a part of the insurgent cavalry set out for Canalejos. San Geronimo was now "consolidated." It belonged inside the red line on the map in General Fombombo's study. Strawbridge decided he would go back with the squadron.

During these three days the drummer's wounded hand had been steadily growing worse. Coronel Saturnino tried to persuade the American to remain in San Geronimo until his wound healed, but Strawbridge declared he had important business with General Fombombo. He said he was afraid that the capture of so many federal rifles would ruin his trade with the general.

Saturnino assured him the acquisition of the rifles in the *casa fuerte* would not influence the general in the slightest degree. But Strawbridge was far from convinced. He had seen Saturnino's word tested often enough to doubt it. He knew the colonel's Latin penchant for a pleasant falsehood rather than an unpleasant truth.

But behind his anxiety about the rifles, Strawbridge was homesick for Canalejos. He really wanted to see the señora, to sit with her on the piazza in the evenings, and hear her play the piano. Thoughts of her came to him with an ineffable charm and sweetness.

So on the third day he set out with the troops, with a wounded hand and with the vision of a slender music-making figure in a nun's garb, moving before him like a mirage over a desert.

The drummer had not traversed twelve kilometers before his wound took a wicked turn. With the jolting of his horse the aching increased, and the arm swelled clear up to his shoulder. He grew feverish, then somehow, in the furnace of the llanos, he imagined that he was in the cavalry charge again. He suddenly began spurring his horse and waving an imaginary carbine at a roof full of Federals. Then the Federals seemed to capture him. He struggled terrifically, but the Federals pinioned him and were going to execute him, just as Rosales had been executed.

Thereafter Strawbridge's delirium was broken by intervals of clarity. Several times he became rational, to find himself bound fast to a litter which was swung between two mules. Then he would be about to be executed again.

For a long time, when the drummer emerged into an interval of clear thinking, he found himself in the furnace of sunshine on the llanos; an eternity or two later he regained consciousness shuddering with cold, and saw the sky above him filled with stars. The squadron had gone on ahead, leaving the sick man with Father Benicio, Gumersindo, and the pack-mules.

On the morning of the second day, Strawbridge thought he heard the priest say they would soon be at home. The next thing the drummer knew he lay in a great bed, with cold packs on his hand and arm and all over him. And he saw what to him was the most beautiful face in the world, looking down at him, weeping silently. The American had barely the strength to extend his good hand.

"Señora ..." he whispered.

The woman suddenly sobbed aloud.

"Oh, señor, they have told me what a hero you were!"

Then the señora suddenly flickered out again.

CHAPTER XIX

Strawbridge could understand only snatches of Benavente's satire which the señora was reading. When the Spanish girl read, she reverted to the soft Castilian pronunciation of her childhood, and Strawbridge's ear was accustomed to the hard colonial accent of South America.

Benavente has a leaning toward the theme of unfaithful wives, and the comedy which the señora had chosen to read was of this type.

As the reading progressed, the mood of the satire, the quirks and turns of Benavente's wit played over the girl's face as if from some delicate, changing illumination, as indeed it was. Presently, in the sheer pleasure of watching her, the sick man gave up the effort to follow the text. He had never before observed such a radiance about her, such a fine, ardent life in her. The drummer's nationality evoked the thought that some artist ought to paint Dolores sitting thus reading. It was his American instinct to commercialize the moment, not for its monetary value but for its pleasure value. He was under the abiding American delusion that pleasures are somehow bottleable; that a pleasure can be commanded to stand still in the heavens, somewhat after the fashion of Joshua's sun. It is the command of these American Joshuas which has inflicted on the world the phonograph, the kodak, the college annual, place-card collections, and the family album.

As the drummer studied the señora's face, he observed, when she smiled, a little dimple in her left cheek. Somehow this tiny discovery stirred the sick man in a subtle way. With a feeling of peculiar intimacy he watched it come and go. It seemed to advertise, ever so delicately, veiled and exquisite reserves in the nunnish figure. It amazed him that he had not seen, until just now, how lovely the señora was. It seemed as if beauty had been spilled over her.

He lay warming himself in this miracle, when the girl looked up, studied his face a moment, then accused playfully:

"*Cá!* señor, you are not listening to a word I read. What are your thoughts?"

The sick man was taken aback when he was thus brought to a realization of the vague compound of admiration, sensuous longing, and wistfulness which moved his heart, for the wife of another man. He moistened his lips to say something, when the señora assisted him:

"I dare say you are lying there thinking about your business."

The drummer accepted the suggestion:

"Perhaps I was."

"You mustn't worry about it."

At this negative suggestion, Strawbridge did begin to worry:

"I think I have a right to, señora, when my trip down to San Geronimo spoiled the very thing I went after."

"How is that?"

The sick man tossed his head on his pillow.

"Oh, you know I wanted to sell the general rifles. Well ... I helped him capture all he can use ... ruined my own sale." The salesman laughed a little, but he was not amused.

The girl did not smile.

"Has your trade really fallen through, after all you've done?"

"Sure! A sale can slip away from you just so easy." He stared at the ceiling, with hollow, troubled eyes.

With a faint, tender smile, the girl looked at her patient.

"Tell me, Tomas: why do you place such great stress on selling, selling, selling?"

He looked at her, weakly surprised.

"Why, that's my job!"

"Yes, I know, but you will sell to some one else if not to the general."

"But the idea is not to miss a sale; to get everybody; to do a big business."

The señora laughed outright but kindlily.

"Yes, but what is the object of your big business, that you work at it with such fury? You already make the money you need."

"I didn't know I worked at it with such fury."

"*Cá!* You do!"

The drummer pondered a moment.

"Well, a man just naturally wants a big business, and, besides, my old man expects it. I'll lose my job if I don't."

"*Pues*, your 'old man,' then: why does he want a big business? What does he mean finally to do with it?"

Strawbridge, with a sick man's suggestibility, stopped fretting about his own sale and lay pondering gently what his old man meant to do with his business. He could not imagine his old man *doing* anything with his business except running it, expanding it, beating down competitors with it. Just then he recalled an explanation which is current with every American, and which finds expression in every American paper and magazine, so he repeated it:

"Why, business is a game with my old man, señora; he never will stop, because that's his game. He takes a pride in seeing how big a business he can develop, just as he tries to make a low golf score. Business is the American game."

The señora smiled at such naïveté. She might not have smiled had she known that Strawbridge had sounded for her the depth of American popular philosophy on the point; but, not knowing that, she put it down to the drummer's general childishness.

"Tomas," she said gently, "do you really think that a game, any game, is the whole of a man's life? Would you be willing, Tomas, to spend the whole of your life playing a game?"

"That's what everybody believes in America, señora."

"Surely Americans must be wrong!"

"I don't know. What do you think?"

"I have wondered. You are the only American I have ever known, Tomas, and you were so big and strong and restless, I could not help saying to myself, 'Why is he so restless? He is not poor; any one can see that. What does he mean to do with his fortune that he rushes so to get?'" The señora quoted her thoughts pensively, and then added, "Still, I suppose I do know."

"Why, why?" blurted out the drummer, greatly surprised.

"You wish to make your fortune equal to that of some wealthy girl's."

"A wealthy girl's...." The drummer looked at the Spanish girl quite blankly, then, as her implication penetrated him, he was moved to a somewhat abrupt denial:

"No, señora, no girls for mine ... at least not yet." He shifted his bulk a trifle and lay looking at her defensively; then he saw where her logic had led her. "Why, the idea! We were talking about why all Americans work so, and you think they work because they want to get married. What an idea!"

"But doesn't that explain a great many, señor?"

"Mighty few business fellows. When we are boys we have our sweethearts, of course, but when we get out into business, women sort of drop out of our lives for eight or ten years. We chase 'em a little, but not much. Later, when our business justifies it, we buy us a motor, a bungalow, and a girl,—I mean, we pick out a girl and marry her,—but getting married is just a symptom that a man is getting on in his business; it's not the aim of his business, at all. The business clicks away just the same, whether he marries or not."

It would be difficult to say just how much the señora was moved at this reversal of ordinary human motives. She looked at the drummer for several moments, and finally asked in an odd voice:

"How do you decide you have the reached a position to marry, Señor Tomas?"

"Oh, that depends on your ideals. When I was a kid I thought fifteen a week and a flivver would do. As I got older my ideals went up, and now I've got to have ten thousand a year and a twelve-cylinder."

"And you have no particular girl in view?"

The drummer laughed weakly.

"When you've got ten thousand a year, you don't have to have any particular girl in view. You've got to keep out of view, or some flapper 'll land you."

The señora shook her head.

"I don't understand it, Tomas," she said gently. "It seems to me you deserve something finer than what you say. It's so ... like a machine." She flushed faintly, and arose, saying that she must make the sick man some broth.

"You'll be back soon, señora?" he asked anxiously.

She smiled at him, picked up a salver from a table, and went out.

With the departure of the señora, the sense of pleasure which had enveloped Strawbridge also vanished. It gave him the same feeling of loss that he experienced at times when he stepped out of the glow and romance of a theater, into a dull, prosaic street. Still, after all, it was in dull, prosaic streets that money was made and ambitious young fellows gained headway. A query trickled into the drummer's mind. He wondered if it would be possible, if it were in the scope of things to take some of the glow and romance of the theater out into life, to keep it there, always to have this dear warmth in his heart ... if the *señora*.... A quiver went through the drummer at the direction in which his musing had led him. He came to a sudden stop, deserted the theater which his fancy had built, and walked slowly out into the prosaic street once more.

When his door opened again, Strawbridge saw, to his disgust, that it was the *griffe* girl who had brought him his broth. The girl had had a serious part in nursing Strawbridge over his wound and the solar fever which exposure in the campaign had caused. This had bred in her considerable authority. So now, as she entered, she narrowed her black eyes, nodded firmly at her patient, and said, "You are to drink this, señor."

The salesman was outraged that the maid should have come instead of the mistress. He turned on his side away from her.

"Don't want any."

"But the señora said you were to drink it."

"Don't believe it's time."

"You can look at your watch, if it hasn't stopped running. You never remember to wind it. Have you wound it this morning?"

The drummer fumbled under his pillow for the watch. It was still running, and stood at eleven minutes after his broth-time. He wound it with the sensitive fingers of the sick. As he did so, he stared ill-temperedly through the window and observed a number of banners waving in the plaza. He broke out:

"Look here! Are they going to have another damn fiesta? What's it for? Good Lord! the time they waste on fiestas!"

At this outbreak the *griffe* girl stared at him, then wrinkled her freckled snub nose, and went off into such a gust of light-headed giggling that Strawbridge was irritated anew.

"What the hell you whinnying like that for?"

The maid caught up the corner of her apron and stuffed it into her mouth as a mirth-extinguisher. The American received the tray on the side of his bed, glaring at the girl, who plainly was about to burst out laughing again. A sudden plan came to him.

"I'm going to get up," he announced.

The maid was horrified.

"Oh, señor, you are not!"

"Oh, señorita, I am!"

"But you mustn't. It'll make you worse!"

"I'm all right. I feel all right. I'm going to get up, so get out of here!" He began tumbling his big body around under the sheets.

The *griffe* girl became desperate.

"But, señor, the señora has not said so; the doctor has not said so; nobody has given you permission...." She was trying to shoo him back under the cover with her hands.

"Are you going to get out or not?"

"Señor, you must not get up!"

"Oh, all right! Stick around and get an eyeful...." He began heaving himself up, tumbling back the sheet.

The *griffe* girl started backing out of the room. She resisted him morally to the last ditch, motioning him back into bed, but being gradually expelled as larger and larger segments of his pink pajamas came into view. The queer part was that in Strawbridge's extreme weakness the *griffe* girl had assisted one of the guards in the drummer's necessities; now she was whisked out of the room by the sight of his pajamas. Such is the power of matter over mind.

Strawbridge made a sorry mess of getting his clothes on, until Pambo, the guard who had served him during his illness, came in—sent, no doubt, by the *griffe* girl—and helped. Pambo was a pleasant little fellow, and instead of discouraging the invalid's effort he congratulated him on his improvement, and suggested a walk down into the plaza.

After the dressing, the two men left the palace and moved very slowly through the sunshine to a seat in the plaza. The guard placed the invalid's chair in the deep shade of a *mamone* tree, then, promising to return in half an hour, went back to his duties.

Already a crowd of idlers were gathered in the plaza, watching the preparations for the fête. The invalid sat in the color and stir, with that feeling of soft, weak pleasure that comes to a man after the pains of the sick-bed have vanished. All things were very grateful to him—the sunshine, the movement of the crowd, the calls of the venders, the heroic statue of

General Fombombo offering on a scroll to the State of Rio Negro, Liberty, Fraternity, Equality.

Presently the firemen's band in red coats and blue trousers began gathering, with their instruments. Pleasure-seekers grew thicker, and commenced renting chairs and placing them around a band stand which was shaped like a huge conch-shell. Girls in mantillas began with their fans to conduct discreet flirtations. Certain bolder women moved among the crowd, waiting for some one to accost them. Two or three priests from the cathedral mingled with their flock. One father moved about with his eyes riveted on a little Bible, having selected this strange place for his religious meditations.

A number of persons saluted the drummer, which rather surprised him, for the upper-class Venezuelans are usually reserved toward foreigners. Strawbridge was thinking over his sudden popularity, with the mildly amused superiority of a North American, when he saw approaching him a negro in a white linen suit. As this figure came nearer, the sick man recognized Gumersindo in gala attire. The negro bowed deeply, congratulated Strawbridge on his early convalescence, then took a copy of "El Correo del Rio Negro" from his pocket and pressed it upon his friend.

"Have you read my description of the battle of San Geronimo, *mi caro señor*?" he asked warmly. "*Caramba!* I do not say I have excelled, but Father Benicio, a man of excellent judgment, assures me these pages—" he tapped the paper—"will go down to posterity as one of the great battle descriptions of history. You will find your own name mentioned, *mi amigo*. I have taken the liberty of comparing you to the Swiss Guard at Versailles and the English regiment at Carabobo—a wounded lion, señor, crouched before the shield of Rio Negro!"

All this was uttered in a tone of impassioned eloquence, and now the black editor astonished Strawbridge by suddenly wringing his hand and hurrying away, leaving the paper with the invalid.

The drummer was amused at this emotion in Gumersindo, which he did not understand, but his sickness had brought with it a certain pensiveness, and he sat pondering on the springs of Gumersindo's enthusiasm. To write a history that would be handed down to posterity! What was the use of it? The American wondered what he would like to hand down to posterity, and he thought of life-insurance. Strawbridge glanced through his "Correo." Gumersindo had written six columns of closely printed matter. The American folded the paper and laid it across his lap.

The crowd in the plaza grew more interesting. Government dignitaries, merchants, and professional men began to arrive. Men collected in knots and conversed with excited gestures. Presently a great cheering went up, and Strawbridge saw General Fombombo traversing the plaza, in the presidential motor. At his side sat the peon girl Madruja. She held up her chin like a queen, and the line of her olive throat against her furs might have been a stroke of Raphael. Even in the brief glimpse of their passage, Strawbridge got an impression that the general was fondling her hand.

The outrage set up in the sick man's head vague fancies of liberating Dolores. He thought of divorce. The Spanish girl ought to get a divorce. She had every provocation. But of course there were no divorces in Roman Catholic Rio Negro.

The sound of a chair being dragged close to his own caused Strawbridge to glance around. He saw Lubito smiling and settling a chair in the turf by his side. On the other side of Lubito, Esteban was unfolding another chair. The peon youth seemed thinner and more care-worn than on the night when he had attacked General Fombombo.

The bull-fighter was very cordial.

"*Caramba!* I'm glad to see you alive, señor! I read in the paper how badly you were wounded, and what a hero you were." At the drummer's demurring gesture, he persisted with renewed force: "Oh, we know all about it. I said to Esteban, 'You called Señor Tomas a *cobarde* because he did not choose to assist you that night in the *palacio*. Nothing could be farther from the truth.'"

The peon youth stopped his steady stare into the plaza, to ask:

"But why did he turn against me?"

Lubito shrugged and made a gesture.

"How should I know? Am I as deep as the sea? Perhaps to save you. Had he not used his influence on *el Presidente*, no doubt you would have been rotting to-day in La Fortuna; but instead he had you turned out, and here you are, as free as a bird."

"I don't understand why he turned against me in a fight," repeated the peon, doggedly.

"*Caramba!* If you had a head to understand that, Esteban, you would not need to sit here gnawing your fingers now. I am far brighter than you, Esteban, but this Señor Strawbridge is a dark man to me. He moves in his own way, Esteban. He is like a cayman in the Orinoco; no man can tell when or where or at what he strikes."

The drummer followed this panegyric a little uncomfortably.

"Look here," he inquired: "how did I get such a swell reputation for double-crossing?"

"How! *Caramba!* Did you not despatch poor Lieutenant Rosales to his death at the *casa fuerte* in San Geronimo? He would have failed, but you gave him the strength to go on—but how far?" The bull-fighter held up a stubby forefinger and whispered an answer to his question: "Just as far as you pleased that he should go—and then he fell. But you: did any blame attach to you? None at all. You had a wealthy ship-owner sail up the Orinoco and bribe the insurgents in your behalf. Oh, we have heard everything, not through this paper, but—you know—from mouth to mouth. *Caramba!* this ship-owner poured out gold for you—box after box. It was easy enough to see whose gold it was!"

"Whose?" cried Strawbridge, quite amazed at so grotesque a misinterpretation of the facts.

"Whose! Whose! *Diantre*, Esteban! such a man! Why, señor, whose should it be but your own! Would any ordinary sailor have so much gold to fling about? No, it was your own gold, and only He who looks down upon the doings of men—only He knows how many other ways you are reaching out, raking this poor country of Rio Negro into your power. You had poor Rosales killed; he would have been a rival of yours one day, for he had the pride of Satan. You have a warm friend in Señor Tolliver, and yet he has been the enemy of all *revolutionistas* for years. You have twisted *el Presidente* around your finger, and—" Lubito paused and winked delicately—"and I hear that *la señora* is no bitter enemy of yours, either! *Caramba!* What a man!"

Strawbridge flushed and dropped his amused look.

"Say, just leave the señora out of this, will you?"

"How?"

"She is a lovely girl in the most painful position. I have done nothing more than any gentleman would do if he had a spark of manhood."

Lubito looked at the American rather blankly.

"*Seguramente*, señor, any *caballero* would do what you have done ... if he had a spark of manhood. *Seguramente!* I ... I hope you will allow a friend to ... to.... *Cá!* ... to congratulate you, señor."

This equivocal sentence brought the conversation to an impasse. The drummer was on the verge of taking offense at the innuendo, when Esteban interrupted in a very miserable voice:

"Señor Strawbridge, you are a wise man. Tell me what I can do to regain Madruja."

The drummer was touched at the peon's unashamed desolation.

"Esteban," he said seriously, "I don't know what you can do. I have been thinking over your very question—in a general way. There are no courts to separate her from ... from him. There is no public opinion to force him to give her up. There is no—"

"But, señor," interrupted the peon, "she—*mi Madruja adorata*—is not with *el Presidente* any more!"

Strawbridge leaned forward and peered around the bull-fighter at the peon.

"Not with him any more? What do you mean, Esteban?"

The youth made a desperate gesture.

"May the lightning strike God, but he has flung her out into the streets, señor!"

Strawbridge stared.

"Are you crazy, Esteban? I saw Madruja and the general drive past in a motor, not ten minutes ago!"

Lubito interrupted:

"No, you did not, señor. That was another girl he has picked up. Madruja is ... well, to speak plainly ... Madruja is growing heavy after the manner of women, and really, now—" the bull-fighter shrugged and opened a hand—"really, now, what could *el Presidente* do but turn her out?" He looked from one of his friends to the other and said intimately, "Now, really.... I dare say we have all been fathers at one time or another.... What else could he have done?"

Strawbridge did not hear this observation. He sat perfectly still in his chair, and said in a shocked tone:

"He really did!"

Lubito answered again:

"*Ciertamente*, señor; but any one could have foretold that. Do you not recall, Esteban, I told you that in advance? Do you not recall my saying, 'Esteban, *mi bravo*, cheer up. Presently *el Presidente* will grow weary of your Madruja, and you will have her back'?"

The drummer sat pondering the facts, in a benumbed manner. Somehow this Madruja affair touched him painfully. Presently he looked at Esteban and asked:

"Well, ... did you get her back! Do you want her back?"

Lubito replied for his friend:

"*Diablo!* no, he didn't get her back! *El Presidente* has a way with women. The poor girl is completely mad. She lives alone in a big house, and weeps night and day. She says the general will come back to her as soon as he grows weary of this new mistress. 'But, Madruja,' I argued with her, 'he will always have a new mistress! He always has had. Now take back poor Esteban. Look at him. See how he loves you. Your poor Esteban!' But she curls up her pretty mouth. 'Esteban! Esteban!' she says. 'Stupid as a donkey, dull as an old hound's tooth! Do you think I would take a poor lout of a peon in this house which *el Presidente* has given me?'

"'*Pues*,' I said, for I always did admire her, '*Pues*, take me!' She gave me a straight look, for we were talking to her through the bars of her window. 'You! What do you know, Señor Lubito, about the grand super-civilization of the future republic of Rio Negro? Do you know how to make all these wide sandy llanos bloom and bear fruit! Your sword has never carved an empire—nothing but bulls!'" The bull-fighter looked at the drummer in a puzzled fashion, shrugged, and finally added, "She is utterly mad."

CHAPTER XX

Strawbridge did not know why the general's second infidelity stirred him so deeply. For some reason it sent him hurrying weakly back, through the heat, to the palace. What he meant to do when he got there, what he could do, he did not know.

The drummer reached the side door almost exhausted and rang the bell. He waited several minutes in the intense heat of the sunshine. At last the door was opened by the *griffe* girl. She gave just one glance, then swooped on him, caught him about the waist, and helped him inside.

"*Caramba!* Señor Tomas, you are as white as a sheet! You are about to fall! You must go to bed at once. I told you—"

"Where is your mistress?" panted the drummer.

The girl was dictatorial.

"*Cá!* What do you want with the señora? I tell you to go to bed! I told you never to...."

The maid's question helped temper Strawbridge's impulse. After all, what did he want with the señora! What did he mean to say to her! There was nothing to say, much less to do. He began to realize how empty his impulse was of any possible action.

"What do you want with her?" repeated the maid, holding him up and leading him inside.

The drummer fumbled for an answer, and then explained lamely that they were reading a play together.

The freckled maid looked up at him, amazed.

"A play! *Caramba!* it must be a wonderful play!"

"Look here," frowned the American, recovering his dignity, "can't you answer a simple question without making remarks?"

"*Pues*, was I making remarks? You told me you were reading a play!"

"Yes, you do make remarks! Damn it! you talk all the time! If you've got to chatter like that, beat it!"

She would not let go her patient, for fear he might really fall and hurt himself, but she was offended.

"*Seguramente!*" she snapped. "If I ever get you in bed, trust me, I'll never lift another finger to get you out! *Caramba!* after all I've done!" She seemed about to cry. "As for the señora, she is in the music-room, and when you rush in through this heat, all white and trembly, to read a play, I think you are crazy; that's what I think!"

"Well, damn what you think! Here, let go; I can walk without you!" He shook himself loose and walked on in weak irascibility.

The girl stood looking after him with angry tears in her eyes and much anxiety for his welfare as he passed through the transverse corridor and turned down the main hallway.

He moved more and more slowly past the old doors which lined the corridor. There were no guards in the passage; they had been drawn away, no doubt, by the fiesta. The palace seemed rather empty without them. He was thinking of this when the door of the music-room opened and a man stepped into the hallway. He stood holding the door ajar and looking back into the room. The drummer was surprised to see that it was Coronel Saturnino. The salesman had thought the colonel was in San Geronimo, but no doubt he had come to Canalejos for the fiesta. The expression on the officer's face struck Strawbridge. For once his look of satire had vanished, and it left exposed what must have been the real Saturnino beneath all his quips and mockeries. He was speaking through the door, in a low tone:

"When a man has only one desire in life, señora, would he not be a fool to sacrifice that! Why should he sacrifice it! Shall his one brief glimpse of existence be entirely empty?"

There came a gasp from the music-room, and Strawbridge caught the phrase, "But, Pancho, that is sacrilegious!"

"Sacrilegious!" echoed the officer, in a sudden passion. "Sacrilegious! A word to trap fools with! To give up the very heart of this life, here, expecting another which will never come.... Dolores, can you imagine the immeasurable unconcern with which Nature views us! And then expect me to give up the very essence of my little glimpse of existence, for fear, forsooth, that the hand that made me will not precisely approve my squirmings toward the ends for which He framed me! Puh! it's too absurd!" With pallid face he stood looking through the doorway; then came a return of some of his old pococurantism: "Well, señora, I leave you now, but I will come back one day, you might say as a missionary, to convert you to a happier view of life and the Deity. Until then, *adios.*" He bowed gracefully and turned up the passage toward the front of the palace.

With considerable surprise, and also a certain questioning, the American watched the colonel go. The officer evidently had concluded a tête-à-tête with the señora which was unsatisfactory to him. Strawbridge was secretly glad of this; he had always been glad that Saturnino was persona non grata with the señora.

But what set up a questioning in the drummer were the tones of the man and the woman, and the nickname, "Pancho," which the señora had used. This diminutive and just such overtones the drummer recalled hearing through the hedge as he stood in the plaza outside the cathedral garden. The idea that those quarreling lovers in the garden had been Saturnino and Dolores came to him with a shock. All along, had Saturnino been a suitor for the señora's favors? Was the officer attempting intimacies with the wife of his employer and general? Such duplicity filled the American with disdain. He was shocked at Saturnino. Then, as he stood thinking about it, he asked himself why he should be shocked. The colonel was no Anglo-Saxon, with a restraint cultivated by long generations of controlled ancestors. He was a Latin, a Venezuelan.

The door of the music-room was still ajar when Strawbridge reached the entrance. He had meant to express, in a roundabout way, his deep moral approval of what the señora had just done, but what he saw in the music-room put completely out of his head any sentiment he meant to utter.

The señora half knelt before the window-seat, with her head in her outstretched arms and her rosary clutched in her fingers. As a sharp accent in the picture was her hair. Her nun's cap had fallen off and revealed a great jet corona wound about her head in a complexity of cables. The glint and sheen of the light from the window fell over this luxuriant coiffure, and the slender white nape of her neck curved up into it. The loveliness of it clutched at something in the drummer's chest as if with physical fingers.

At his continued gaze the girl stirred, looked about, saw him, and made a little defensive movement toward her nun's bonnet.

The American protested involuntarily:

"For God's sake, señora, don't hide it! What makes you want to hide your hair?"

Her eyes showed she had been crying, but such an outbreak of admiration moved her to a brief smile; immediately she was grave again.

"It is a vow I made for my sister, señor."

"A vow to what?"

"To Saint Teresa."

"To a saint! Are you hiding your lovely hair just to keep a vow to a saint?"

"*Sí*, señor."

"Well, I declare! think of that! Wait, don't put it back on right now...."

Nevertheless she replaced the bonnet, smiling faintly at his protesting face. Then she became concerned about him.

"I didn't know you were out of bed. You ought not to be, Señor Tomas. You look quite worn out. Come over here, on this couch by the window."

She was swiftly becoming herself again, pleasant, softly gracious, and remote. She crossed the room, took his arm, and helped him to the wicker couch she had indicated. Her mere presence and touch wove a deep comfort about the sick man. Whatever were her relations with Saturnino, they faded into a small matter in the atmosphere of her delicate charm. Strawbridge leaned back against the end of the couch, looking at her.

"What were you crying about when I came in, señora?" he asked simply.

She looked at him with dark eyes that appeared slightly unfocused.

"I would rather not tell you, Señor Tomas."

"You might tell me, señora. I'm a mighty good friend of yours."

The girl sighed with some comfort of her own.

"Yes, you are. You are so ... nice. But you don't want to be my confessor, do you, Señor Tomas?"

"I wish I could be. Who is your confessor, señora?"

"Father Benicio."

"Sure! it would naturally be him."

She noted his tone, with surprise and a delicate amusement in her face.

"You seem really aggrieved. Do you want to be a priest?"

"I wish I could sit in a little box with you and hear you talk what is really in your heart, señora. I wish I could find out what is in your heart. I think it must be a pure and lovely place, señora, like one of those chapels in the cathedral, with an alabaster cross and a soft rug to kneel and pray on."

She seemed almost startled.

"Oh, no, Señor Tomas," she denied hurriedly, "it is not like that, at all. Holy Mary! I wish it were!"

"But it is!" affirmed Strawbridge, warmly. "Why, señora, the very first morning I saw you going to chapel I thought—"

The Spanish girl arose abruptly.

"Listen," she interrupted. "Don't talk to me of chapels and crosses and souls!" She stood looking down on him, with tragic eyes. "I am not a person who should speak of such things. I ... I...."

The American looked at her in dismay. He thought of Saturnino.

"Why ... what do you mean?" he asked in a lower tone.

She studied him a moment longer.

"I was a girl when I came here to Venezuela, Señor Tomas, a little girl of sixteen, just out of a convent; and then ... I was dropped in a place like this!" She made a quick gesture, spreading her hands as if to fling something from her fingers.

A rush of pity caught the sick man.

"Whatever made you come here?" he questioned gruffly, then frowned and cleared his throat.

The two understood each other with remarkable economy of words. The girl answered the implications of his question:

"Because he was rich! He had millions of pesetas, millions. My parents said it was a wonderful opportunity, and I—" she touched her breast sharply—"why, I knew nothing of life or love or marriage! They said he was a wealthy Venezuelan who owned a territory almost as large as Spain itself. Well, he does ... but nobody said what he did in that territory!" She gave a brief, shivering laugh.

The sick man arose unsteadily.

"That's the damnable point!" He trembled. "That's what I can't endure. I think about it all the time. I was sitting in the plaza thinking about the shame he puts on you—"

The girl looked up at him.

"Señor, what do you mean?"

"I mean the shame and disgrace of it. I can't endure staying here seeing you continually disgraced in your own home by one stray woman after another!"

The señora stared.

"Señor, do you fancy I want it to be different?"

The drummer was astonished.

"You don't! Do you mean you condone such offense? Do you mean?..."

The señora's black eyes grew moist at the reproach in his voice.

"Dear Señor Tomas, that is something you do not understand. You don't know how glad I am to be free of him—such a brute! Oh, señor, you can't imagine how horrible it was—the very sight of him. It seemed to me I could not endure it another day. A murderer, a robber...." The expression on her face moved the drummer. "At last I went to Father Benicio. I told him I would jump in the river and let the caymans eat me rather than ... continue."

Strawbridge was trembling as if he himself had been tormented; yet how much of this was from sympathy, and how much from this heady topic of sex which had suddenly sprung up between them, the youth himself had not the faintest idea.

"And what did he do? What did Father Benicio say?"

The girl exhaled a sick breath.

"Oh ... duty ... sacrament. *Sacrament*—with him!" She stood breathing heavily through her open lips. "When Father Benicio saw I really meant to kill myself, when he saw I was desperate, then, finally, he told me to wear this." She touched her black nun's robe.

"To wear what?"

"This robe."

The drummer looked at the robe as if he had not seen it before.

"What has that got to do with it?"

"*Pues ... cá!*" The señora began to laugh hysterically. "When I wore this nun's robe, he stayed with other women all the time. He would not touch me. He ... he.... Father Benicio said he would not!"

She laughed till the tears stood in her eyes. Strawbridge stared at her. There was something dreadful about her laughter. Presently she sobered abruptly.

"Why ... why was that? Why-y?" The drummer was utterly at sea.

The señora shook her head.

"Father Benicio told me to wear this robe and conceal my hair."

"What an extraordinary thing!"

"Father Benicio is a very wise man."

"But there is no sense to it. Still, if it worked...." The drummer cogitated, and presently made the observation, "So, you are not wearing it for your sister, after all?"

"Señor, I have never had a sister."

Such an extraordinary ruse required thought. The salesman sat down slowly, and the girl followed his example. She was perusing his face while he puzzled over the unaccountable quirk in the dictator's amorousness.

"Why, señora," he said at last, as if coming to a conclusion, "that doesn't seem possible. Why, I think you are lovelier in your nun's robe than.... Why, you look as pure and tender and as fair as the stars of heaven. If I—"

The Spanish girl reached out an impulsive hand and gripped the American's.

"Ah, Señor Tomas, that is because you are a dear, dear boy; it is because you, yourself, are pure and tender and fine!"

At her caress a force apparently quite other than himself moved him, to his own fear and dismay. His unwounded hand went groping beneath the voluminous sleeve of the robe, up the soft naked arm of the girl. With his other arm he caught her as she swayed against him. She gave a long sigh, as if utterly exhausted. The touch of her body to his set Strawbridge quivering and trembling. His bandaged hand groped over her with delicate pains until it touched the warm supple mounds of her bosom; there the sheer pain in his fingers mingled with his passion and edged it into a sort of tingling ecstasy.

The two lay relaxed together in the corner of the couch, without a sound. The music-room swam before the man's eyes, in the melting madness of her warmth and passion. She wore no perfume—no doubt by the wisdom of Father Benicio—but the faint, intimate odor of a woman's hair and body ravaged his senses with its provocation. He drew her closer. He was trembling as if with sickness. He passed his lips over her temples, cheeks, nose; their lips met.

He had desired her subconsciously for so long; he had repressed his passion for her so endlessly into the very form of propriety that now it suddenly burst loose like a flood and rushed over his senses. The two clung together quite silently except for an occasional sob, an intake of shaken breath, and the rapid murmur of their hearts.

Strawbridge first recovered himself. Her embrace had whisked away all his feeling of futility and doubt. He knew now precisely what he must do.

"First," he said, "I've got to get you out of here."

She looked at him with misty eyes and a faint, sad smile.

"Out of the *palacio*?" she whispered.

"Out of Rio Negro, out of Venezuela, to the States." Her sweet puzzled face amused him, and made him feel tenderer than ever.

"But, dear Tomas, I am married."

"We'll get a divorce."

"But that is impossible in Rio Negro."

"It's easy in the States."

She studied his face so intently that he grew a little afraid of what she might say about the divorce. Finally she asked:

"My own dear life, when did you first *know* you loved me?"

After that the sequence of their plans to elope was continually broken by caresses and the wistful interrogations of a newly revealed love. Mixed in with these they planned with what coherence they could their elopement. They discussed horses, a motor, but finally decided on a small boat down the Rio Negro. Strawbridge would get one that afternoon, and the next night they would start from the piazza in the darkness. By daylight they would reach San Geronimo and the Orinoco.

The señora tried to make her lover realize the gravity of the undertaking, the danger and certainty of punishment if they were discovered, but the whole affair glowed on the American in a rose-colored light. They would escape, of a certainty. He had never failed to do anything he set out to do, and he wouldn't fail now. Luck was always with him, and he was predestined to win. He was in gala mood. He commanded fortune! Once the girl put up a hand to his mouth.

"Eh, hush! don't say that! It ... it reminds me of ... him."

Their talk came down to the odds and ends of the affair—how large a bundle of clothes she could smuggle out of the palace; the food they should carry, hammocks and *mosquiteros*. In the midst of these trifles came the sound of many feet in the corridor. The man and the woman got away from each other quickly and sat on opposite ends of the couch, looking at the door a little anxiously, when there really did come a sharp rap. With a glance at Strawbridge, the señora sprang up, crossed the room, and opened the shutter. In the entrance stood General Fombombo in full uniform. Banked behind him were ranks of men, most of whom were in uniform. After an instant the blur of color defined itself as Coronel Saturnino, a number of other officers, several of the governmental dignitaries, some of the alcaldes from the surrounding villages, Gumersindo in his white linen, and behind them ranks of the palace guards, in dress uniform. It was a fiesta assembly.

The drummer stared at the processional in the utmost amazement. A wild suspicion shot through his head that somehow General Fombombo had learned of his dalliance with Dolores, and that all this pomp was a movement to arrest him and send him to prison. The American moistened his lips. He could feel the blood leave his face as he stood looking at Dolores's husband.

But the general was smiling. Indeed, the faces of the whole group of dignitaries wore expressions of mysterious kindliness and good-will. The black man Gumersindo seemed to labor under some beneficent excitement. The dictator began speaking, not in ordinary conversational tones, but in the somewhat over-emphasized articulation of an orator.

"Señor Strawbridge," he began, "we, the admiring citizens of the independent republic of Rio Negro, have chosen during this fiesta and on this historic spot to express to you our never-dying respect, gratitude, and affection for a man, who, impelled by no selfish motive, but moved only by a flame from the very altar of freedom itself, by the purest love of human liberty and the world-wide brotherhood of man, has hurled himself upon the field of battle and, at the risk of his own life, made safe the social and political securities of a young and struggling people. Amid the defiance of cannon and the flashing of swords, you, Señor Tomas Strawbridge, led the forces of liberty to complete and glorious victory. It is with tears of gratitude that we, the representatives of the free and independent state of Rio Negro, bestow upon you this token of our love and appreciation for your heroic act in saving the insurgent army on the bloody field of San Geronimo. There will come a time, Señor Strawbridge, when our beloved valley will be decked with great and smiling cities; when men and women will live with no tyrant to make them afraid; then, carved in letters of gold in the pantheon of that happy people, will shine the name of Tomas Strawbridge, hero of San Geronimo!"

The President was moved. His eyes were misty as he drew from his pocket and pinned on the drummer's lapel a little gold decoration pendent from a rainbow-colored ribbon. It was the Order of the *Libertador*, for heroic action. Strawbridge had seen dozens of these decorations in Venezuela, but he had always put them down to the South American's love of fripperies. Now there was something about these men and their solemn, admiring faces that moved him.

A play of incongruous emotions kept harassing the American's nerves. He alternately flushed and paled. How grotesque it was that the general should have given him this medal just as he was planning to abduct the general's wife! As the dictator bent toward him to pin on the decoration, the drummer caught a strong odor of musk.

After the presentation other dignitaries delivered orations reviewing Rio Negro's heroic past. They pointed out, from the very music-room windows, spots where martyrs had perished.

When the officials had finished, Gumersindo read his whole six columns describing the battle of San Geronimo. The black man seldom glanced at the paper, but recited the whole from memory, in an agreeable resonant baritone.

After the ceremony the whole audience shook hands with the drummer, and each man expressed his admiration with a suppleness of phrase that was very graceful and yet seemed sincere. Perhaps it was.

CHAPTER XXI

There are certain moments in the lives of men when the only course of action morally possible lies along immoral lines. By dint of hard necessity such moments lose the reproach of bad faith and assume the simple pathos of misfortune. Perhaps three-fourths of the crimes committed because of women fall into this unhappy class.

Long before convention softened the rape to its symbol, the marriage ceremony, men abducted the women they loved. There must have been a time when the highest social virtue was for a passionate swain to steal a girl from her jealous guardians. Upon this broad corner-stone of passion have arisen daring, stalwart, and reproductive generations, and that is the final word of approbation with which life lauds conduct.

Since that simpler era, minor moral obligations hinging on property, society, friendship, nationality, and former marriages have confused but have not transformed the issue. To-day, when any of these obstacles are swept aside by passionate lovers, one feels its pathos but not its sin.

It was precisely in this dilemma that Strawbridge labored. The little gold medal fastened on his lapel by the dictator reproached him continually as he worked in his room, packing in a canvas roll those of his belongings which were absolutely indispensable. He meant to carry them inconspicuously to the river. General Fombombo was his host; he had been a prospective customer until the capture of the rifles at San Geronimo, and he still was a trusting friend. And now he, Thomas Strawbridge, was about to steal the general's wife! The big American sickened at the thought of it, but the complementary idea of resigning Dolores never once presented itself to his mind. This would have been a desertion of something exquisitely more dear and intimate than his own flesh. Since the señora's embraces, her body seemed more native to him than his own. There was something shrine-like about her.

With Hebraic simplicity the Bible says of a man and wife, "Ye are one," and this was meant for lovers. Strawbridge tingled and thrilled with this amazing oneness. Some miracle had occurred within him to extend his sentiency into the señora. As he worked, she rushed upon him at intervals with such poignancy that he would lay down his packing and sigh and tremble at the sudden and sweet transfiguration. He was not himself any more. Body and soul were impermeated, somehow, with the sweetness of Dolores.

In the midst of one of these epiphanies came a tap at his door. The drummer had a sense of being waked out of a sleep. He saw his canvas pack under his hands and made an effort to conceal it by thrusting it hastily into an open cabinet drawer. Some of his toilet articles and clothes lay scattered about, and he tried to cover them under the sheets of his disordered bed. It seemed to him that his jumble of packing must advertise to the world his intention of eloping with the señora. When the American had concealed enough to give his room an aspect of innocence, he went over and opened the door. The *griffe* girl stood in the hallway. Her freckled face seemed screwed up with some internal tension. Her black eyes sparkled.

"*Ola*, señor!" she whispered, and stepped inside with her air of excitement and her glittering eyes. Strawbridge looked at her in dismay. Plainly she knew his plans, and he thought to himself that they might as well have been published in the "Correo."

The maid burst into ejaculations:

"*Caramba!* How well you look! You have been cured by magic!" She reached out and gave his arm a sudden squeeze, giggled, then, with an effect of legerdemain, thrust into his hand a little green-gold watch.

The American looked at it blankly.

"What the hell?" he asked in a low tone.

His profanity shook the girl into a hysteria of choked giggles; then she produced, also apparently out of nothingness, a blue envelop directed to himself. Instantly Strawbridge knew that it was from the señora, and his heart began to beat. His fingers trembled so that he could not get into the envelop with his one good hand. He was forced to ask the girl to open it.

The half-breed went at the matter in her own way, moistening an edge with her little red tongue and picking open the damp crease with a hair-pin. The big American stood with his good hand gripping her plump shoulder and delaying the operation by his impatience.

The note was exceedingly brief. It said simply:

<blockquote>Set my watch with yours. Piazza, 11 P.M. to-morrow.

DOLORES JUANA AVILON Y BUSTAMENTE.</blockquote>

The implication of the señora's maiden name written in full moved Strawbridge with a delicate tenderness. He looked at the letter, then at the watch. It was an old-fashioned timepiece, carved on the obverse side with a faint landscape which was worn smooth in places; on the reverse was an antique coat of arms with its quarterings colored by a worn but exquisite enamel. The drummer did not know that he was looking at an heirloom of centuries; he had no idea that on the back of this watch he saw the combined coats of arms of two of the most ancient houses of Spain. A sense of pathos moved him at its evident age.

"Poor little girl!" he thought to himself. "The first thing I'll do when we get to New York will be to go to Tiffany's and get her a wrist-watch." He set the timepiece, with care, and returned it to the *griffe* girl.

In the afternoon Strawbridge went down to the native market to lay in provisions against his voyage down the river. Among the little market stalls the only prepared food he could find were the cart-wheels of cassava bread. The sick man looked at this bread dubiously. He knew that at one stage in the making of cassava it is a rank poison, and he wondered if the Indians in making this bread had extracted all its bane. The sight of the loaves which had once been poison filled him with foreboding. He imagined himself and the señora going down the river in a small boat and becoming poisoned on this bread. What a horrible end to their romance!

The possibility depressed him. However, he purchased a loaf, had it wrapped in a palm-leaf, and recalled wistfully the little delicatessen shops in Keokuk where he could order a lunch with a word. He wished keenly for them, as he bought some wood-like yammi and two or three big plantains shaped like rough bananas. When he started back home with his bundle, a dozen porters besieged him begging to be allowed to carry it.

Later in the afternoon he went to the fish-wharf, to bargain for a boat. He found clumsy crafts, each one carved out of a single log, leaky, greasy, and smelling overpoweringly of fish. The drummer walked slowly from one end of the quay to the other. The notion of embarking Dolores in one of these vile boats filled him with disgust. At last he chose the least loathly of the dugouts, and began dickering with its fishy owner, to buy it. The fisherman was a barefooted, chocolate-colored peon, who carried a paddle about with him as a sign of his calling. He was naked from waist to sombrero. His legs were thin, but his torso rippled with muscles developed by his boating. His face, his inch of forehead, and his coarse hair were just a few centuries this side of the pithecanthropus. He could scarcely believe the *caballero* could want to buy his fish-boat. He stared and scratched his head at the marvel.

"You are no poor man, señor. Why should you fish?"

"I fish for sport."

"*Caramba!* sport! Do you think it is sport to bake in the sun, to be flung into the rapids, to fight the crocodiles that eat your catch? Do you call it sport to pack a *tonelada* of fish on your back, trying to vend them when no one will buy?"

Some fellow fishermen drew about the two at this curious conversation. One of them interposed:

"Perhaps *el caballero* is going to fish as a penance, Simon. Perhaps he has committed some grievous sin and *el padre* has imposed—"

"*Basta!* Are you blind, Alessandro? Do you not see this *hombre* is an *Americano*, and not a Christian at all? The padre is nothing to him."

Another voice in the fish-scented crowd took up the argument:

"An *Americano*! Perhaps he does fish for sport. They do the maddest things for sport; they run and walk and jump and fight for sport. This one went to the battle of San Geronimo and won a ribbon. There it is; you can see it for yourself on his coat."

One of the older fishers shrugged a naked shoulder:

"Sport never sent the *Americano* into the battle, brothers. I was talking to an *hombre* named Lubito, a bull-fighter, and what he said ... what Lubito said about this *Americano*...." The old peon nodded, and thumped the butt of his paddle on the ground.

"What did he say?" asked Alessandro.

The ancient lifted a shoulder, pulled down his wrinkled lips, nodded at the palace up the river and at the gloomy bulk of La Fortuna down the river, made a clicking sound with his tongue, and went silent.

These clicks and glances seemed to explain something. Simon, who owned the boat, looked at Strawbridge, with his small black Indian eyes stretched wide.

"*Cá!* Then you don't want to fish, after all?"

"Look here!" rapped out the drummer, feeling very uncomfortable. "Do I get that boat or not?"

Simon shrugged, and mentioned a price which no doubt was grotesquely exorbitant, according to his peon sense of value. The drummer reached into his pocket and drew out a roll of Venezuelan bills.

"I'll take it provided you'll scrub the damn thing with sand and get it clean."

The whole crowd stared at this amazingly swift trade. Here and there came a sharp intake of breath at such an amount paid for such a boat. Only the peon who owned the boat kept his head, but his excitement was shown by the sharp dints in the sides of his sun-blacked nose.

"Señor," he jockeyed, breathing heavily and staring at the bills, "it is impossible for me to clean the boat at such a price. Already I have given the boat away; I have pushed it into the rapids. I am a poor man, señor, and I cannot possibly clean the boat for less than ... for less than—" he stared fishily at Strawbridge, fearing to name too small a sum—"t-t-two, t-three ... *sí* ... t-t-three more bolivars, señor, and it will be cheap as mangos, at that!"

The drummer drew out the three extra bolivars and tossed them to the fellow. Three bolivars are sixty cents.

"Scrub it with sand, and hitch it below the *palacio* when you finish."

One of the fishermen shook his fist violently in the air, a peaceable Spanish gesture to work off unusual excitement. The oldish peon leaned forward on his paddle.

"No one must speak of this unless all of us want to...." He drew his finger across his throat, made a clicking sound, and nodded toward La Fortuna.

It was sundown when Strawbridge returned to the palace. In coming up the river bank the drummer took a short route behind the cathedral. As he came closer he saw that a nest of little adobe houses were built like lean-tos against the sides of the church. These little mud huts clinging humbly to the soaring walls of the great fane, and the whole illuminated in the deep yellow of sunset, formed a picture which arrested even the drummer. It drove away for a moment the permeating thought of the señora. It extinguished his desire and his sense of hurry, in the timelessness of beauty.

Beyond him on his left lay the wide vacuity of the river. The terrain on which Strawbridge walked was high above the river and was grown with patches of thistles, cactus, and a thin, harsh grass. Through this wound a number of paths leading to this or that little hut. The scene was animated with a scattering of naked brown youngsters who played silently and seriously after the manner of Latin children. They almost blended with their background of sand and adobe.

As the drummer walked through this quaint place, an old woman, with her apron full of charcoal, came out of a little shop. She hobbled along a path, evidently meaning to intercept the American. Her intention became so obvious that he stopped and waited for her.

"Can I do anything for you, *vieja*?" he inquired, running a hand into his pocket.

The old creature crossed herself with her free hand.

"May the Holy Virgin guard you, señor!"

The sick man got out a centavo, but to his surprise the crone did not extend her palm.

"*Señor Americano*" she whispered, "when do I get my Josefa back!"

The question sounded so pointless that Strawbridge thought she must be slightly unbalanced.

"Your Josefa, señora?"

She pointed with a trembling hand.

"The poor *joven* you sent to La Fortuna, señor."

The drummer was nonplussed. She seemed to be rational; indeed, she had shrewd wrinkled eyes and a high-bridged, aristocratic nose. She might have been a kind of dowdy dowager.

"*I* sent a youth to La Fortuna, señora!"

She glanced up at the yellow-green sky.

"Holy San Pablo! Has he forgot! Is it so little to him, that he forgets my poor boy Josefa, the *dependiente* in 'Sol y Sombra,' whom he loaded with irons and hid away in La Fortuna!"

The drummer regarded the old creature with troubled surprise to find that she was connected with the unhappy clerk in "Sol y Sombra." Indeed, he had almost forgot the incident of the little monkey-eyed clerk; or at least it no longer disturbed him. The battle of San Geronimo had somehow cut a gap in his life, and all things antecedent to it seemed in a remote past. Now this woman had abruptly crossed the gap, and had bound one of the keenest indiscretions of his old life with his new. Somewhere under the black hulk of La Fortuna, which glowered against the sunset, Josefa still existed. Strawbridge felt that thrill of discomfort which a sportsman feels when a quail flutters in his coat hours after it should have died. He hardly knew what to say. Finally he asked:

"Are you Josefa's mother!"

"His grandmother, señor. He lived with me, but when he fell into misfortune, I had to give up my house, and Father Benicio found me a place here in the cathedral, to scrub the brasses. I live in the third *casa* yonder, under the transept." She pointed it out, and, from her tone, the little hut seemed part of her griefs.

She stood looking at Strawbridge expectantly, evidently waiting for him to do or say something. He grew more and more uncomfortable. He put his hand irresolutely into his pocket and drew out some coins, regarded them doubtfully, and made a suggestive movement toward the crone. She held out an old hand, raw in places from her unaccustomed work in the cathedral.

"When do I get my boy back, señor!" she repeated in a low tone.

"Señora, ... I don't know."

"You do not know when you are going to sack La Fortuna!" Her whisper was astonished.

"I ... sack La Fortuna!"

"*Seguramente*, señor! Lubito said you had all your plans laid. He said you had men everywhere, ready to leap upon Canalejos at a word from you; that you would set all the prisoners free and put the tyrants in their own dungeons. But he said you were a North American, and that when you gained power you would not oppress the people as General Miedo and General Fombombo did."

Strawbridge was annoyed and a little anxious at this continual bobbing up of the bull-fighter's gossip.

"Look here," he said. "Lubito is going to get me into serious trouble, spreading that sort of rumor."

"Oh, no, señor! the peons never betray the *hombre* who comes to fight their battles. No one spoke a word when General Miedo marched against Canalejos. He was in the city before *he*"—she nodded toward the palace—"knew a breath of it. No one will speak against you. Lubito has arranged everything. The whole town will rise up when you lift your sword. I shall be happy, señor, when you stand *him*—" another nod at the palace—"in front of the rifles."

Strawbridge was shocked at her bloodthirstiness. And he saw that nothing he could say would shake her in her delusion. And why should he shake her? Why not let her draw any comfort she could from an imaginary revenge? He promised to do what he could for Josefa, and started on for the palace.

That evening Strawbridge did not sit with the señora on the piazza. Their plan to elope had made the lovers chary of being seen together. The drummer sat in his room and from his window watched the vestiges of sunset darken into night. He was ill, and the reaction after all of his walking and talking and love-play with the señora made him weary and despondent. Thoughts of Josefa and the old charwoman bedeviled him. Through his window he could see the dark reproach of La Fortuna blotting out the residual umber in the east. Somewhere in that pile Josefa lay manacled because he, Thomas Strawbridge, had conceived a hardware display for "Sol y Sombra." The salesman got up and moved about his room in weary restlessness. In his thoughts he cursed the country. He recalled Rosales standing before the firing-squad; the little Austrian operator whom Saturnino had corrupted; the centaurism of General Fombombo. It was the country: there was something about this country that got a man. Then there insinuated itself into his reverie the fact that he himself was planning to elope with the dictator's wife.

Strawbridge's thinking stopped abruptly and he stood staring at nothingness, with widened eyes. He did not want to yield to wickedness. He wanted to stay decent. And even as he was thinking these things a profound justification arose in his mind. It was his duty to deliver an unhappy woman from such a mad, immoral land. It was his duty and his deepest desire. He had the widest license to protect her that any man could possess: he loved her.

But as to the others—there was something about this country that got a man.

CHAPTER XXII

The next morning Strawbridge awoke with a brisk feeling that some important and happy event was pressing into his life. The sight of his roll of canvas, packed and ready to go, and the bundle of cassava bread gave substance to his mood. He felt stronger than he had since his sickness. No doubt the caresses of the Spanish girl had infused vigor into his big body. He sat up on the side of his bed, pushed his feet into alpargatas, and then got up and went flapping into his bath-room. He got out of his pajamas and walked carefully down the slippery steps of his marble bath, turned the key in the silver nozzle overhead, and stood gratefully in the faintly cool shower. It was his first self-performed ablution since his sickness, and when he had finished he set about the ticklish experiment of toweling himself with the aid of his wounded hand. He managed a very light friction without pain, and this pleased him keenly. His big body was growing softly pinkish again. He ran his good hand along the slight growth of hair on his chest and down the curve of his abdomen with the frank narcissism most men possess and which the thought of marriage enhances.

To-night he and the señora would embark on the most tinglingly romantic adventure of their lives. At the thought his heart began to beat. She was only a little way from him at that moment, only a few doors distant.

He went back into his room and began touchy efforts to dress himself. He did his underclothes well enough, but his socks were troublesome because his feet were still faintly damp. Suddenly, through some compulsion, he dropped this task midway, jabbed his feet into alpargatas again, stood up, and looked out the window. He did not know what had prompted him. In the gray light he saw the slender figure of a nun passing from the palace to the cathedral.

The sight filled the drummer with an extraordinary turbulence. He made a step toward the window and called to her sotto voce. She did not hear, and he drew an intake of breath on the verge of calling more loudly, but the caution of lovers silenced him. After all, why should he call her? He stood watching her, repressing the imperative which had moved him to attract her attention. He did not even know what he had meant to say. His excitement calmed him a little, and even amused him. He pressed his face against the window bars and watched her as far as he possibly could, until the ornamental evergreen with its tassels concealed her from his eyes. Then he turned back to his toilet, with a faint sense of deprivation.

Only then did the drummer think definitely that the señora was going to early mass and confession. In a few minutes she would enter the little double stall in the cathedral and would whisper through the aperture, into the ear of a priest.

The thought brought him a pang, and that, perhaps, was the reason of his distress at her going. He had instinctively wanted her not to go. In the confessional Dolores would whisper of their passionate moment in the music-room; she would lay bare every nook and corner of her heart. The thought of any other human being knowing what was in her heart filled him with a vague jealousy. The idea grew into a mysterious and painful emotion. He could not get rid of it. The priest would explore the señora's heart more intimately than he. And he saw no end to such conditions. He could never get as close to Dolores as could her spiritual adviser. One day, no doubt, she would hold him in her arms, she would give him all that she was, and yet somewhere within the woman's soul would remain privacies which he, her wistful and passionate lover, could never know. Such a reservation filled him with a kind of despair. He felt that in the holiest places of her soul he must remain a stranger. The man's self-torture brought sweat to his face.

He went back to his dressing, but kept glancing through the window, watching for the girl's return. He recalled that he had set his watch with the señora's. He got it from under his pillow and looked at it. The hour was eleven minutes after five. In seventeen hours and forty-nine minutes he and Dolores would be out on the rapids in the night. It seemed to him as if everything were waiting for that hour to come. The whole mechanism of day and night tapered to this event. A little quiver went through him.

In the east the sun must have cut the horizon, for behind the cathedral and the prison spread a pale-gold fan. From the top of the prison came the flash of a cannon dimly picked out, like the flare of a firefly against the light. Two seconds later came the flat crash as if some power had delivered a terrific blow and had lapsed instantly into silence. It advertised the dictator's will over the llanos. The drummer looked at the prison against the east, with his old feeling of dismay.

The stir and rattle of early morning brushed away this unhappy impression. Came a tap at his door, and the *griffe* girl brought in his coffee. She still wore her air of suppressed but joyous excitement, and presently volunteered the whispered information that the señora had not as yet returned from early mass.

"She is usually back by this time." She nodded.

"Wonder what's keeping her," said Strawbridge, as naturally as he could.

"I do wonder," echoed the maid, turning, with her silver urn in her hand, to look through the window.

The drummer felt an impulse to talk to the girl about his coming adventure. It was clear that she knew all about it, but he decided regretfully not to. It would be imprudent. The maid stood close to the window now, looking at an angle into the plaza. Suddenly she began jiggling up and down.

"Oh, there she is! I see her black gown coming through the shrubs!"

Strawbridge knew that he ought to remain sipping his coffee, but he jumped up and strode over to the girl's side. The two stood with their heads almost together, getting glimpses of the black gown through the shrubbery. The little maid unconsciously caught and squeezed Strawbridge's arm.

"Oh, isn't she the sweetest, dearest señora! Oh señor, isn't she lovely and beautiful and just too sweet!" The little servant was caught up in a paroxysm of a woman's love for lovers. She might have been Strawbridge himself glowing over his sweetheart; or perhaps it is truer to say that she was glowing toward him through the vicarious love of her mistress. In the midst of it her spirits suddenly fell.

"*Cá!*" she pouted. "It's Father Benicio!"

Her disappointment was so intense that the drummer laughed. He patted her rubbery shoulder.

"Oh, well, that doesn't destroy the señora completely," and in good spirits he finished his thimbleful of coffee.

The maid went out with the coffee things and left Strawbridge standing at the window with a feeling of well-being. The romance surrounding the way he would gain his wife moved him pleasantly. It reminded him somewhat of the film he had seen in Keokuk called "Maid in Mexico." At the time he had thought such a romance impossible, and yet he had vaguely wished that some such thing might happen to him. And now that the fact that his own life had fallen into lines rather resembling that cheap melodrama, profoundly increased his pleasure in this passing moment at the window. So, American slap-stick movies found a remote justification.

The drummer was brought out of his reverie by a rustling of skirts in the passageway and a tap at his door. His thoughts instantly warmed to the señora and in a low tone he called to her to enter. He moved toward the door, with a fancy to take her into his arms and kiss her. When the door opened, Father Benicio entered. Then the American recalled that Dolores was still at the cathedral.

Strawbridge, rather curious as to what had brought the priest here, pushed forward a chair, and chose one for himself. He pulled his around so he could see out at the window. Then he drew his cigar-case and offered it. The father accepted a cigar and rolled it gently between his thin fingers.

"How is your business, Señor Strawbridge?" he inquired casually.

The drummer was surprised. This was the first time a Venezuelan had ever volunteered the topic of business. He lighted a wax match and held it to his cigar.

"Why, ... so-so," he answered in a muffled voice, out of the corner of his mouth. And he got his cigar going.

"Will you sell as many rifles as you hoped?"

Strawbridge looked at the end of his weed to see if it was burning smoothly.

"Think not. You see, the capture of San Geronimo has given the general a large number of rifles. They're out of date, of course, but then ... you know this country."

Father Benicio nodded paternally.

"A little behind the times in warfare, as in everything else. However, Señor Strawbridge, if I can bring my influence to bear in any way to promote your interest, I hope you will not hesitate to call on me."

The drummer was genuinely touched.

"Why, thanks, Father Benicio; I appreciate that."

The priest gave a rather bloodless smile.

"I am glad to assist you because, if you will allow me to say it, your sincerity of purpose deserves assistance. I have always admired the enterprise you North Americans exhibit. For instance, I cannot think of any other man than a North American who would have the moral courage to put by every incentive to misuse his position for his own personal advancement, and remain true to his employers."

The American blew out a puff of smoke, removed and looked at his cigar, and said in a tone that varied by a hair from his normal hearty voice:

"That's a very nice compliment, Father; I hope I am worthy of it."

"I am sure you are. You know there are so many temptations, in this country, into which a man can fall and forsake his business obligations."

Strawbridge drew thoughtfully at his cigar.

"Well, ... yes, probably so." Back of this by-play he felt a little uncomfortable with the suspicion that Dolores had told the priest of their proposed flight. If so, here was still another person in Canalejos who knew of it.

Father Benicio did not answer at once, but sat for perhaps half a minute gazing out into the plaza; his silence showed the priest did mean something very personal and intimate in his general remarks. Presently he began again:

"Your company sends you out at a great deal of expense, Señor Strawbridge. Your employers place high confidence in you. In fact, have you ever stopped to think that the commanding position of Anglo-Saxon commerce in the world is founded directly upon the devoted self-sacrifice of its agents, just such men as you? There is a moral solidarity among the English peoples, Señor Strawbridge, which I should like very well indeed to see in my own people."

It was very evident to the drummer that he was about to receive what traveling salesmen call a "bawling out." He knew the priest meant to "bawl him out" about Dolores. And he considered quickly what line of resistance to take. In the meantime the father talked on, smoothly and sympathetically:

"And, Señor Strawbridge, I am a priest. I am, I trust, a vicar of God to all mankind." He crossed himself. "And if I, as a priest, could help you over any little obstacle in your path, I should be deeply pleased. If you could frankly discuss with me any little difficulty that may have come into your life—I mean ethical difficulty; some clash between your private desires, for instance, and the duty you owe to the company which sent you here...."

Strawbridge reddened at this very clear statement that the priest knew everything, and he answered in the rather flat tones of nascent irritation:

"Really, Father Benicio, there is no clash whatever between ... er ... anything I propose to do and my business duties."

"I am glad to hear you say that, my son?" But the sentence was an interrogation.

The drummer remained silent. He did not mean to discuss with Father Benicio his affairs with the señora. He smoked stolidly, staring into the green and gold of the plaza. The early morning sunshine gave it a tender glow. The cleric placed his unlighted cigar gently on the edge of the table, and did not pick it up any more.

"Whom I am really thinking about, Señor Strawbridge, is my daughter, Dolores Avilon Fombombo."

Strawbridge frowned slightly as if at some disagreeable flavor in his tobacco.

"Did she go and tell you everything?"

"Naturally, señor. What else could she do?"

The drummer flung his head about and looked at the father.

"Good Lord! in a case like this—" He broke off abruptly. "Well, what are you going to do about it?"

"I? Nothing. I advised my daughter not to do this rash thing which you and she contemplate."

"Rash! After six years of insult and abuse!"

The priest bent his head gravely.

"*Sí*, señor, very rash and very wicked."

The big salesman straightened in his chair and with outraged eyes regarded the cleric.

"Wicked! How do you get that answer? Wicked to get rid of an empty marriage? Call that wicked? For Dolores to leave a man who shows by every move he makes that he doesn't give a damn about her! Don't your reason tell you it would be damn sight wickeder for her to remain in such a shameful connection with a man she detests?"

Father Benicio sat measuring the salesman, with small black eyes.

"Do you gauge shame and honor and duty purely by the personal pleasure one receives in obeying one's vows and obligations, Señor Strawbridge?"

"I'm not measuring anything. I'm stating facts."

"Does it cease to be your duty to attend to the business of your company, merely because it would be pleasanter to run off with your customer's wife?"

The drummer lifted a hand and laid it flat on the table.

"Look here, you can cut out that line of talk. She's not his wife. He's given her up. And, besides, folks do marry to make life pleasanter on the whole. Yes, they do. You know they do. And if their life on the whole is unpleasanter after marriage than before, why, then they've failed. They are not a going concern. They are not declaring any dividends, and the only thing to do is to quit; to get a divorce and quit."

Father Benicio sat reflecting on this to such an extent that Strawbridge thought he had convinced him, by mere power of argument; however, at last the priest began again:

"But, Señor Strawbridge, there are some duties which you will always perform at great inconvenience and even pain to yourself. These duties are not what you could call dividend-bearing duties. They will never pay you anything; they will always bring loss and pain and yet ... you do them."

"What sort of duties are you talking about?" asked the drummer, suspiciously.

"Well, ... your business obligations to your house."

"But I tell you that isn't in this. The order's gone—"

"But if it were, and in the midst of your enterprise you were moved to desert your firm by some sharp and sudden passion, which, if you resisted, would cause you pain as long as your memory held its seat, still ... would you not stand by your obligations? My son, when I look at you, I believe you would."

Strawbridge started to speak, then paused to clear his throat.

"Look here, Father, that's different. When it comes to business—"

"But business is only a duty, an obligation among other obligations."

"Yes, I know; but you see, business depends on team-work. A hundred, a thousand, a million other men are in the game with you. You can't lay down on your own crowd. Why—good Lord!—if we all got to laying down when we liked, the whole commerce of America would go bluey!"

The priest smiled faintly and kindly.

"So you will stand by business coöperation at expense to yourself, but not social coöperation, or spiritual coöperation?"

"About the last two—" the drummer shook a finger—"I don't know."

"Now let us see," said the priest, evidently becoming more comfortable. "You owed your time to your company. Why did you not spend your time with the general, trying to get an order, instead of with the general's wife?"

"I did try to, but he wouldn't talk business, and that's the only kind of talk I can talk with a man. When I talk anything besides business or politics, it's got to be with a woman. Then when I saw how badly treated the señora was—why, any man with a spark of manhood—"

"Would assist her," finished the priest. "But do you think it fair or honest to your employers to give up their business in order to rectify wrongs which don't concern you? And was there as much suffering as you fancied? You found things here exactly as they had been for six years. It was a status quo, a method of existence, and then you came in and broke it all up. You persuaded a frail girl into the belief that happiness lies not in following the law of God but in yielding to her impulses and passion."

"Well, she will probably get happiness that way. Most women do. At least, she'll have a chance. If a woman's first marriage is a failure, maybe she'll have better luck next time."

"But you say, yourself, one ought not to break business obligations."

"Sure not!"

"Don't you think vows taken before God are as binding as a trade between an employer and a salesman?"

Strawbridge shook his shoulders in irritation.

"Oh, damn it! you twist everything to suit yourself! I don't know anything about this vow-to-God stuff. Business is business. As to marriage vows, we go before a justice of the peace at home and we don't vow to God.... Well, now, anyway, you come right down to it and, don't you know, business *is* the most important! You know not a thing in the world depends on your religion. Your house doesn't depend on it for their sales; your national trade balance stays right where it belongs, no matter who's got religion and who hasn't. But all that sort of thing slumps the minute you neglect business. Now, you'll excuse me for putting the plain dope to you. I know you are a priest and all that, and it's very seldom anybody talks plain horse-sense to a preacher. But instead of anything depending on religion, you know and I know that if the business interests of America should neglect the church for just six months, why—bluey!" Mr. Strawbridge snapped his fingers, waved his hands, and nodded, then concluded in an ordinary tone: "So it is very important that business comes first, and then ... other things."

The priest arose slowly, turned toward the door, and then hesitated.

"Señor Strawbridge," he asked carefully, "what would you do if your order for rifles really did depend upon your going back to New York and leaving this unfortunate girl in peace?"

"Well, since the order has gone to the bowwows, that is out of the question."

"But what would you do?"

"Hell! there wouldn't be but one thing to do! What makes you ask?" He turned around and looked at the father.

The black-robed figure reached inside his cassock and drew out a legal-sized document. It was dignified with a big red government seal. The priest opened it with a crisp rattling and spread it on the table before Strawbridge. It began with a sounding preamble:

> By order of his Excellency, el General Adriano Caspiano Guillermo Fombombo y Herrara, Constitutional President of the Free and Independent State of Rio Negro, Señor Don Tomas Strawbridge, representative of a corporation bearing the name of Orion Arms Corporation, located and doing business in the City of New York, State of New York, is hereby empowered to purchase from his said Company fifty thousand rifles of the caliber and specifications stated in the attached sheet of specifications, and a million and a quarter rounds of cartridges for said rifles. The same to be delivered f.o.b., at the steamer in the harbor of New York and to be billed to Senhor Dom Sebastiano Carupano in Rio de Janeiro, Brazil, not later than six months from the date of this order.
>
> JUAN DELGOA,
Minister of War.

The drummer stared, open-mouthed, at the order. He licked his lips and with a sick face looked up at the priest. His voice came thickly:

"H-how came you with this, Father?"

"I asked for it, my son."

"Does he ... does the general know ... everything?"

"I suppose so, Señor Strawbridge," said the priest, drily; "he has a fairly competent intelligence department, and you were right here in the *palacio*."

Strawbridge nodded numbly.

"Did ... you tell him why you wanted this?" he asked in a strained voice.

"The general has confidence in me, señor; I simply requested the order, and received it. You, yourself, would have received it in due time if ... you had been available."

The salesman's shoulders felt heavy. Perspiration broke out over his face.

"Well, ... after all ... I can't accept this."

"What do you mean?"

"You kept it too long: I can't break my word to the señora."

"But it is a duty you owe your company."

"No, we made arrangements when I thought the trade was off. That finishes this." He pushed the contract away.

The father walked over to the big drummer and laid a translucent hand on his shoulder.

"You seem unhappy over this, Señor Strawbridge."

"My old man will think I double-crossed him—for a woman. He'll never believe the real facts."

"My son—" Father Benicio's voice softened—"Dolores is just as unhappy as you are. She feels just as keenly the vows which you do not comprehend, as you feel the duties which she cannot understand. She still says she will fly with you, even after I have reminded her of the holy commands of the church; she will still fly with you because of her promise; but she is very unhappy about it."

Strawbridge looked up.

"Is Dolores unhappy about ... eloping?"

"Very."

"Why—Good God!—I don't want to make her unhappy!"

"I know you don't, my son; I think there is something very high and fine in both of you. Suppose we walk over and see Dolores, and talk it over with her."

"Where to, Father?"

"To the cathedral. Dolores is still in the cathedral. You can have privacy there."

The salesman got up unsteadily. The priest took his arm, and together the two men walked out of the palace. As they passed out at the east entrance, Strawbridge glanced down at the river. Just beneath the piazza a little fish-boat lay moored to the bank. It had been scrubbed and sanded until it gleamed in the sunshine, as white as a bone.

An intermezzo of thoughts danced through the drummer's head as he accompanied the priest, for his final talk with Dolores. He began to suspect that Father Benicio had used the order for the rifles quite as adroitly, to separate him from the señora, as he had used the nun's gown to withdraw the Spanish girl from the bed of General Fombombo. It was the same kind of stratagem, the same kind of hateful cleverness in pulling just the right strings in human beings to move them toward his own ends.

As the two men walked toward the cathedral, Strawbridge looked at the ascetic face of the father, the precise stock about his neck, and his delicate fingers smoothing down the girdle of his cassock. The drummer studied him angrily, and made mental surges to shake loose from this order for rifles and recover his moral right to Dolores again. Moreover, he was uneasy about the approaching interview with the Spanish girl. He began thinking what he would say. He massed his arguments for elopement just as he always massed his selling points before calling on a prospective buyer. He would bring her to his side by the verve and swing of his attack.

In the entrance of the cathedral, the priest dipped his finger in the shell font and crossed himself. Then both men reduced their footfalls almost to silence and moved along the left aisle in front of a row of chapels. The drummer could half see their crosses and passions in the dusky light of the church. Here and there, over the shadowy building, knelt men and women at their devotions. The pleasant smell of incense filled nave and aisles. From the high altar came the monotone of a priest at his prayers. The ensemble softened the drummer's mood. Involuntarily his thoughts began to throw out those filaments of sentiment toward the past, toward the future, which religious buildings invariably evoke. It loosened his self-centeredness. It tended to strew his entity through time and eternity. It whispered to him that he had not always been what he was, nor would he always be. His excited nerves felt this influence, and he tried to resist it. He tried to brace himself against it. He swore mentally and told himself that he ought to stop where he was, that he ought to go no farther into this softening, deorienting building. He tried to re-collect his arguments for elopement.

Father Benicio was pointing.

"She is there, in the chapel of the Last Supper."

The altar of the chapel of the Last Supper was a rich dull sheen of gold from carpet to ceiling. Strawbridge was dimly aware of a soft harmony of color on the left wall leading to this altar. It was the great picture which illustrates the chapel, but the drummer did not observe this. His whole attention was concentrated on a slender black figure which knelt before the center of the huge altar. The golden background seemed to set forth with an exquisite pathos her sadness and sweetness and trustfulness. Strawbridge felt a profound impulse to stop and pick her up in his arms and bring all of her unhappiness to an end. She had been so miserable in her loveless marriage, her lonely life in the palace, the savage and cruel milieu into which she had been cast; and now, just as love and opportunity had come into her life, for the church, the church which she had clung to for succor, through all these years—for this church to lift its hand and forbid her—that was too much; that was more than human nature could endure!

The drummer caught the priest's arm.

"Look here, Father Benicio," he whispered shakily, "this don't go. I'm going to take her out of here! You needn't talk. I don't give a damn what you say; not a damn! Not a damn!" He accented each oath with a grip in the tender place inside the priest's upper arm. Tears stung the drummer's eyes.

Hearing the murmur, the girl turned. Her face was tremulous, and, at the sight of the priest her poor composure gave way. She stretched out her arms.

"Oh, Father, I ... I can't do it! Oh, kind Father, forgive me this one great and mortal sin and I will be the meanest servant of our holy church all the rest of my life! Good Father Benicio, you know I am no wife! Sweet Father, do pray for me and let me go!" She caught the priest's hand, kissing it over and over and wetting it with her tears.

"Listen here!" gulped Strawbridge. "Just go, Dolores! Why—God damn it!—just get up and go!"

The priest made a gesture.

"Listen, my children. Let us think seriously. You are passion-torn now, but have you not heard that he that loseth his life shall find it? Neither of you came into the world of your own will, nor for your own pleasure. You came in God's good time, to serve His ends for His glory." The father crossed himself with his right hand while his left retained the fingers of the kneeling girl.

"My dear daughter Dolores, have I not explained to you time on time the depth and sweetness of renunciation? Only that which you renounce shall you preserve.

"We Spaniards, my child, have always lived by a great mystical apprehension of God through the spirit of renunciation. It is the life-breath of the greatest nation in the world. You, my daughter, are a Spanish woman and a Catholic communicant. It is impossible for you to act in any other way and gain happiness. The anguish which you feel this moment is nothing to the lifelong fires of remorse which would burn in your heart. This moment is the parting of the ways in your life. It is impossible for you to do aught but remain pure and faithful and loyal."

The father paused a moment and continued:

"And this good youth who loves you, Dolores—he comes from a distant people, and the teachings of his people are very like our own. They instill into the hearts of their men their duty to support one another in the market-place, just as it is the precept of us Spanish to support one another in the temple. But with him, as with us, this is a religion. It is the object of our renunciations. It is that for which we deny ourselves, for which we would give our strength, our patience, our sacrifices, our lives. If you cause this boy to break faith with his market-place, Dolores, you will have destroyed the man you worship. And, my dear son Tomas, if you take away from Dolores the holy sacraments which support her life, you can never have one unsullied caress from the woman you adore. How well I know it is not in your hearts to blast and destroy each other!"

Father Benicio looked with sad eyes at the lovers. Then he lifted the cross which hung about his neck, and concluded solemnly:

"Now may the Holy Saints guard and direct you, my most dear children, and lead you into paths of final peace and happiness." He made the sign of the cross above their heads, turned, and moved silently from the chapel.

The drummer stood mute near the altar where the girl knelt. In his heart he acknowledged the rightness of the priest. He essayed some clumsy words to express what he felt.

"Dolores," he whispered, "do you think?... Is what the father said?... I don't mean myself; I mean you.... It doesn't make any difference about me, but ... oh, Dolores!..."

The girl was pallid but quite composed. She seemed to be staring into some far distance with her slightly unfocused eyes.

"*Sí*, señor," she whispered, with a long exhalation, "Father Benicio is a very wise man."

Above the two on the left wall of the chapel shone the sad radiance of Michelena's "Last Supper." In the center of the picture stands the Christ, and behind him, seen through the archway of an open window, gleams the soft radiance of a moonlit landscape. The rising moon forms a halo for his head. He is breaking the bread and giving it to his apostles to eat; to James and Jude, to Peter and Thomas, and to John, his beloved. And as he giveth it he sayeth unto them, "This is my body which ye eat, and this cup, which I give ye to drink, is my blood."

CHAPTER XXIII

Father Benicio had, as men say, convinced the head of Thomas Strawbridge but not his heart. As the drummer moved about his room in the palace, packing his belongings, the thought of resigning Dolores, on whatever moral grounds, filled him with a sense of ghastly loss. The thing seemed impossible. It seemed unbelievable that Dolores was in an adjoining room, and that presently he would go away and they would never see each other again.

He went on with his packing, mechanically, with a kind of shocked sensation at this impossible thing. His hands did their work with the meticulous care of a traveling salesman, a part of whose trade is to pack well. He folded each tie, shirt, sock precisely so, arranging them in his suitcases in smooth layers, with their accessibility determined by their frequency of use.

At Father Benicio's suggestion, Strawbridge was moving his quarters from the palace to the priests' house in the rear of the cathedral. It would save the lovers the pain and stress of seeing each other daily, so the father explained, and Strawbridge was going. He would remain with the ecclesiastic until the flotilla arrived, and then he would embark for Rio with the gold and barter which had been conscripted in San Geronimo.

The *griffe* girl helped him in his packing. She assisted where his wounded hand failed. She knelt on his bags and pulled home their straps. For some time the two worked silently, then the servant broke into sounds that resembled low, quick laughter. The drummer looked at her with a feeling of dull reproach, when he perceived that this was her method of sobbing. Her sympathy unmanned the convalescent. He touched her shoulder as she worked beside him, and said in uncertain tones:

"Don't cry, *chica*; it's all right; it's for the best; it's all for the best." And his sympathy, reacting on her, drove the little creature into more uncontrollable outbursts than ever.

Half an hour later the porters came for his bags. He possessed five bags, and five men were conscripted to carry them. They filed into the palace and stood for a moment looking at the room, at Strawbridge, at the bags, evidently speculating on the size of their gratuities. Then they hoisted the bags atop their dirty red caps and moved single file out through the corridor, down the transverse gallery, and so through the side entrance toward the plaza.

As one of the palace guards closed the door behind them, Strawbridge lingered a moment, looking back at it. His mood invested the door with something unusual. It seemed to have developed a personality of its own. It closed him out definitely. It shut in Dolores. Its finality swamped an irrational hope which, until that moment, Strawbridge was not conscious had existed in his heart. Until that very moment he had hoped for some unexpected event to occur which would prevent his final departure. He did not know what he had expected, but something, somehow, a softening, an amelioration.... The bolts of the palace door rattled noisily into place.

The porters moved slowly away, single file, through the sunshine. The drummer turned and followed them. He thought of the priest, of the priest's homily, but nevertheless as he walked along there grew in his mind a feeling of guilt, of some sort of basal unrighteousness. He ought not to do this thing—walk away and leave Dolores like this. It was a kind of desertion. During his stay at the palace both he and the girl had come to base their whole structure of future happiness upon their mutual relations. Now he was judging and condemning them both, the half judging the whole.

And it was more than Dolores whom he was banning. The Spanish girl had come to imply to him a home. He was deserting that, too. It was no such home as the salesman had ever known. As child and boy he had been reared in the hurly-burly of a middle-class home in Keokuk, wherein he found the bustle of a market stall. It was a place of endless work and tasks and runnings to and fro. He had supposed homes to be by nature rattling and bustling, until Dolores and her Latin surroundings brought to him intimations of a place of quietude and sweetness such as he had never imagined.

Strawbridge had been, as they say, in love before. But his American sweethearts always suggested to him comrades in sport, partners at a dance, fellow enthusiasts over moving pictures and jazz; they did not suggest quietude, or homes, or babies. Indeed, their hotly pursued pleasures made babies seem rather the absurd accidents of dual living than the end of matrimony.

With Dolores Fombombo, Strawbridge felt the continual implication of motherhood. In the tenderer moments of his passion, he built a sort of romance home about this dark-haired woman who could read Spanish plays and talk with curious wisdom about marriage, life, and art. These were minor charms. In the heart of his vision always shone a picture of Dolores with a baby at her bosom. He always saw, as clearly as in a hallucination, the soft contours of her breast yearning to its little pink mouth, and the bend of her dark crowned head above its dimpled tininess. It was this and all the long covenant of grandchildren and great-grandchildren which Strawbridge was abandoning as he passed through the side exit of the palace, and the doors shut to and the bolts shot fast, after him.

The salesman walked slowly after his porters, around the public gardens, to the priests' house. He was a drummer again. Once more he had lapsed into the raw, nomadic life of a traveling salesman, with its hurry, its careless and casual acquaintances, its mechanical optimism, its worn jests, its empty routine, its devastating dullness, and its petty obscenities. In point of fact, he was a wealthy drummer, one who at a lucky stroke had sold a large order and had gained a swollen commission. He was rich enough now to buy the home and the motor and the woman which he had described to Dolores.

The priests' house was the largest and finest of that proliferation of buildings which clung about the skirts of the cathedral. It was two stories in height, and built of stone. Its flat roof reached to about one third of the height of the cathedral walls. The motif of the green carving over the big double door was a cross. A horse and cab always stood in the sunshine before the house, for the use of his Grace the Bishop, Father Honario. Almoners and donors came and went, all day long, to and from the priests' house. Here the bishopric received fees from the rents of ecclesiastical properties, tithes, the church taxes, endowments for masses, and what not. It was a clearing-house for the ghostly ministrations which the priests performed in the parish; it was the go-between twixt the market-place and the millennium.

The look of the house managed to convey an impression of this dual service. Its façade was a flat, dignified stone, plastered in yellow and relieved by the single dull-green carving over the door. The windows were small, barred, and as unrevealing as the face of the priests themselves. The place had, somehow, a look of wealth and penance. One felt that dignitaries and beggars, pain and pleasure, death and riches were received with an equal hand in this imperturbable house. The most casual glance told that no woman lived within its walls.

Strawbridge rang the bell, and his porters lined up patiently in the sunshine. An old man with a twist in his neck opened the door, glanced obliquely at the visitors, and inquired what was wanted. Strawbridge gave the name of Father Benicio. The wry-necked one nodded, and closed the door, and Strawbridge could hear him shuffling down the hall. The sick man stood silently in the heat outside the enigmatic façade. At a faint clinking he looked around and saw the cab-horse swinging its head for a momentary riddance of flies. The drummer continued gazing vacantly at the swarming pests as they resettled in the corners of the horse's eyes and on the sag of its tremulous lips.

The door opened and Father Benicio stood to one side to allow the file to enter. The porters got under way patiently. The priest spoke to Strawbridge, in the tones one uses to a man who has suffered some great calamity. He told him his room was ready and that he hoped the drummer would feel that the bishopric was his own home.

The priest led the way through a short passage, to an interior doorway. This gave on a large, hot room screened off from a patio. Through an open door on the left, Strawbridge saw a large, somberly furnished room with an altar occupying one end and on the side walls old-fashioned paintings of men in ecclesiastical garb. He followed the priest past this door and along a very narrow passage flanked on both sides by small monastic cubicles. Into one of these the father ushered the drummer. Its interior was finished in roughly dressed stone covered with plaster. An iron bed, an unpainted table, bowl, pitcher, and an extra calabash of water for bathing furnished the cubicle. Over the bed hung a little bronze crucifix with a half-burned candle in a sconce under it. One narrow window, set high and deeply recessed in the stone wall, and with the flat iron bars of a prison across it, furnished light and air.

As the porters set down the bags, they crossed themselves, and they reverently bowed and kissed the father's hand as they passed out. When they were gone the American stood in the middle of the floor, looking grayly at his new quarters. He smiled faintly at the priest.

"This is a funny place for me to come to, Father Benicio."

"I hope you may find peace here, my son."

"Why, ... ye-e-s ..." assented Strawbridge, vaguely. The words lingered in his thoughts a moment. "Find peace...." The phrase really held no signification for him. Weary from his exertions, the sick man sat down on the side of the bed. When he touched the mattress he was surprised to find it stuffed with straw.

"That," explained his host, gravely, "is to remind us of One who was born in a manger, my son." He glanced toward the crucifix and bowed his head.

The drummer looked at the little bronze carving and the half-burned candle below it. The world of thought and emotion which the image symbolized was utterly foreign to him. Now this supporting symbol of the straw in his bed aroused in him a faint curiosity. He put a question to the priest, with the simplicity of his kind:

"You talking about this bringing me peace.... How can it bring anybody peace? What's the idea?"

Father Benicio answered him just as simply and fundamentally:

"You must know that Christ died for your sins, my son."

"M—y-e-s," admitted the American, without conviction. He had heard that phrase all his life, from Salvation Army workers, from revivalists, from country preachers. It seemed to him to be something they interjected into their homilies at intervals, which meant nothing at all.

Father Benicio stood studying the drummer. He went on carefully:

"Now that you are so deeply hurt, my son, you can carry your wounds to Him in meditation and have them healed. You remember that He healed the maimed, the halt, and the blind on the shores of Galilee. He forgave the woman of Samaria. He is just as great and merciful at this moment, my son, here in this cubicle, as He was two thousand years ago. If you will only break your heart before Him, if you will acknowledge yourself sinful and unworthy, then the blessed saints will take away your griefs, and into your heart will descend the dove."

To Strawbridge this mysticism was simple confusion. Doves and broken hearts—they conveyed no idea whatever. He said to the priest:

"I don't see what my sinfulness has to do with the señora. Anyway, I am not particularly sinful. Outside of smoking and cursing ... I do curse a good deal, but it is just a way I have. I don't mean anything by it."

"I know you do not steal nor commit perjury, Señor Strawbridge, and your profanity is perhaps venial, but you were about to commit a mortal sin; and, to judge from your state of mind, I believe you have already."

"I have already what?"

"Surrendered yourself to the desires of your body."

The drummer's voice became instantly angry:

"With the señora?"

Father Benicio held up a hand.

"I should loathe to think that. In fact, it would be impossible for me to think it. I have known Dolores for years, as her confessor. God in His providence has seen fit to visit her sweetness and gentleness with great distresses...." The priest's voice wavered. For a moment he ceased talking, and then explained simply: "I meant you had received other women into your life, Señor Strawbridge."

Strawbridge laid his hands down in his lap and moistened his lips. The silence became uncomfortable.

"Well, ... yes ... naturally."

"You have persistently sinned."

"Oh, I ... I haven't been so bad about women," defended the drummer, earnestly; "just one now and then. I'm willing to put my record against most men's. I think you'd say I was a pretty decent sort of chap."

The priest looked at him.

"You seduced a woman now and then—and don't think you have sinned...."

Strawbridge had an uncomfortable feeling that his face was growing hot.

"They were not the sort you *seduce*," he accented in annoyance; "they were the sort you pay. I wouldn't seduce any girl who ... who was a virgin. That ... that would be a little too bad."

He was trembling internally. Under the priest's questioning there gradually compiled within him a sense of guilt. It was an extraordinary feeling. For years at a stretch he had never once thought of his goodness or his badness. Now, in Strawbridge's ache for the señora, the priest brought up this utterly irrelevant and painful experience. The ascetic, however, continued to regard the drummer gravely.

"It seems to me, my son, if you thought your acts were harmless heretofore, yet surely, in the light of your affection for Doña Dolores Fombombo, you must see that you have lived sinfully. Do you not know that at heart these women whom you paid were much like the señora, only they were weaker, and tread bitterer paths? Is there any real difference between giving a woman her first stain, and giving her the last pollution that destroys her! If you can imagine the señora flung about the streets, defiled, mocked, and paid for, do you think she would be any more pitiful than any other woman? A human soul is a human soul, my dear son."

A distressful feeling arose in Strawbridge at this renaissance of his transgressions. For some reason the priest's words aroused with painful distinctness the memory of his first impurity. It had been with a hoyden, boyish girl with whom he had been skating at dusk on the cement walks in the park. He recalled the heavy syringa bushes, and how suddenly she had begun to cry, and how frightened and ashamed he had been. He remembered how he took off his skates because they made too much noise, and hurried silently home by back alleys, under a profound sense of shame and guilt. And that girl had been a virgin. He had deceived the priest. Now, as he sat on his bed in the cubicle, he felt a renewal of all the shame and guiltiness occasioned by that distant act of his boyhood. He wondered fearfully what had become of Daisy. He could see her distinctly, sitting on the grass, twisting her hands together and sobbing heartbrokenly for the evil which had befallen her.

Father Benicio stood watching his face during these melancholy memories.

"When you reflect on these transgressions, my son, then you will thank God a hundred times that you escaped leading the woman you love into a life of adultery."

"But, Father," asked Strawbridge, unsteadily, "what is going to become of her!"

"What do you mean!"

"I mean, in this land of murder and crime what will become of Dolores?"

"Ah, my son, that lies with God." The priest crossed himself.

"Yes, I know, but...." To Strawbridge the priest's phrase meant it lay with chance, that nothing watched over the Spanish girl, but he could not profess such a sentiment to Father Benicio.

"She will be safe, my son."

"Are you sure, Father?"

"I am quite sure, my son."

"But something could so easily happen to her. Everything is so uncertain here. You continually feel that it is all going to ruin. Why, in San Geronimo I saw women shot—shot down. I saw a girl killed in her window. How in God's name am I going away and leave Dolores where—"

"Stop! Do you think yourself more powerful than God? Do you doubt He can protect her body if it pleases Him? Or if He chose to lay her body aside, would she not be still more safe?"

The priest's earnestness and simplicity brought Strawbridge a brief illusion that life did not end with his body, but that it stretched out in some mysterious sunshine beyond the physical facts of Canalejos, of Rio Negro, and, indeed, of the whole world. The bodies of men and women had an appearance of shells which contained reality and timelessness. And as for Dolores's body, that was a small and a passing thing.

Father Benicio moved toward the door, and again invoked Strawbridge to meditation and repentance. When the priest had vanished, the drummer's apprehension of the other world lingered a few minutes like a mirage; then it too disappeared. The sins which Father Benicio had recalled so vividly and which he had counseled Strawbridge to meditate upon presently faded into subconsciousness as having no connection with his present life, and his thoughts came back to Dolores.

For some time these thoughts held no definition, but formed a vague, miserable mood, with the señora as the central association.

The American restlessly pulled his straw bolster to the foot of the bed, lay back on it with his legs hanging off, and gave himself up to staring at the little bronze Christ and the candle. The crucifix held dull high lights which focused his gaze.

Presently he found himself reconstructing his whole intercourse with the señora, from the very first night they had met. He wondered what he could have done to save their relations from this shattering wreck. It all appeared natural and inevitable.

It seemed to Strawbridge that their undoing really began with Dolores, when she confessed their plans to the priest. The American had had an idea that a priest merely heard a confession and remained entirely inactive; just as one might drop a note in a letter-box, that would end the matter; but Father Benicio had acted promptly and with extraordinary insight. He had seized on exactly the implement to persuade the drummer. Only now did Strawbridge realize how astute the priest had been in hitting on the rifles. The drummer pulled his bolster, to give his head a cool place to lie on. He drew a deep sigh, and began once more at his point of departure, searching for a flaw in his conduct. The meeting ... the breakfast ... the piazza.... Here his brain skipped an interval, and he wondered if he could not have eloped with the señora and still have obtained the order for rifles. He took the point up carefully. The dictator needed the arms; Dolores was a matter of indifference to the dictator. He would hardly have allowed her abduction to stand in the way of a trade.

The drummer began casting about in his mind for a safe way in which he might have abducted the señora and still have sold the rifles. The Tollivers might have helped him. If he and Dolores had been able to reach the English ranch, they could have slipped into federal territory while George Tolliver negotiated the trade. Strawbridge moved his pillow restlessly, and wondered why he had not done that. He lay thinking hard, with his eyes fixed on the shining points of the crucifix.

Lubito had been a possibility. If Strawbridge had explained everything to Lubito, with the bull-fighter's help he could have pushed the whole matter through during the afternoon before, instead of waiting over-night and allowing Dolores to trap them by a confession to the priest. With Lubito they could have fled to San Geronimo, and the torero could have brought back a letter arranging the order for rifles. But because he had not thought of these simple expedients, he would have to travel to the ends of the earth, while she, the woman he loved and who loved him, would be kept by the dictator to shame, or to use, as he saw fit.

The drummer writhed and clutched an edge of the straw mattress. He stared with a suffering face at the crucifix. Out of the depth of his soul he was repenting his sins. For what are sins but the mistakes which have worked pain in a man's life? And what is repentance but grief and a turning away from those mistakes? The only difference between the repentance of a saint and the chagrin of a cutpurse caught in the toils of the law, is the class of mistakes in their lives which brings them pain, and from which, in spirit, they turn.

CHAPTER XXIV

At some point in his vigil Strawbridge must have gone to sleep, for at some other point he awoke with a start. He thought that he was in a small-town hotel, and that the night clerk had allowed him to oversleep. He reached out, expecting to touch a chairful of clothes, when he discovered that he was already dressed. Then in the darkness above him he saw a lighted candle and a crucifix. Only these two objects were visible, and they stood out, swimming in a black immensity. They put to flight all theories of locality. He sat staring at the candle and the cross, trying to orient himself when, eerily, the darkness about him seemed to move, to fashion itself into his true surroundings. He was again in a cubicle in the priests' house.

Now that he had placed himself, he knew what had aroused him. It was his engagement to fly with the señora, which the priest had set aside. In the profound stillness of the stone chamber he sat brooding on the fact that on this very night he would have embarked with Dolores on the black reaches of the Rio Negro. Perhaps he would already have started.

At the thought he fumbled beneath his pillow, drew out his watch, then got up, pinched the shroud off the candle, and looked at the time. What he saw was the result of the simplest psychology, but it filled the American with a sense of the uncanny. He had waked precisely on the dot of eleven, on the very moment of his engagement to meet the señora. The coincidence seemed to the drummer portentous. It was a signal, from some ghostly influence, for him to pursue his plans; why else should he have awaked at exactly the appointed hour!

He stood beside his bed, watching the minute hand creep slowly past the dot. He knew that at the palace Dolores also was looking at the hand of her watch; he knew that she, too, was filled with the same violent urgency which moved him, that her access of formal morality must, like his own, have waned under the surge and desire of the night.

In the dim light he saw his bags which the porters had brought. He moved across, chose the one which contained the canvas roll prepared against his voyage, and silently opened it. He drew out the package. His heart beat; his lips grew dry. He listened as if he were robbing the suitcases. Once or twice he hurt his sore hand, but he hardly noticed it. When he had his roll he looked at the watch again. It was two minutes past eleven.

The drummer wore American shoes with rubber heels. He stepped noiselessly into the passageway and moved toward the entrance. He saw a dim illumination in the large room latticed off from the patio. The air in the house was still warm. He moved forward carefully, hoping to find no one in the faintly lighted chamber. He was perhaps half-way down the narrow passage when suddenly a tremendous clangor filled the whole house. It roared and boomed with gigantic reverberations. The very walls seemed shaken with it. Strawbridge almost dropped his bundle. It was an alarm because he had stolen out of his room. It was some damnable device of Father Benicio, who would shock the whole city with sound if he but moved. But a moment's saner thought told him it was the carillon of the cathedral, ringing for some nocturnal mass.

The clangor had hardly died away in heavy, monotonous strokes when the whole house was filled with a sense of movement—a rustling of straw mattresses, the shuffle of alpargatas, the faintly vocalized yawns of waking men. A little later, robed figures came out of the different cubicles, bearing candles.

Each sleepy priest bore his candle high, so its rays fell on his shaven poll and on the shoulders and breast of his cassock; the rest was lost in shadows. They might have been a company of heads and shoulders floating about in darkness. Some yawned patiently; others stretched, rubbed their eyes, and otherwise dispelled their drowsiness. They whispered a little among themselves, and soon an air of concern animated the whole brotherhood.

As Strawbridge stood with his bundle, hemmed in by priests behind and before, a hand was placed on his arm.

"Are you going into the cathedral, my son?" asked Father Benicio's voice; "we are going to hold a mass for the dead."

The salesman was taken aback.

"For the dead?" he aspirated.

"Some one has died in La Fortuna. Father Jaíme was on watch, and he has just seen a corpse thrown into the river."

Strawbridge was shocked; he was more deeply shocked that this thing had happened on the very night and at the very hour when he and the señora would have made their flight. He fancied the soldiers coming down to the water's edge with a dead man at the moment he and the Spanish girl were passing in their boat. What a grim precursor of their honeymoon!

"Did they murder him?" he queried.

"I don't know. He may have died of disease or as a result of former torture."

The American moistened his lips.

To torture, to murder, to fling their victims into the river! The horror of Rio Negro, the misery of all Venezuela jellied around the drummer's heart.

"Are you going with us into the cathedral?" questioned the priest again.

The drummer was seized by a revulsion to all his slynesses and unstraightforwardness.

"Why, no, Father," he said in a tired voice. "I'm going back to the *palacio*. I can't stick it out any longer. I was just going back when those bells broke loose and—"

"What are you going to do there, my son?" interposed the priest.

"I ... well, I'm going to try to get the señora to go with me, after all...." He paused, looking at the father, and added with a touch of defiance: "All this stuff about heaven and hell—that's all right for them that like it. I don't mean to be disrespectful to any man's religion. I was brought up to respect every faith—Christian, Mohammedan, Buddhist. They're all all right if a man lives up to 'em," the American finished his strange declaration of catholicity. He felt better now that he had told the priest of his intentions. He let his bundle down frankly into his good hand, and nodded at the father. "Well, good-by, and good luck. I thank you for what you tried to do for me. I know your intentions were of the best. So long," and he turned away.

The priest had stood perfectly still through this outburst, looking with an impassive face at the American. Now he took a step after Strawbridge and touched his arm.

"My son, you can't take her now," he said in a strange voice.

Something in his manner stopped the drummer, puzzled him and filled him with a vague apprehension.

"Why?"

"She is out of your reach forever."

The drummer's eyes widened, his mouth dropped open.

"You ... you don't mean she is dead?" he whispered.

"She is to you. This afternoon she entered her novitiate as a Sister of Mercy."

The American's bowels seemed to sag inside of him. A weak feeling flooded his body and shook his knees.

"Dolores is going to be a nun!"

"My son, what other place was there for so bruised a heart? Only our holy church can offer her peace."

Strawbridge stood breathing heavily through his open mouth. The priests had formed a line, and now they were marching through a door which led directly into the cathedral. Father Benicio bowed his head and turned to fall into the last place in the rank. The line of candle-bearers disappeared one by one into the dark vastitude of the cathedral. The American stood motionless in the faintly lighted room, watching them go. Presently from afar off he could hear the first melancholy responses of a mass for the repose of the dead.

CHAPTER XXV

The novitiate of Dolores Fombombo was Fortune's shrewdest thrust at Thomas Strawbridge. After that he stayed on at the priests' house because it ceased to make any difference to him where he domiciled. He spent most of his days there with the priests, sitting in the patio or lying on his straw bed in the cubicle. Now and then, when he saw his bags, he would think to himself, "I ought to take some samples and my order-book and canvass this town again." At other times he would think, "I ought to write a report to my house." But his feeling of "oughtness" applied to a perfectly empty motor-impulse for execution. It was precisely as if he were a figure without any will whatsoever.

Strangely, he did not think over-much of Dolores. Occasionally, when his mind made a movement toward her, he had a terrifying feeling as if some chasm were opening before him. Then, almost immediately, it seemed as if his brain closed gently shut, the chasm vanished, and with it all thought of the girl. To say that he grieved for her would be untrue. He had been numbed.

The most trifling things were sufficient to catch the drummer's unanchored attention. His eyes would follow the priests' cat across the patio, or he would watch the slow march of the cathedral's shadow over the flagstones in the *calle*.

He became acquainted with the priests who were domiciled in the building. These were his Grace the Bishop, Father Honario, a big, sleek, solemn man with swinging jowls that were bluish from a closely shaved beard. Father Roberto was a close-lipped man with a disapproving expression. Then there was Father Pedro, a fat, unaspiring priest, who drank enough wine at his noon meal to make him sleepy all the afternoon. There was still a fifth priest at the house who was not attached to the cathedral at all. This was Father Jaíme, a sort of itinerant guest who had come to the Canalejos cathedral from a Trappist monastery on Lake Titicaca in Peru. The bishop allowed Father Jaíme a few pittances for holding mass at the funerals of his humbler parishioners, and this was the only stipend he received. When Strawbridge knew him he was trying to save sufficient money to purchase the churchman's half-fare passage from Canalejos to Port au Spain in Trinidad, where the Benedictines had a monastery. As far as Strawbridge could gather, Father Jaíme was a sort of ecclesiastical tramp.

The man who rang the cathedral bells, an office which occurred at almost every hour of the day, was called the "Cock." His nickname came, perhaps, from a thin, beak-like nose protruding from under the dirty visor of an old cap. He had a Jewish appearance. He was the only object which aroused to wrath the lethargic children of the cathedral settlement. When the Cock appeared, the children spat at him and called him "bloodsucker" and all manner of insulting epithets. The reason for this contumely was that the Cock lent money in a small way, and the hatred poor people have for a parsimonious money-lender was reflected in their children.

The Cock lived with a very industrious Indian wife, in one of the adobes at the back of the cathedral. He seldom spoke to any one, but moved gloomily on his way to and from his bells. However, once Strawbridge did observe a visitor in the bell-ringer's hut. One day as the salesman was walking slowly along one of the paths on the terrain of the river, a gay figure stepped out from the blackness of the hut, drew off his sombrero, and bowed to the American with undeniable grace. As he bowed he exhibited a knot of hair at the back of his head.

"How goes *el señor, mi General!*" he called warmly. "Be assured Lubito knows your unhappiness, señor, and that you have but to lift a finger and the sword of a bull-fighter will leap from its scabbard." He went through the pantomime of drawing his sword, and his bold figure, set against the darkness of the doorway, formed a picture.

The sick man looked at him, thought of his walk with Lubito in the plaza, Esteban's attack on General Fombombo in the palace, Madruja. Such reminiscences were leading him straight to the señora, when some involuntary check in his mind softly closed that stream of thought and left the drummer staring emptily at the torero's posturing. He turned away along the path, vaguely disturbed and unhappy. The bull-fighter looked around and nodded knowingly to some one inside the hut.

"*Caramba!*" he praised. "What did I tell you? Deep! Why, you can't tell by his face that he even knows me, and yet ... we are as brothers! What a dictator that *hombre* will make!"

The cathedral itself was a kind of labyrinth through which Strawbridge sometimes wandered with a sort of dulled attention. He understood little of the ecclesiastical symbolism in the chapels and on the high altar, or the allegorical frescoes in the dome and pendentive. He did peruse the fourteen stations of the passion which spaced the interior walls of the church, and while he could not follow the details of some of the cartoons he understood their general purport. He never entered the chapel of the Last

Supper. Something warned him from the place where he had stood with Dolores under Michelena's great masterpiece.

This, unfortunately, was the only worthy canvas which the cathedral of Canalejos contained. The other chapels held staring images of one saint or another, and near the entrance of the pile, on the right side, was a crude picture of souls in purgatory. It was so badly done it was not even hideous.

The altars of the more popular saints were piled with ex-voto offerings. These were all manner of little images, made of tin, silver, or gold, and not much larger than a tobacco-tag. They were images of legs, hearts, arms, feet, a little tin mule, or a tiny house. Each one commemorated a miracle performed by the saint on whose altar it lay. A little silver leg was probably the gift of some rheumatic whom the good saint had cured; a mule would illustrate the gratitude of a peon for finding a strayed burro. The simplicity and childishness of these little gifts touched even Strawbridge; and, moreover, such an accumulation of testimonials lent a certain air of credibility to the power of the images in the chapels.

Besides these offerings of gratitude, on each altar were piles of letters asking the saint for further interventions. Once, as Strawbridge was looking at the missives, he wondered if any real power lay back of these stiff images of saints. Could it be that behind them was ranged some sort of spiritual reality, with a power and a will to soften human unhappiness? The thought stirred the benumbed heart of the American. He stood staring up at the wooden effigy, with a notion of adding a petition of his own to the pile on the altar.

The thought moved him. He walked out at the side entrance of the cathedral, into the priests' house. His legs trembled with his idea. In his cubicle he got out pen and paper and sat down to write, when a strange thing stopped him. All of his stationery bore the letter-head of the Orion Arms Corporation. It struck the drummer as somewhat incongruous to write a note to Saint John in heaven on New York letter-heads. And now that he had started to use his own envelops, he could not go out deliberately and purchase the big, square Latin-American envelops such as the peons used in writing a letter to Saint John. In brief, the sight of his matter-of-fact American paper shattered his transitory mysticism and made it impossible. However, the dying of this hope left the drummer grayer than ever.

The wood-carving in the cathedral next offered itself to Strawbridge's faint interest. The circular balustrade which led up and around one of the columns of the nave, to the pulpit, and the canopy over the pulpit were carved out of mahogany with the motif of pineapples and yucca-palm. The wood was black with the centuries. Strawbridge thought this was a defect, but when he recognized the two plants intertwined in the carving, his discovery gave him a childish joy. It led him to look at other work—the choir-stalls, which were not half so well done as the pulpit; the reredos; the altar panels; the pyx. Everywhere his eye fell he saw the labor of generations. Some were the carvings of the Spanish artisans who came to the New World not long after Columbus; others were the work of the Indian and negro apprentices of those original wood-carvers. The whole rise and decline of a folk-art was epitomized in the cathedral at Canalejos.

About a week after Strawbridge came to the priests' house he was walking in the cathedral one afternoon and wandered through an open door into an anteroom full of the images which the priests used in their processionals. It was a strange sight—the Madonnas with dust on their gilt halos; Saint Peter holding up a tarnished key; Saint Thomas reaching a broken finger toward the far-off wounds of Christ. These and perhaps a dozen other dusty figures, all as large as life, were placed helter-skelter in the storeroom, some facing one direction, some another. Over in a corner lay three or four litters on which the images were borne. One had a glass frame, another was draped in silks.

The drummer stood looking curiously about him, when he heard a rustling among the images. He moved toward the sound, and after a moment saw an old woman dusting the statues with a brush. A second glance showed him it was Josefa's grandmother. This dusting no doubt was a part of her labor as a charwoman in the cathedral.

Presently the old crone observed Strawbridge. She recognised the American, and put down her duster.

"*Cá!* It is you, señor. I thought it was Filipe, come in to help me. Have you come to tell me something?"

Strawbridge explained that he was merely idling in the cathedral; then he asked her how she liked her quarters by this time.

"It keeps the rain away. Then you have nothing to tell me of poor Josefa?"

"No, Doña Consolacion—at least not yet," he added, in order to give some crumbs of hope.

The old woman mumbled her wrinkled mouth with nervousness.

"But you will soon?"

"I hope so, Doña Consolacion."

"Very soon?"

"I hope so."

She nodded.

"*Sí, sí*, I hope so. I pray so every night, señor, at my *oraciones*." She gave a Virgin a stroke with her brush, then added in a whisper, forming the words very plainly with her thin wrinkled lips, "Who—was—it—the—soldiers—dropped—in—the—river—the—other—night?"

The question brought the drummer a wave of surprise and revived pain.

"I ... I don't know, señora!"

The old woman gave up her dusting and came nearer, so she could talk in a whisper.

"You don't think—you don't believe i-it could h-have b-been—?" She gasped and cut off her sentence.

"You mean...."

She nodded mutely, with a terrified expression in her old eyes.

"Why, no, Doña Consolacion, I am sure it was not ... not your grandson!"

But Doña Consolacion was peering at him, and his face was too full of apprehension to reassure her. On the contrary, with the suspicion of the aged she read tragedy there. She suddenly dropped her duster and her face screwed up into the tearless grimacing which stands for weeping with the aged.

"Oh, *Dios mio!* my Josefa, my poor little Josefa is gone!" She rocked to and fro with her hands crossed over her dried breast. Suddenly something flared up in her and she pointed at Strawbridge: "And you did it! You killed him! It makes no difference to me if it was all a part of a plan to free this country. I would rather have my little Josefa than free a thousand countries!"

Strawbridge made a gesture.

"But listen, señora; there is no reason to think it was Josefa! He was young and strong. He wouldn't have succumbed so quickly. There must be hundreds of other prisoners in that jail. It is more likely one of them has died than ... than your grandson.... Some old man whose strength had broken down!"

The old woman grew quieter at this reasoning, and stood looking at Strawbridge, with her toothless lips moving in and out with her agitated breathing.

"Holy Mary! I hope you are right! If I only knew he was alive! But he was young and strong, as you say.... *Cá!* but I don't see why you should have chosen him, Señor Strawbridge, to cast into prison, even if it is all a part of your terrible plans."

"But, dear Doña Consolacion," remonstrated the drummer, "it was no part of a plan. There was no plan to it. It was simply an unfortunate move, an accident."

The old charwoman shook her head.

"*Cá!* señor! there is no use deceiving me! I am not a spy but an old woman cast down by a tyrant. And my family have always been lovers of freedom. My father was a Rosales." Her old voice gathered dignity at this reference to her family, and then, nodding her head to accent her words, she added, "And poor Ricardo, whom you had shot, Señor Strawbridge—he was my grandnephew."

The American stared in amazement.

"Ricardo ... whom I had shot!"

"*Sí*, señor—Lieutenant Rosales, whom you ordered shot in San Geronimo. *Pues*, you need not stare so. I understand all. Lubito has explained your deep and mysterious plans that reach all over the world. And also Lubito explained that one cannot make an omelette without breaking eggs. Napoleon first said that, señor; all cruel men say it. But I do not complain. I was born a Rosales, and more than one of us has given himself to die."

The old woman's persistent delusion that he was some sort of arch-plotter, assigning this and that man to his fate, filled the drummer with dismay.

"But señora," he began hopelessly, "how many times have I said that I have nothing, nothing whatever to do with all this butchery! I would not harm a soul in Rio Negro—no, not for the whole government. I would not—"

But the old creature shook her head, with her mouth quirked in withered satire.

"*Ola, señor!*" She wagged a finger. "I know, I know." She started to stoop for her brush, but the drummer forestalled her. "I know one little thing that tells me all, no matter what you admit or deny."

Strawbridge looked at her.

"What's that?"

"I refer to...." She wagged her head vaguely and looked at the American with narrowed and disapproving eyes.

"What are you talking about, Doña Consolacion?"

"I was down at the riverside on the night when the soldiers flung the body of the dead man into the water."

The salesman stared at her, with his brows drawn in a faint frown.

"Well ... what of that?"

"Oh, what of that! I was at the riverside just below the *palacio*, Señor Strawbridge, where the white boat lay. I went down because the Cock told me I could find some driftwood there, and I had no money to buy charcoal...."

The phrase "white boat" moved some memory that was battened down in Strawbridge's heart. It gave him a ghastly sensation, as if an arm were reaching out of a grave. And there was something disconcerting in the rancor in the crone's voice, in the circumstantiality with which she began her account. He stood looking at her, wondering and rather fearing what she was about to say.

"What's the point to this?" he hesitated at last. "What if you were at the river—under the *palacio*?"

The charwoman found enough spirit to shrug.

"No matter how grand your final object may be, señor, I think that was going a little too far. There are certain things a Spanish *caballero* will not do, señor—no, not though he gain all Venezuela by it!"

The drummer took a step nearer the old woman, and looked hard at her.

"Look here, Consolacion," he uttered in a strained voice, "what—in—the—hell—are—you—talking—about?"

The ancient shrugged again, and the nostrils of her hatchety old nose dilated momentarily, then she burst out:

"*Dios mio!* I am talking about the señora, poor Doña Dolores, whom I found down there—poor lamb!—frightened almost to death, and weeping.

She started to fly as I came up, but I called to her and she knew I was a woman...."

A horripilation went over Strawbridge. He clutched the old creature's arm.

"The señora!" he whispered, staring with distended eyes. "My God! you can't mean Dolores was down there that night, on the river!"

The hag broke into sardonic, clacking laughter.

"No, you didn't know that! You didn't know you had a poor frightened girl go down to the river bank and wait and pray for your coming until it grew so light she was forced back into the *palacio*! No, you didn't know that! Oh, to be sure, I explained to her your plans. I told her that she was just a tiny little part; that you had killed my grandnephew and my grandson, and now for some reason you had flung her down in the river mud, like an old rag—you, and your great plans!"

The old crone's tirade seemed to break loose something hot and seething in Strawbridge's brain. The enormity of his delinquence, the pitifulness of the girl, the rapture which might have been his! His legs shook so that he caught at the effigy of the Blessed Virgin. But all that remained of his mutilated hand were two fingers. These gave way instantly, he staggered against the wooden figure, and the thing swung slowly over and crashed on the tiles.

The ancient shifted from the dowager back to the servant again.

"Look! Look!" she squealed. "Oh, look what you've done! You've broken her head!"

The American neither saw nor heard the fall of the effigy.

"But, señora," he stuttered, with a salty taste in his mouth, "he ... he told me ... Father Benicio told me that she ... she had gone to a convent!"

The hag came out of her servant's concern for the statue and fell to lashing again:

"A priest told you! *Diantre!* You believed a priest in a case like that! Poor little dove! She did join the sisterhood, Señor Strawbridge, but it was on the afternoon after your cruel desertion of her. What else could she do—poor little dove!"

CHAPTER XXVI

With legs that shook and hands that clutched at nothing, Strawbridge got out of the image room into the cathedral. He screwed himself to sufficient self-control to be silent as he shivered along the aisles, peering into every chapel and niche for Father Benicio. He raged internally, thinking what he would do to Father Benicio. He syncopated his thoughts with clenching of fists, spreading of nostrils, and muttered blasphemies. When he found the priest, he would throttle him, beat his shaven head on the stone flags. Vibrations of wrath shook through his chest and belly.

He made the entire round of both aisles, and then turned automatically into the priests' house. Opening a door, he stepped quickly into the big room with the latticed side. He glanced about with a beating heart and saw it was empty. He got to the entrance of the bishop's room and looked in. Only the Christ on the cross, and the darkened pictures of former bishops looked down on him. The drummer turned and set out up the narrow passage, to search among the cubicles.

At that moment a loud ringing of the gong at the outer door caught his attention. It came in a succession of three clangorous peals, loud and imperative. It suggested an interruption and sent Strawbridge trotting up the passage, looking hurriedly into each cubicle. All were as obviously empty as a cigar box. Some smelled of burned candles, one of medicine, one or two of stale bedding. The only difference between them was in odor.

The doorbell clanged again, three times. Then it suddenly occurred to Strawbridge that this might be Father Benicio, asking entrance. The thought sent him flying to the door, with titillating nerves. He began whispering through his dry mouth:

"Good God, let it be that devil Benicio!"

He stepped into the entrance and closed the inner shutter behind him. At that moment the gong filled the closed passageway with a great uproar. It was imperative, excited, and held the prolonged clangor of a visitor who is at the end of his patience.

The drummer rushed to the door and laid noiseless hands on the bolts. He had a sensation of immense strength. He wanted not to frighten the priest, but to let him come unwarned into his grip. Not until Strawbridge set about drawing the bolts did he remember that he had but one hand. A thought flickered in his head that he might need his automatic, but it was gone almost instantly.

The bars were hot. He could feel the heat, reflected by the panels, of the sunshine outside. With a painful surge of expectancy he swung open the outer shutters. In the dazzle of sunshine stood a figure who the drummer could see was not Father Benicio. His murderous impulse had been so sure of the priest, that he stood batting his eyes in the glare, when he heard an excited voice gasp:

"*Gracias á Dios!* it's you, Señor Strawbridge! *Diantre!* I thought I would never get you! But—*caramba!*—you know it already! Look, look, Esteban, how white his face is, and how bloodshot his eyes! We were two great fools, Esteban, to imagine we could tell *el señor* anything!"

A second figure stepped in front of the door-casing and shrugged.

"*Naturalmente*, Lubito, if *el Señor General* ordered these boats up here, he knew when they were coming."

"But what shall we do, *mi General?*" demanded the bull-fighter, excitedly. "Are you ready for us peons! Just a word, and we will flame up like a bonfire!" The torero made a swift upward gesture.

Such ejaculations and questions were enough to seize part of the attention of the homicidal drummer.

"What are you talking about!... Boats ... men ... peons!"

"*Demonio!*" roared Lubito, in admiration. "Is he not as deep as the devil's pit, Esteban! What are we talking about? *Pues, mi General,* we are talking about your men and your boats, your guns; they are below the rapids. They are gathering in from God knows where. When we saw them coming, Esteban and I came running here as fast as our legs would carry us, to know when you wanted us, here in Canalejos, to strike. Is it now? Is this the day? Shall we set fire to hell now? How is it, *mi General?* Now?"

The bull-fighter's cries vibrated with a curious edge. He whipped out an imaginary sword and saluted, tossing up his head and knot of hair.

"What part of Canalejos do we sack first! Send me where there are plenty of women!"

Esteban, with his stupid peon face, stood nodding.

"And me ... send me where I can find Madruja, *mi General.*"

By this time Strawbridge had fathomed what had set off the imaginations of his self-appointed henchmen. He made a heavy gesture.

"That isn't my flotilla. It's the dictator's boats, come up from Rio at last." He stood staring at his two followers, with a new and profound depression coming over him. "So this is the end of it! This is the end of everything!" A great sigh burst from him. He struck his palm miserably against his breast. "Oh, Good God! Well, I'm ready to go."

He stumbled out of the priests' house. Each of the bewildered peons took one of his arms, and the three men set out around the buttresses of the cathedral and the adobe lean-tos, toward the terrain of the river. The pain of a complete and final leave-taking of Dolores was upon Strawbridge. The peons had not the least notion of the cause of their master's despair.

"But, *mi General*," demurred Lubito, uncertainly, "there are too many canoes for the trading party; the river is black with them. *Caramba!* if they are not your men—"

"*Es verdad, Señor mi General*," put in Esteban. "There are too many—"

The peon's words were interrupted by a sharp, crashing blow from the direction of the river. It smote the ear-drums of the three men terrifically, and was followed by an abrupt silence. It was a cannon-shot. At the moment the three men trotted around the last obscuring adobe that stuck to the cathedral. On La Fortuna they saw a puff of smoke dissolving into air, and far down below the rapids they saw a crawling of men from a multitude of canoes—so far away that they looked like insects. Among these insect lines forming on the shore, Strawbridge caught the gleam of a banner.

The cannon on La Fortuna crashed again. Soldiers went marching out of the fort, toward the foot of the rapids. They went down the terrain of the river at a double-quick.

A feeling of movement and stir spread over the city. Almost before Strawbridge knew it, the whole terrain on which he stood was covered with denizens of the adobes. The Cock came out, peered through the sunshine, then darted back into his inky hut and reappeared with an extraordinary single-barreled, muzzle-loading pistol and a dagger. Men and women came running out of the plaza, to the riverside, for a view.

Lubito clutched the drummer's arm.

"You see, *mi General*, it is your men attacking. What shall I do? Gather up my men and advance?"

Some obscure cerebration caused Strawbridge to answer, "No, ... no, not now. Wait till we see how this goes!"

The bull-fighter snapped his fingers in admiration.

"*Caramba*, Esteban!" he cried above the noise of the gathering crowd. "What calmness! This is the strategy of a Napoleon!"

By this time the gun on La Fortuna was firing regularly, and far down the river, among the insects, little plumes of smoke showed where the shells were bursting.

Strawbridge left the river bank and made his way through the crowd, toward the plaza. He was filled with a rising anxiety for the señora. He wondered where she was, to what convent she had retired. He supposed that she would be safe, but she would surely be frightened. The drummer went hurrying eastward through a small *calle*, glancing to right and to left, half expecting to see the señora's face at some barred window.

Along the thoroughfares natives were darting about, salvaging their household goods as if from a fire. Women and children, with burdens on their backs, turned out into the streets and went hurrying along, urged by the groaning of cannon and an occasional dry rattle of musketry.

This continued from street to street, and by the time the drummer reached the plaza, the square was already crowded with fugitives, all of whom were flowing westward, past the palace and the state buildings, toward the outskirts of town and the llanos. The mass moved slowly and in great disorder. Mules and donkeys went past, laden with household goods; carts containing food, *mosquiteros*, calabashes, invalided persons. Pedestrians struggled along under huge bundles done up in ponchos; old women carried their belongings twisted up in their skirts, with their bare legs and feet exposed. It was an astonishing, frantic procession, with every one struggling, pushing, cursing unfortunates who could not move quickly. Perched on top of many a bundle rode pet game-cocks. The shrill crowing of these fowls added a curious stridor to the turmoil of the refugees.

Almost every shop around the plaza was shut now. One or two doors had been forced by looters, and the riffraff of the street eddied into these magazines as if by some law of nature, and streamed out again with their arms filled with spoil.

In the midst of this pillaging and flight, a murmur, which swiftly rose to cries, oaths, and shouts of anguish, came from the direction of the palace. It grew louder and louder, and presently the drummer was aware that the crowd about him was solidifying and surging backward. He tried to find out what was the matter, but in the uproar he could ask nothing. Within the space of a minute he was caught in a dense jam and had to struggle merely to keep his feet. He held his sore hand up, to prevent its being hurt, and tried to push his way in some direction, but men and women were crushing into him on every side. Then, owing to his height, he saw the danger.

Down the square the palace guards were coming at a double-quick in the direction of the fighting. The front ranks had leveled their bayonets to force a swift passage through the mob. Before the steel the crowd flung itself back, shrieking in terror and pain. The masses crushed blindly toward the sides of the square, lost their bundles, upset carts, bastinadoed their burros, and flung themselves, in compact masses, away from the line of march.

As the guards plowed down the plaza, Strawbridge felt himself crushed one way, then another; and then suddenly a line of division opened and left him with half a dozen others directly in the middle of the way. He was in a narrow alley through which the bayonets were double-quicking. He had that terrible sensation of being unable to move in either direction. He stood dodging in a mad contra-dance, then he seemed lost; he dashed to one side and tried to press his body into a solid wall of flesh. He might as well have tried to sink into a bank of rubber. He stood out; he was still exposed. The bristle of bayonets was right on him. He made a last convulsive effort to merge himself, when an arm thrust out of the mass, hooked about his waist, and from some leverage, pried the American into a niche at the very moment the bayonets skimmed smoothly past.

The crush stood perfectly immobile as the rifles went by. A sweat broke out on Strawbridge. He twisted his head to look at the palace guards. Only a few days before, they had been little better than servants who fetched and carried for him; now, at a cannon-shot, at a volley of firearms, they had formed a machine which, accidentally, almost casually, had transfixed him.

The moment the soldiers were past, the crowd filled the *calle* again, struggling with greater violence than ever. A voice shouted in Strawbridge's ear:

"Where are you trying to go?"

Strawbridge looked about and saw a bearded and somewhat familiar face. It belonged to the man who had wedged him into the crowd. Then the drummer recognized him as Dr. Delgoa, the minister of war, whom he had seen once or twice at the palace. The doctor's face had a strained look, and now in the press he still held Strawbridge's arm, perhaps with an idea of directing the drummer's steps.

"I wasn't going anywhere, specially," shouted the American. "Trying to find out what's the trouble."

The doctor shook his head.

"*Diantre!* This is terrible! Come with me; I am going to the *palacio*. Here! Let's get into this side street. This crush!" These exclamations were jogged out of him as he edged his body into this and that aperture. He made way for the drummer, who followed him body to body, and at last succeeded in pushing himself into the mouth of a stinking little side *calle*.

In this place the crowd dwindled to small groups and single pedestrians who hurried back and forth with ant-like aimlessness. Dr. Delgoa rested a moment. He wore a high hat; now he took it off, drew out a silk handkerchief, and mopped his face and hair. Somehow he had managed to preserve his silk hat; his black frock-coat and his pearl-gray trousers were unrumpled despite his struggle.

"We'll have to get away from here!" he said in a breath. "This *calle* will be untenable in thirty minutes.... The machine-guns...." He started walking along the *calle*, with the stragglers. "*Caramba!* I wish I knew which way the cat'll jump," he puffed, drying his hatband as he went. "One never knows what to do. I left my wife at home. Of course the telephones have been seized, and I can't talk to her. Where are you going, Señor Strawbridge?" He had evidently forgotten the drummer's answer to this same question a minute or two before.

"I'm trying to find out what caused this." The American looked back and listened to the inarticulate roar of the mob thundering in the tympanum of the narrow street.

Dr. Delgoa started to explain, but at that moment out of a back door of a shop bundled an old woman with a great pile of fiber hammocks. The men collided with her. The old creature spat invectives. She twisted about, saw who had struck her, and became more furious.

"It's that thief Delgoa! That bloodsucker Delgoa! May a ray of God blast your entrails! You stole every centavo my shop could earn, you and your cursed police! May you be bayoneted through the liver!"

Her anathemas were finally lost in the uproar. They struck coldly on the drummer's nerves in so perilous a situation, but Delgoa paid no attention to her. He began shaking his head, with his distressed look.

"If a man could only tell which way it is going to go."

"Who is it fighting us?" called Strawbridge. "Have the federal forces suddenly got up here?"

Delgoa looked around at him, rather surprised.

"No, it's Saturnino."

Strawbridge stared, thunderstruck.

"Saturnino—fighting us!"

"Yes, yes. Been brewing a long time. Very ambitious man. Heretofore the general has handled him somehow, through the influence of the general's wife. Now I understand she has entered a convent, and of course—" the Minister made a hopeless gesture—"of course that unchained hell."

A wide dismay suddenly swept over the drummer. He felt that he and all the people in Canalejos were caught like flies in the web of Coronel Saturnino's endless calculations. He knew that back there, in San Geronimo, the colonel had worked out, night after night, precisely how he would conquer this point and that redoubt; how many men it would require to take that coign of vantage, and so on, step after step, all the way to his goal.

Suddenly the drummer turned to the minister.

"Why didn't Fombombo throw the colonel into prison years ago?"

Dr. Delgoa looked at him, his mind evidently coming back from some painful abstraction.

"Oh, yes.... He couldn't. Saturnino has always been a favorite with the army. Besides, the general needed a tactician. *Diablo!* I wish the general had kept his wife in the *palacio!*"

By this time the two men had come to the mouth of the little side street, where it emptied into the main thoroughfare opposite the palace. Delgoa held out an arm to warn the drummer, then advanced carefully to the limit of the protecting walls and peered down the plaza. The place was a litter of scattered goods and broken carts. Here and there a human figure darted across the wreckage, making for some place of safety. The crowd had struggled past and were gone.

Just across the street the doors of the palace stood open. Four soldiers were posted by each shutter, whose duty, evidently, was to close the building at a moment's notice. On top of the palace roof were lined a number of guards, and in the machicolations above the architrave shone the muzzles of some rapid-fire guns.

Dr. Delgoa stood in the *calle*, peering at the scene before him and listening with all his ears. He said to Strawbridge in an apprehensive voice:

"The cannonading at La Fortuna has stopped."

The drummer listened. It was true, but he had not observed the fact, under the ceaseless tearing sound of the small arms, which was growing louder and louder. It sounded somewhat like an approaching storm. Delgoa waved a hopeless hand.

"*Dios mio!* which way will this battle go! *Canastre!* this deciding for your life, your property and your family!" With a tortured face he turned to Strawbridge. "Just think, if I fail to guess the victor just once, I go into La Fortuna, my property confiscated, and my wife...." He snapped his fingers and flung out his hands.

Such frank opportunism amazed the American.

"Why—damn it, man!—stick to the side you think is right!"

"Right! *Right!*" Delgoa laughed in a very access of irony. "My dear *amigo*, I am a politician. I have nothing to do with—" He interrupted himself to listen to the increased ripping and tearing of the gun fire; then, with his head cocked sidewise, he looked steadily at Strawbridge and whispered, "I believe Saturnino is winning...."

The drummer was outraged.

"Well—by God!—between the two I stand by the general!"

"But look yonder!" The minister pointed down the plaza. "Yonder are the guards falling back!"

At that moment a flurry of men that looked like leaves before a wind, whirled out of a street into the plaza and instantly settled into every niche and crevice they could find. Almost immediately came another whirl of men, falling back behind every makeshift ambuscade. The minister gripped the American's arm.

"Your general is losing; we are going to change dictators!"

The American burst out in profanity:

"I don't give a damn! I've always been against Saturnino! He's nothing but a rascal, a damn clever rascal! Hasn't got a principle in him!" The drummer shook off the doctor's arm, and next moment darted out of his covert, toward the long flight of steps at the entrance of the palace.

The big American's flight might have been the signal for the whole regiment of palace guards to retreat headlong toward the *presidencia*. Immediately a company of insurgents deployed into the square, and knelt to fire. Even in the drummer's short sprint across the *calle*, the attackers discharged a volley. The crash, pent up between the houses, roared down the *calle*, and a shower of leaves and twigs fell from the ornamental greenery in the plaza. Stone flakes leaped from the façade of the palace; spots of dust floated up into the air along the *calle*; the air was filled with a whining. Here and there a flying guard stumbled in the plaza; two or three of the less severely wounded went crawling on their hands and knees toward the side streets, to escape the steel storm. Strawbridge dashed up the long flight of steps and was hardly inside the recessed doors when the van of the retreating guard began to pour up the steps into the building.

The moment the drummer entered the palace he stepped into quietude and order. The heavy walls reduced the rifle fire in the streets to a mere popping. Along the passage were stationed several officers, who directed the returning soldiers to march back into the building, toward some objective unknown to the American. One or two of the officers recognized Strawbridge and saluted as he entered.

An odd feeling of home-coming visited the salesman as he stood near the entrance. His painful week at the priests' house seemed to have dropped out of his life. It seemed to him that the señora was still in the music-room, that he might walk back, tap, and have her come to the door.

Bullets were now snapping regularly at the stone façade. They reminded Strawbridge of the first scattering drops of rain at the beginning of a summer shower. Another batch of soldiers came running up the long steps. One of them even laughed, and waved his cap to some one on the roof, when at that moment he fell forward and lay twisting on the sharp corners of the stone steps. Suddenly the drummer saw that it was Pambo, the little brown guard who had nursed him through his illness. His comrades had left him on the steps. An impulse sent the drummer leaping down three steps at a time through the whining air. He seized Pambo in his arms and came back up. The little soldier recognized the American, for he gasped out, "*Cá! Señor Americano*, tell Juana...." Then he began bending his body backward, thrusting out his chest in an effort for breath. When Strawbridge laid him on the floor, he continued these convulsive movements, bowing up his torso, his mouth open, gasping, and his eyes staring.

The next moment the officer nearest the door looked out and gave a command, and the four soldiers swung shut the heavy metal doors. Instantly the hall was blanketed to silence. The only sounds were the footsteps of the guards walking briskly to the rear of the building and the clinking of balls striking the doors of the palace.

The drummer fell in with the last soldiers who went down the hallway. Along the sides of the passage hung the dark portraits of former dictators, men who had usurped and lost power, and who had been done to death in just such another eruption as now raged outside. With a beating heart the drummer hurried past these ironic pictures.

He meant to fight for General Fombombo. Why? He did not know. Perhaps it was because of the order for rifles. Perhaps because he sensed in the arbitrary general something finer than what he found in the cynical colonel. Or, more likely, it was the result of the salesman's discovery that Saturnino was a lover of Dolores; the general was only her husband. Strawbridge fell in with the soldiers.

The recruits turned in at a side door of the passageway, and this gave upon a flight of stairs that led to the roof. Guards were pouring up and down this staircase; the upward-bound were laden with ammunition boxes; the down-bound were empty-handed. This was the general's ammunition, hoist from some donjon in the palace.

The moment Strawbridge stepped into the stairway a din of firing and shouting broke upon his ears. The salesman ran up the steps beside one burden-bearer. As they emerged on the roof, one of the soldiers reached over and jerked the big American down to a stooping posture. Everybody was stooping. The palace guards crouched and sprawled inside the waist-high wall that surrounded the roof, and fired through the machicolations. Stationed here and there among the riflemen were machine-guns. Each gun was handled by two men. Now and then one of these guns would break into a hard yammering, then abruptly cease. The riflemen were firing in the same careful way. They sighted and fired with murderous concentration. Like all Latin-American revolutionists, they never used volley-firing in the hope of making a hit. Every bullet was aimed at somebody.

A dead man or two and a few wounded men were scattered over the tiled roof. Stone splinters snapped out of the merlons from adverse gun fire. The smell of smokeless powder filled the air with a headache-y quality. The drummer saw a rifle and a bandolier of cartridges beside a motionless figure. He crawled to it and salvaged the gun. He got to the wall and settled himself beside an aperture, in line with the whole wallful of reclining riflemen.

Peering out between his merlons, he found himself looking into the westering sun. Saturnino had flung his forces on top of the houses directly west of the palace. This screened his men in the yellow glow of the declining sun. The whole outline of the opposite buildings was an indistinct purple. The drummer stared fixedly at this purple outline, then he thought he glimpsed a movement. He leveled his gun and fired. At the same moment a machine-gun near him began a sudden chattering. Just where the drummer had seen a movement, the black figure of a man lurched up against the yellow light and disappeared backward.

A thrill of triumph shot through Strawbridge. He thought he had hit his man. He lifted himself for a good look and another shot, when a bullet flicked a bit of stone out of his merlon and cut his forehead just over his eye. The salesman dodged down, put up his fingers to the sting, and saw that he was bleeding a little. It made him angry, and he fired his rifle viciously several times at the blank purple rim of the opposite wall.

At that moment a hand was laid on his shoulder. Strawbridge looked around and saw that it was General Fombombo. The dictator was patting his shoulder warmly and encouraging him as a father might encourage the first efforts of a son.

"That's the idea—two or three quick shots, then get down."

The general himself did not keep down so carefully. He seemed sure that he would not be touched, and was careful only of his men. A contagious power surrounded the commander. His hand on Strawbridge's shoulder filled the American with warmth and confidence. He felt a passion to do some striking thing in the general's service. Standing up quite as high as the dictator himself, he suddenly cried out:

"Look! Yonder are some fellows down on the street level! Watch me get—"

The general pressed him down.

"Guard yourself," he ordered; "you are too valuable to be in this firing-line. You must go to New York for me. Report to the magazine and help send up ammunition. Descend quickly, señor!"

The drummer was about to crawl off toward the manhole, when abruptly the whole rank of rapid-fire guns began a steady shrieking. At the same moment half the riflemen reared up to shoot at something on the street level. As they did so came a cracking from the opposite building. The guards fell backward from their barricade, some wounded, some finished. Perhaps half remained standing, firing solid volleys down into the street.

Fombombo bellowed for the riflemen to remain down and let the machine-guns clean the streets. The big man's roars seemed to fling the soldiers back into their niches. The machine-gunners, with their steel shields protecting them, depressed their guns and began a vibratory screaming at something below.

Strawbridge, with a nervous spasm in his throat, peered through a machicolation. Out from behind the nearest building came a swarm of ghastly scarlet figures armed with heavy timbers. The machine-guns whipped the *calle* about them. Groups of the ragged red specters were struck to the ground about the timbers, but others of the rabble leaped to their places. They were the "reds." Saturnino had collected these wretches from the canal camps all over the survey, and now flung them at the dictator. There was something sickening in the charge of the "reds" across the *calle*. The machine-guns could not beat them back. They sowed the street with filthy red canvas bags; but still they came on and rushed their timbers under the overhang of the building, where the machine-guns could not reach them.

The drummer turned and scuttled toward the manhole. As he straightened and went flying down the steps, he heard a great booming echoing through the palace.

It was the "reds" thundering with their wooden rams against the doors of the building. When Strawbridge got below, the whole palace shook with the blows. All the inner doors along the central hallway stood open, and soldiers darted in and out of the rooms to fire through the windows. Rifle-shots roared through the place, and the stinking haze of smokeless powder floated out into the corridor through the tops of the doors and settled against the roof.

Some impulse sent Strawbridge running to the señora's room. As he dodged inside, he saw two groups of soldiers crouched in the corners and raking the windows with their fire. Some of their bullets bit pieces out of the iron window bars. At regular intervals the end of a heavy beam crashed against the bars and slowly bent the heavy grille inward. One by one the anchorages in the stone casing broke loose.

The two squads of peon soldiers were barricaded behind delicate dressing-tables and exquisitely wrought chairs; half a dozen guards knelt behind a canopied four-poster. Their rifles were leveled across an embroidered silk coverlet. Everything in the room still looked incongruously feminine, even with men firing across it and a dead soldier sprawled on a couch. Now and then a bullet drilled a neat hole in an old-fashioned thin glass mirror in a dressing-stand. And notwithstanding the sharp stench of powder-gas, still a faint feminine sweetness lingered in the señora's apartment, a gentle wraith that would not be exorcised.

Abruptly the whole of the bending bars broke loose and clanged down inside. Instantly the window was filled with crashing rifles. The concussion tore the drummer's ear-drums as he crouched behind the massive bed. Guards crumpled up out of both firing-squads. Bottles, brushes, and silver containers on the señora's dressing-table leaped to splinters. The next moment the window was full of the heads and shoulders of men, struggling to climb inside. They were the most ghastly human beings the drummer had ever imagined.

The few guards left in the room fired point-blank into these terrible creatures. Strawbridge caught up a gun and was on the point of firing. He was aiming down the barrel at a skull-like head when he recognized the tortured features and the burning monkey eyes of Josefa.

Such a revulsion swept over the American at the semblance of the little clerk that he dropped his rifle and crouched behind the silken bed. The prisoners in La Fortuna had been released. The mere horror of their faces must have shocked the remnant of the guard into flight. Those who were unwounded leaped from hiding and bolted for the door, shouting above the din, "*Los presos!* The prisoners are upon us! La Fortuna has fallen!" They rushed pell-mell into the hallway, still shouting their warning until their voices were lost in the din.

Strawbridge stared at these animated cadavers. Whether they recognized and spared him as an American, or whether they overlooked him among the wounded and dead, he never knew. The disinterred wretches streamed past, with unshaven faces, with yellow skins sticking to the very bones of their skulls, with eyes lost in bony pits, with lips stretched across teeth in wrinkles. Their clothes were torn filth and sores. Into the boudoir with them gushed the smell of rotting flesh and latrines. This was the very dung of Venezuelan society; it was the cesspool of the prison regurgitating into the palace; it was human sewage flowing backward. It was inexpressibly obscene.

Nausea overcome Strawbridge; yet as they passed into the hallway he struggled up and followed them. The corridor was a haze filled with flashing rifles. Out of half a dozen rooms poured other assailants, who had succeeded in breaking through the windows—other prisoners, other "reds," other insurgent soldiers, all mixed in the maddest confusion. They collected themselves under some leader; they formed themselves into a regiment and then went pouring through the doorway onto the staircase leading to the roof.

The drummer stood watching the scarecrow fighters as if hypnotized. He watched them swirl into the passage that led above. Suddenly, above the tumult, he heard the hard, shuddering reports of the machine-guns. A storm of steel burst down on the ghastly assailants, bearing them backward: the skeleton regiment recoiled, bent low, and started climbing again, struggling up over their fallen comrades straight into the muzzles of the guns. Ghastly croaking shouts; thin, rattling huzzas; the clatter of the guns;

the reek of ordure and sores; the inferno roared on. The rattle of the machine-guns was dwindling. Strawbridge heard hoarse coughing cries: "Down with Fombombo! There he is! Strike him! Stab! Shoot! Here he is, over with him!" The drummer wondered what thoughts burned through the dictator's mind as he faced his horrible enemies. The cesspool of the prison had belched back, clear up to the roof of the palace, and General Fombombo was inundated.

Strawbridge was deathly sick. He tottered back to the boudoir and clambered out at the broken window, unopposed. Assailants no longer encircled the palace; they had drained inside. The tumult on the roof was rapidly subsiding. Here and there cries of "*Viva* Saturnino!" began to sound. Presently a few soldiers came running out of the palace, waving their rifles and shouting, "*Viva* Saturnino!"

Viva Saturnino! The battle was over.

News of the victory spread through the plaza and the adjoining streets with extraordinary swiftness. Strawbridge could hear cries for Saturnino as they were repeated in every direction—near, far, now from all parts at once—"*Viva* Saturnino!"

By common concert men and women appeared, coming in from every direction. Crowds might have formed out of the air. They came shouting and huzzaing for victory. They took up the cry, "Liberty! Justice and Saturnino!"

A group of peons began dancing in the evening shadows which fell across the plaza. Some tatterdemalions ran with ropes, lassoed the head of General Fombombo's statue, and began pulling it from its pedestal. The marble seemed to resist. It held out its scroll bearing "Liberty, Equality, and Fraternity," but at last it swung slowly outward and smashed down on the pavement.

At its fall a ferocious joy-making boiled up in the crowd. Some one lighted a fire in the center of the square, and immediately every one flung the litter from the refugees upon the pyre—broken carts, smashed furniture, rags, all manner of waste. The fire boiled up in a great white smoke, and presently flames began licking through it. The revelers began to sing; half a dozen voices, a score, others and others, until a great sounding chorus roared up from the plaza. Some rimester had improvised the words:

Viva el Coronel Saturnino,

   Son of Freedom and Rio Negro!

Save our daughters and our niñas.

To Hell with General Fombombo.

The crowd danced about the bonfire to this absurd chant—men and women, embracing, kissing, singing, whirling in and out like brown vortices of sand blown up by the winds on the llanos.

The drummer stood near the façade of the palace, watching the growing saturnalia. He thought of the señora, and he thanked God she was safe in some convent, out of all this fury and madness. Greater and greater crowds gathered in the plaza; they streamed in from everywhere. An old woman passed Strawbridge, with her arms about a filthy skeleton-like creature. In the gathering gloom of evening, Strawbridge recognized the old charwoman of the cathedral, Doña Consolacion, and her grandson Josefa. These two had been reunited. The drummer watched them pass. The strange thought came to him that he had brought them down to their poor plight.

The bonfire was leaping high by this time, and with the delicacy of an etching the ornamental trees stood out against the flames. Below circled the dark figures of the peons, singing of liberty, justice, and Saturnino. Amid the rhythmic intervals of this uproar, the American heard a solitary sobbing. The sound was so consonant to his own mood that he looked about for the mourner. He found the weeper in the gloom beside the long stairway that led up into the palace. He walked slowly around the curve of the marble balustrade, and in the shadows he saw a misshapen woman bending over some object on the pavement and weeping vehemently. Strawbridge drew closer until he could see her face, distorted with grief. It was Madruja. The peon girl was heavy with an unborn child, and in her arms she held the body of the fallen dictator. The dead tyrant looked curiously small as he lay on the pavement, where he had been thrown from the roof of the palace. Occasionally the girl would pause in her sobbing, to stroke the dead man's face with her puffed fingers; then she would break out afresh.

As Strawbridge stood blinking his eyes a street vender came running along, lifting his hands in an attitude of prayer and shouting a priest-like singsong at the skies. Strawbridge listened to him. He was chanting in a frenzy of satire:

"O Saint Peter! O good Saint John! Guard well your eleven thousand holy virgins; General Fombombo is on his way to Paradise!"

CHAPTER XXVII

The dead man's fate oppressed Strawbridge, and the irony of all the rejoicing at the rise of Saturnino filled him with bitterness. He turned away. He meant to go back to the priests' house. He would leave this anarchic land as quickly as he could. As he turned, a girl came running down the steps of the palace. She stopped half-way down and peered at the man on the pavement. Next moment she called his name, under her breath:

"*Ola*, Señor Strawbridge! is that you?" She started quickly down the rest of the steps to him. "*Cá!* Señor Strawbridge, come to my señora at once; she needs you! Quick! *Pronto! Ehue*, señor, hurry!"

The drummer recognized the *griffe* girl. The urgency in her voice brought him up sharply.

"What is it, *chica*?"

"Oh, *Madre de Jesus*! The soldiers are searching the convents! She has slipped into the garden and hid! The poor angel! I came flying for you! Señor, hurry! For love of the Virgin! Would you have a heretic like Saturnino seize a nun?"

A terrible feeling came over Strawbridge.

"Seize her! Is that hell-hound...." The monstrousness of it throttled him. The girl pulled at his sleeve, and by this time both were running diagonally across the plaza. They were not conspicuous: they might have been new merrymakers, hurrying to sing, around the bonfire, of the rise of Saturnino and of his protection to "our daughters and our *niñas*." But these two angled into one of the narrow *calles* that emptied into the plaza. Even from this little run the convalescent began to breathe heavily. He caught his breath to ask:

"How do you know they are searching the convents?"

"I was in the convent of Saint Ursula with her."

"What did they do there?"

"The soldiers surrounded the place, and allowed no one to leave."

"That might be to keep you from getting hurt," gasped the drummer, with a ray of hope.

"Oh, no; they are searching other convents. One of the sisters escaped and told us. Everybody knows who Coronel Saturnino is hunting."

The drummer mended his lagging trot a trifle.

"God almighty!" he breathed in despair; then, "Aren't we almost there?"

The girl pointed ahead at the upper story of a big convent that rose above the poor huts which surrounded it. It was hazy in the gathering shadows of night.

"She is hiding in the garden on this side."

"Were you in there with her?"

"*Sí*, señor."

"How'd you get out?"

"I climbed the limb of a tree and dropped out."

The drummer was filled with apprehension.

"Good Lord! we'll never get in, that way!"

The *griffe* girl suddenly began to whimper.

"Oh, señor, don't say that! It is the only way we can get back! We can't let the poor señora be caught in the garden!"

At this moment the two rounded a corner and came upon the dark wall of a Venezuelan garden. It was quite as high as an ordinary adobe house, and was finished in the same way, with plaster masonry. It had not a foothold from top to bottom.

The girl caught the American's arm and drew him to a standstill.

"*Ola!*" she breathed. "There they are now!"

The drummer paused to peer through the gloom, and saw two peons with rifles, standing half-way down the length of the garden. He looked at them, ransacking his brain for some plan. Then he moved forward again, with his shoulders back and with a certain air of authority. The soldiers heard him approach, clicked their rifles, and called him to halt.

The big man stepped out of the shadow of the wall.

"I am the *Americano* who is backing Coronel Saturnino's rebellion with money," he stated briefly. "I suppose you saw me give him a chest of gold in San Geronimo; at least you heard about it."

One of the guards saluted.

"*Sí*, señor."

"The *coronel* has reached Saint Ursula now; he told me to come out here and send in you two guards to help him search the place."

One of the soldiers looked at him suspiciously.

"Why did not the *coronel* ask you to help him, señor?"

"Me? Why, I'm no Catholic. I am a Protestant. You don't imagine the *coronel* would allow a Protestant to go searching through a Catholic convent, do you? He respects the decencies of life."

The doubting guard touched his cap.

"Very well, señor." Both of them turned about, shouldered their rifles, and marched off down the garden fence toward the convent.

When they were some distance away, Strawbridge turned and beckoned. The *griffe* girl came to him. She was doubled up with stifled explosions of laughter.

"*Caramba!* what a man!" she gasped. "Send those two donkeys trotting off like that! *Cá!*" She put her hand on her stomach and doubled again.

Strawbridge shook her out of her mirth.

"Here, cut it out! How can we get into this garden?" He looked up the sheer wall. "How in hell are we ever going to get in?!"

The girl looked up.

"I got out on that tree." She pointed at an overhanging bough.

"Well—damn it!—you see you can't reach it now. You couldn't reach that from the top of the wall!"

"No, señor."

The drummer took the girl by the arm as if he meant to throw her over, and moved distractedly back along the wall.

"I wonder if you could hold on to that Bougainvillea," he speculated hurriedly. "The only thing I see to do is to boost you up to it. We can try it."

They hurried up under the bush. Strawbridge picked her up bodily with his good hand and the elbow of his bad arm. He got her to his shoulder, put one hand under her, and shoved upward with his whole strength. The smell of the kitchen enveloped him. Her sandaled feet were on his shoulders; then she stepped on his head. Flickers of flame danced before his eyes as she kicked off and grabbed the down-hanging bush above them. The next moment she was scrambling toward the top of the wall, clinging to an armful of Bougainvillea stems.

Strawbridge watched her, with his arms straining upward, as if he still bore her weight. He stood thus, as the half-breed girl gained slowly upward and wriggled her body over the top of the wall.

The drummer stood for a monotonous age in the gloom beside the garden, waiting for the reappearance of the maid and her mistress. As he stood there the stars came out among the overhanging branches. A faint perfume of some flowering tree sifted down to him, and its fragrance alternated with the smells of a Latin street. A rumor of the turmoil in the plaza still reached his ears, but it was overpowered at regular intervals by the sharp trilling of some insect in the wall. This tiny creature repeated its love-trill over and over, until at last it caught the drummer's attention. He thought what a strange thing it was for this little living speck to send out its love-cry thus and to expect, out of the immensity of the night, some final satisfaction. And there was he, Thomas Strawbridge, on precisely the same quest of love as the midge in the wall.

It was a fantastic thought. The drummer shuddered, and moved about. It seemed to him the insect had been trilling for hours, when he heard a movement on the top of the wall. Then the voice of the *griffe* girl whispered:

"Señor, we went to the gate. There are four guards there. How will the señora ever get down?"

Strawbridge was at the edge of his nerves. He thought in irritation: "You fools! wasting time to go to the gate!" He said aloud: "Dolores! Are you up there, Dolores!"

"Oh, dear Tomas, how can I get down?" came the girl's whisper.

"You'll have to drop!" He braced himself for a violent strain.

"I'll catch you!"

The salesman heard a movement above, then the rapid breathing of women attempting some uncertain feat. Presently he made out an object lowering itself, or being lowered, from the rim of the wall. Then he heard a strained whisper: "Oh, señor, I *can't* let go! Please come up and help me!"

Strawbridge was writhing in a rigor of impatience.

"Drop! For God's sake, drop, Dolores!"

"But I can't drop in the dark! I can't!"

"For Christ's sake, Dolores, drop!" he cried. "*Chica! chica!* Break her grip! Shove her hands loose! Quick! Damn it! here they come!"

At that instant came a flurry of falling skirts; a blow of soft flesh staggered the drummer and almost brought him to his knees. An aura of faint perfume surrounded him. The breath burst from the girl's strained lungs as she jarred through her lover's arms to the ground. The next moment they had straightened themselves and set out running, hand in hand, down the *calle*.

"To the cathedral," gasped the señora. "We'll be safe there!"

From behind them came shouts, then a rifle-shot. A moment later the fugitives ran past the turn in the *calle* and for the moment were screened from rifle fire. They had hardly turned when the *griffe* girl came pattering behind them. She was winged with terror for her mistress.

"Oh, Heart of Pity! They are firing! Run! Run!"

The maid's excitement really hurried them on faster than the shots had done; but the señora already was panting with the exhaustion of the gently bred.

"I—I—how far do we have to run?" she gasped.

"On, on, señora! Merciful Mary!"

"But—but I can't! I—I—"

"Let's carry her!" panted Strawbridge, at the end of his resources, but he knew he could not do it. The run was telling on his own strength.

They were half-way down the *calle* now, spurring on the last of the señora's endurance. They were running between solidly built walls. Behind them the soldiers were shouting commands to halt! The Spanish girl began to sob.

"I—I'll have to stop, I—can't—go—any—"

At that moment Strawbridge glimpsed a little gap in the wall of houses, the slit-like mouth of a tiny *calle*. He gasped to the señora:

"Run into that! Here, to the left! Jump in as we pass. Get to the cathedral the best you can! *Chica* and I will run on!"

The Spanish girl used up the last of her strength to forge ahead of the other two, who ran close to the wall behind her, screening her movements in the gloom. The next moment she disappeared in the narrow opening.

Strawbridge and the *griffe* girl ran on alone. When the whole party, pursued and pursuers, were well past the hiding-place of the Spanish woman, the girl whispered in a fairly controlled breath, "Let's run off and leave them, señor!"

"Can you?" puffed the drummer, surprised.

"*Seguramente*, señor!" There was even a hint of the light-hearted in her voice.

By this time Strawbridge had driven his heart action up to running tempo. He was now good for twenty or thirty minutes of hard running. He answered the *griffe* girl by increasing his pace. She kept even with him, apparently without exertion. Even in the midst of his anxiety about the señora, the drummer sensed the freedom and resilience of the girl's movements.

Nothing but pride drove Strawbridge to keep even with her. He spurted at top speed. His long legs spanned the cobblestones at a furious clip. The girl twinkled along at his side with the effortlessness of a squirrel. She must have enjoyed running; she made little sounds of pleasure. When the soldiers rounded the corner and saw their quarry far down the *calle*, there came a hurricane of distant oaths and shouts, then the sharp crackling of high-powered rifles and a whistling about their ears.

The *griffe* girl had the breath to giggle hysterically, "They—can't—run—or—shoot!"

But the next moment she gave a little cry. With an extra spurt of speed she veered to Strawbridge, clutched his hand, trying to pull him along, then pressed it sharply against her bosom and blubbered, "*Adios, mi amo!* They—my mistress...." Then, abruptly and shockingly, she fell headlong on the cobblestones, out of a dead run. Like some wild animal, she had dashed twenty or thirty yards carrying a shot through her heart

Strawbridge stooped for a moment over the body of the girl, and with a stab of pain realized that she was dead. He lifted her head and shoulders, with an idea of carrying her body to some decent place, but another fusillade of shots rattled behind him. He dropped her on the cobblestones and dashed ahead, bending low to avoid the bullets as much as he might. He had not run twenty yards when he came out on the open plaza. If the *griffe* girl could have gone twenty yards farther....

He turned sharply to the right along the shop fronts, and tried to lose himself among the bacchanalían crowd. He began threading his way as quickly as he could toward the cathedral.

The murder of the servant-girl filled him with terrible apprehensions for the señora. She was alone in this half-mad city. He began reproaching himself for ever having left her. A hundred misfortunes could befall an unaccompanied woman on Spanish-American streets after nightfall. Some of her pursuers could easily have followed the girl up the narrow *calle*. They might be carrying her back to Saturnino at this moment.... A chill sweat broke out on Strawbridge's face. He shoved along through the dancing crowd, past the bonfire, toward the church.

The leaping flames of the fire cast waves of illumination across the plaza and against the cathedral, causing its massive façade to glow and fade in the darkness. From the moment Strawbridge could make out the three dark archways of the triple entrance, he began looking for the woman. He hurried along, peering ahead, hitting his fist against his palm, twisting his fingers. His rapid walk changed into a trot. He forgot that his great height rendered him conspicuous as he shoved along through these low-statured Venezuelans. Once he looked back and he saw a sinister thing. A squad of soldiers were plunging through the singers of liberty, like a plow. They left a furrow in the human mass behind them which required twenty or thirty seconds to refill with revelers. Then from another direction a second body of soldiers pushed their way; these two bodies were converging on the cathedral.

The sight of these squads whipped the drummer into headlong flight again. His apprehension increased as he came to the cathedral. His back crawled with dread of a crashing impact. One little fact comforted his harassed brain: if the two squads were focusing on the cathedral, Dolores must have escaped. If he were killed, Father Benicio would protect her.

At the very moment he thought of the priest, he saw him. The cleric's black-robed figure stood at the entrance of the middle door as if on guard. When Strawbridge reached the piazza in front of the church, he slackened his pace to something a little more respectful.

"Father—Father," he panted, when he was close enough, "is Dolores in the church? Has she come? For Christ's sake, man, tell me!"

The priest waved him sharply inside, then walked quickly to the smaller of the three portals, apparently to shut it. He seemed to have been waiting for the American's arrival. What he did next, the American did not know; he was already hurrying down the aisle toward the chapel of the Last Supper.

Strawbridge knew that Dolores was in this chapel. He turned into the entrance. He could see nothing except the slender dark figure against a glow of gold. The girl turned at his footstep, gave a little cry, and lifted herself to the arms of her lover. The big American bent over her, unable to see for his own tears. He kissed her ears, her chin, with her nun's bonnet in his face. He lifted a clumsy hand to remove it. His shaking fingers felt the coils of her hair, the curve of her neck. He was half sobbing.

"Oh, I ought never to have left you! Poor angel! Did they hurt you!"

With fluttering fingers she got the bonnet off, and it fell down before the altar. They stood pressing their mouths together, clinging to each other with convulsive gusts of strength. They gasped and murmured inarticulate sounds out of the corners of their lips. They had been so terrified for each other, and now their nerves swung back in a crescent and inarticulate transport.

Strawbridge spoke first:

"I saw some soldiers coming this way. I think we'd better go."

The girl lifted her face from his breast to look at him.

"Leave the cathedral!"

"Why, yes, Beautiful! I tell you the soldiers chased me in here. They must be outside. God knows how long we've been standing here!"

She loosed herself and straightened.

"But, my own heaven, this is our sanctuary. We are safe here."

It had never occurred to the drummer to allow the cathedral to be the haven of his flight.

"But listen, beloved: we're not safe anywhere. You thought you were safe in the convent, but—"

"But, *mi adoración*, you know that not even *he* would violate the chapel of our merciful Lady." She looked at him, amazed.

"But he will! I know he will. Here, let's go!" He took her arm and swung her gently about so that she was at his side with one of his arms about her waist.

"But, *mi carino*!" she cried, "don't you know if he should dare come in here, our holy Lady would cast him out of this cathedral; *Cá!* She would call down fire from heaven upon his head!" The girl made a sharp gesture from the image on the altar to some imaginary victim before it.

Such a passion of belief startled the drummer. He had never before sensed this fire in the girl. But his apprehension was rising constantly. He heard a murmur from the front of the cathedral. He made her listen; he began urging her more strongly than ever that they fly while they could. She put a hand over his mouth.

"But listen, *carissimo!*" she insisted passionately. "Our loving Lady brought us together in her chapel; shall we not trust her to the end? Can we wound her feelings by deserting her now?" She touched her breast and forehead and looked at the image. "Oh, *mi corazon*, I prayed and prayed to her for this great happiness! I wrote a letter to my dear Lady and placed it here on her altar so my prayer would go up to her like an incense. And now I have you!" She put her arms around him again and gazed into his face with rapt and tender eyes. "Let us stay here!"

The fact that Dolores had written the letter which he had contemplated writing, moved Strawbridge with a profound intimacy and sweetness. It gave him another of his rare glimpses of the eternity in which his little life momentarily moved. Perhaps supernal powers were indeed ranged back of these altars, with their protecting arms about him and this sweet lady. The thought of such guardianship wrapped the drummer in its glory. It elevated his passion for the Spanish girl; it lifted it from the earth, and set it up in heaven, like a star. He was almost minded to rest his fate with the Virgin, but his mystical mood was broken by the gathering turmoil at the cathedral entrance. The sounds reached the chapel softened and sweetened by arches and domes, but they were sinister. They whipped the American's thoughts from any supernatural help and set him back sharply on his pagan self-reliance. He took the girl's arm again.

"Look here, Dolores," he hurried as the sounds swelled in intensity, "we'll have to go. She—" he nodded at the altar—"she's done enough—all I want. She's got us together. Now we ought to help ourselves!" Strawbridge's voice admitted of no discussion. He was almost dragging the girl away.

The noise at the entrance was resounding as if the cathedral were a bass viol. Dolores moved instinctively back to her protectress, but Strawbridge hurried her along.

As they ran up the aisle, Strawbridge thought swiftly of possible avenues of escape. He remembered the underground tunnels in the crypt, but the idea of flying through a hole in the ground was repellent to him. He would take the night and the stars.

Even while he was planning, he hurried to the side door of the cathedral which let out into the garden. As he fumbled at the bolts with his good hand, came two heavy, drum-like reports from the front of the cathedral. This seemed to loose pandemonium in the church.

The drummer leaped with the girl into the dark garden, and went running down the hedge. They had not gone a hundred feet before they heard men rush out at the side door behind them. Bending low in the shadow, Strawbridge ran at full tilt. His good arm took the strain of the señora's stumblings. In his necessity he upheld her, he almost carried her. He crashed on through the garden. His impact burst open the little postern gate toward the palace. As he ran, he silently cursed his pursuers with every blasphemy he could think of. He could hear the Spanish girl whispering rapid prayers.

He rushed across to the piazza behind the palace. He swung Dolores upon it and leaped up after her. The west side of the piazza was blocked by the palace kitchen. In the cooking-stove a handful of red coals glowered at him. Their pursuers had now filled the thoroughfare between the garden and the palace. Suddenly he saw two or three forms leap upon the platform. The drummer ran to the river side of the piazza. The girl clutched his arm.

"Oh, *carissimo*! we are not going down there!"

"Yes, yes! there's nowhere else to go!"

They stepped upon the steep, dark slope that dropped away to the river. Instantly they were sliding and slipping down, helter-skelter. They went through rotting flesh, bones, decaying vegetables, stenches and smells such as are found nowhere on earth save outside a Latin-American kitchen. They balanced, they caught each other, they fell on their hands and knees. The fetor of the stuff high on the bank changed to the dull smell of dried leavings farther down. Suddenly, from far above them, came the flashes of rifles. As usual with riflemen on a height, the soldiers overshot. A moment later, the fugitives reached the dank smell that marked the river's edge. Not forty yards down the river, Strawbridge saw the glimmer of a white object. He went running toward it, lifting the girl on his arm. The scoured canoe took form out of the night. The drummer swung Dolores bodily over the garboard, then heaved at the prow and began backing it out into the dark, swift river. When it was well afloat, he leaped and landed on his belly across its nose. He wriggled inside, groped for the paddle, straightened up, and began working furiously with his good hand and his elbow, away from the rifle fire.

When he was well away, he looked back. Flashes from the rifles were still visible, but they seemed to be moving rapidly up the river bank. With the rifles drifted the black bulk of the palace, the stately spire of the cathedral, the somber outline of La Fortuna. All moved evenly and swiftly into the west; they dwindled in size and definition until presently they melted into the night. At last all the fugitives could discern were the red reflections of the bonfire against the clouds.

Around the canoe boiled the rapids of the Rio Negro. They were in the midst of the thunder that brooded for miles over cities and villages and llanos. The air was full of flying spray and the peculiar smell of fresh water in great disturbance. The canoe was flung skyward, dropped. It came to sharp pauses, leaped forward, and pirouetted on prow and stern. Strawbridge lay flat on his back in the fish-boat, to keep the center of gravity as low as possible. The stars overhead appeared to him a whirling vortex of fiery points. He gripped the señora's hands in his good palm. He could feel her moving her rosary through her fingers. As they shot through the black thunder, the Spanish girl was praying to the Virgin of Canalejos. Dolores believed the Virgin was guiding the canoe down the perilous channel. Strawbridge's nerves were at tension, but he was not afraid. He believed in his luck.

CHAPTER XXVIII

The distance from Canalejos to San Geronimo is much greater following the meanders of the Rio Negro than the direct route across the llanos. When dawn whitened over the river, on the morning after the flight of the drummer and the Spanish girl, Strawbridge expected hourly to see the campaniles of San Geronimo appear above the horizon. It was his plan, when he came in sight of the city, to wait until night before he attempted to pass in the canoe. He reasoned that Saturnino would telegraph to San Geronimo and order their arrest and imprisonment.

So, as the two fugitives floated down the great muddy flood, they peered through the beating sunshine and the dancing glare from the water, in order to see and be warned by the first glimpse of the distant city. But such a fulgor lay over the water that toward the middle of the morning they were hardly able to see the reeds that marched down to the riverside, or the green parrots that passed over the canoe in great flocks and filled the sky with a harsh screaming.

The river stretched on, mile after mile, a vast moving plane that banished the shores to level lines almost at the horizon. At last Strawbridge came to paddle close to one shore, in order that their tiny canoe might not be utterly lost amid such an immensity. As they clung closely to the left or easterly bank they passed, in the afternoon, what appeared to be the mouth of a small tributary river. Along its banks were a scattering of deserted huts, stakes with rusting chains fastened to them, a stockade of reeds daubed with mud, two or three adobe ovens such as the peons use. Strawbridge looked curiously at the abandoned site, and presently he realized that he was passing one of the branches that would have formed a part of General Fombombo's great system of canals. The work lay abandoned in a furnace of heat; the conscripted "reds" were gone. The only evidences of life were the crocodiles which had taken possession of the waterway and sunned themselves along its sandy rim.

As the man and the woman floated past they looked at the intake and the empty camp until it grew small in the distance and at last melted into the dancing horizon. What the Spanish girl thought as she looked at this ruinous fragment of her husband's great dream, Strawbridge did not know, nor did he dare to ask.

This long reach of water, wrought by the fettered "reds," somehow made Strawbridge, as he floated past it in his little canoe, feel small and uncertain of himself. It brought to his mind keenly the general, his restless planning; working, gathering gold, attacking cities, conscripting labor for vast projects; and now he was gone and this mighty fragment of his work was a harbor for reptiles. Seen from this perspective, the fact that the dictator had abandoned Dolores, who did not love him, for peon girls who did, no longer appeared the high crime which the American had held most harshly against him. It occurred to Strawbridge that there must have been sides to the general which he had missed, or but dimly apprehended.

The drummer's thoughts swung away from the general, to the long line of dictators who had arisen and oppressed Rio Negro. Each tyrant no sooner gained power than immediately he fell into some madness peculiar to himself.

Strawbridge wondered why this was so. Heretofore he had thought such tyranny and oppression arose out of sheer wickedness, but now, looking back on the life of the general, he doubted this judgment. The trend of Fombombo's plans had always been toward some great good for his state. But his efforts, it seemed to Strawbridge, were unbusinesslike. He made a gesture toward projects far beyond his resources. His effort to outstrip his physical resources forced him to conscript the "reds." It was his sensitiveness to any criticism of his unbusinesslike policy that caused him to imprison every critic of his methods. Lack of business acumen was the basic weakness which led to the dictator's tyrannies and to his final downfall.

As Strawbridge sat in the canoe, brooding over it, a strange thought came to him that perhaps all righteousness of conduct was at last resolvable to dollars and cents.

He mused over this curious theory. Gumersindo had told him some of the history of Spain, and all the time the negro editor was relating the expulsion of the Moors and the Jews from the peninsula, the drummer kept thinking not of any abstract injustice of the banishment but of the extraordinarily bad business methods the Spanish monarch used. Likewise, he could not help thinking that while the Spanish Inquisition struck a fine attitude before Heaven, it cut a very poor figure on Exchange.

And now he thought that just as Spain had suffered from lack of business, Venezuela, her colony, had inherited the same curse. The Venezuelans placed religion before business, they placed family pride before business, they placed pleasure before business. It seemed to him that they placed the smallest before the greatest.

Heretofore, when Strawbridge's Venezuelan friends had twitted the American with possessing "monetary morals," the drummer was wounded and inclined to take offense at the qualification. Now, as he thought about it more steadily, it dawned on him that the ability to sift conduct down to its money value was about the only universal standard of righteousness that the world would ever know. This curious conclusion settled many interrogations in the drummer's mind, and brought to him a kind of peace.

Strawbridge felt a man's impulse to share his thoughts with the señora. He glanced up at her, with his theory on the tip of his tongue, but she seemed absorbed in her own musings. As he looked at her through the glare of sunshine, his instinct warned him that he would better not attempt it. It was very precious to him, but it would not be very precious to her. Indeed, as he looked at her, he began to realize that she would never understand it; that she was born on the wrong side of the world ever to understand just these thoughts.

She looked very dear and lovable.

The fugitives did not reach San Geronimo until the third night following their flight. They approached the city in the darkness, as they had planned, but to their surprise and dismay, they saw hundreds of lights moving over the face of the water. From afar off these lights looked like a field of fireflies, but presently they developed into native torches, such as the Orinoco Indians use in hunting alligators at night.

The man and the woman were terrified, and in whispers discussed what course they could pursue. Dolores suggested that they go ashore on the other side of the river and walk down past the town. This was impossible because the city lay in the junction of the Rio Negro and the Orinoco. They would be caught in this V-shaped Mesopotamia, with nowhere to walk except back up the Orinoco. Moreover, any walking at all in such a pestilential country would mean a painful and lingering death for Dolores. Nor was the drummer in any degree a woodsman. He always lost his direction in the open.

It seemed to Strawbridge that their only possible hope was to reach one of the searching canoes and bribe the owner into running them through the blockade. He knew a report of his imaginary wealth had been spread among the peons, and now he hoped by wide promises to slip through Coronel Saturnino's fleet.

He veered his canoe in the darkness and began paddling slowly toward one of the lights. It seemed an ironic thing that freedom, the right to a home and to Dolores should lie just a quarter of a mile beyond those patrolling torches. To accomplish his object, he had scarcely a gambler's chance. Saturnino, sitting in his study in San Geronimo, had worked out every possible combination which Strawbridge could attempt. Now this diapering of lights moving against the darkness was one of his checks.

In the midst of his thoughts, Strawbridge became aware that half a dozen or more lights were bearing down on his canoe. The drummer, in dismay, stopped paddling. He had thought to steal silently up to one of the canoes, unseen by the others, and quietly make his compact with the canoeist to assist him through the blockade. Now, with dozens of boats bearing down on him from every direction, bribery was impossible. He sat staring at the gathering torches, with a profound sinking of the heart. By no possibility could he, a one-handed man, race away from the Indians.

The Spanish girl moved to him.

"Oh, dear Tomas!" she whispered, "are we going to be lost, after all!"

Her helplessness moved the drummer.

"I suppose talking to him, pleading with him, begging him for the love of humanity to let you go—"

Dolores gave his hand a pressure.

"No, we must not despair. I know the sweet Virgin will save us. She would not do so much and then let us be lost." The girl lifted her white face toward the stars and began murmuring her prayers.

The drummer looked at her with a profound pity and tenderness. He knew it would indeed require a miracle to save her now. He swiftly considered what he could do. There was only one thing. He could follow her to Canalejos, and then, when Saturnino had taken her into the palace and wearied of her ... then....

The drummer wondered whether he himself could keep so long and humiliating a vigil. It seemed to him that he could; indeed, it seemed the only thing possible for him to do. Ever again to make a gesture of deserting her was an impossible thing for Thomas Strawbridge. Among all the women in the world she alone was for him; she was a very part of himself.

He put his arms around her.

"Listen, Dolores," he whispered solemnly: "no matter what comes, as long as I have life I will follow you; no matter what happens, I will wait for you." He kissed her gently on the cheek and pressed her face to his. "I will not forsake you, Dolores...."

Amid his murmuring came a shout across the water:

"*Hola, Señor Americano!* Is that *Señor Americano! Canastos, hombre!* you are wanted!"

Strawbridge stood up in the canoe.

"Ho, yes!" he shouted loudly. "Come ahead! I am the American!"

Canoes were gathering now from every direction, and their lights began to illuminate his own boat; still, he could see little of the gathering flotilla, for each torch was set in front of a tin reflector and flung all its light forward. From the dimly seen figures came a voice, saying:

"An order from Canalejos, señor. We are to detain you and *la señora!*"

"Yes, I had supposed so."

A pause, then the voice said:

"We have been watching for you day and night, señor."

The American wearied instantly of this polite Spanish circumlocution.

"Oh, well! Now that you've got us what are you going to do with us?"

"If you will accompany me to my ship, señor! Perhaps you recognize me: we had a very pleasant afternoon together once. I am Captain Vargas of the *Concepcion Inmaculada*." He twisted the light about in his boat and exhibited not a canoe but himself and a number of peon oarsmen, in a jolly-boat.

Strawbridge looked at his good-natured face. That he should have fallen in with this captain who would have been so easily bribed, amid a crowd where such bribing was impossible, was the last touch of ironic fortune. It filled him with such bitterness that he ran his tongue about his mouth as if the flavor were on his palate.

"Yes, I remember you very well. So you are still here?"

"That is true, but I sail at once. I am in the Rio Negran navy now, both me and my *Concepcion Inmaculada*. I am a captain. I am a captain in the insurgent navy."

It was true. Captain Vargas wore a blue coat trimmed with much gold braid. Coronel Saturnino had caught him through his vanity.

A rope had been tossed over the prow of the canoe, and now the whole fleet of small boats approached the lights of a schooner that lay in the harbor of San Geronimo. This was the old schooner *Concepcion Inmaculada*, now the solitary ship in the insurgent navy. Beyond the black rigging of the ship, Strawbridge could see the silhouettes of the long row of palms which stood on the waterfront. The schooner lay exactly where the drummer had seen her after the battle of San Geronimo.

The small boats pulled up alongside, and the captain and the captives went on board. The old tub evidently had been laded during the interim, for now she smelled strongly of balata and tonka-beans.

Captain Vargas led the way briskly across decks and down the little hatchway into the cabin. Two oil lamps lighted this place and when the captain stepped into it the gold braid on his new uniform shone more brightly than ever. He went over to the ship's chest, opened it, and drew out an envelop.

"I have a writ here for you, Señor Strawbridge," he explained politely. "It was very necessary to intercept you; that is why all San Geronimo turned out to be sure you were brought in."

"Yes. You seemed enthusiastic."

Captain Vargas smiled politely. He was a little more polite, a little stiffer, and not quite so friendly now that he was in a uniform.

"Now, if the señora will have that chair.... She must be weary." He drew about a chair and assisted her to it, with elaborate courtesy.

Vargas then bowed again and handed the envelop to the drummer. It was a government official envelop with a large seal. The American opened it, moistened his lips, then held it under the light of an oil lamp and read:

> Señor Tomas Strawbridge,
> Late of Canalejos, Rio Negro.
>
> *Excellentissimo Señor:*
>
> You are hereby instructed to proceed immediately to Rio de Janeiro with the *Concepcion Inmaculada*, taking full command of her cargo of balata and tonka-beans, also of the gold coin and specie on board, as set forth in the ship's manifest. Deliver this cargo to the consignee in Rio Janeiro, and with the proceeds therefor purchase the arms and ammunition as heretofore set out in a contract entered into by the government of Rio Negro of the first part and the Orion Arms Corporation of the second part. This former contract is hereby fully validated by the newly established government of Rio Negro. I have the honor to be, *al mas excellentissimo señor, su muy humilde servidor*,

CPSIA information can be obtained
at www.ICGtesting.com
Printed in the USA
LVHW102002080522
717863LV00022B/331